כִּי בָרֵךְ אֲבָרֶכְךָ
וְהַרְבָּה אַרְבֶּה אֶת זַרְעֲךָ
כְּכוֹכְבֵי הַשָּׁמַיִם
וְכַחוֹל אֲשֶׁר עַל שְׂפַת הַיָּם
(בראשית כב:יז)

I shall surely bless you
and greatly increase your offspring
like the stars of the heavens
and like the sand on the seashore

(BEREISHIS / GENESIS 22:17)

A Jewish History
for Young People

SAND AND STARS

by **YAFFA GANZ**
in collaboration with
RABBI BEREL WEIN

A SHAAR PRESS PUBLICATION

The Jewish Journey Through Time

FROM THE SIXTEENTH CENTURY TO THE PRESENT

Published by **SHAAR PRESS**
and Distributed by **MESORAH PUBLICATIONS, LTD.**
4401 Second Avenue / Brooklyn, N.Y 11232 / (718) 921-9000

Distributed in Israel by SIFRIATI / A. GITLER
4 Bilu Street / P.O.B. 14075 / Tel Aviv 61140

Distributed in Europe by J. LEHMANN HEBREW BOOKSELLERS
20 Cambridge Terrace / Gateshead, Tyne and Wear / England NE8 1RP

Distributed in Australia and New Zealand by GOLDS BOOK & GIFT SHOP
36 William Street / Balaclava 3183, Vic., Australia

Distributed in South Africa by KOLLEL BOOKSHOP
22 Muller Street / Yeoville 2198, Johannesburg, South Africa

Printed in the United States of America by Edison Lithographing and Printing Corporation
Custom bound by Sefercraft, Inc. / 4401 Second Avenue / Brooklyn N.Y. 11232

*T*his volume — which traces the life of the eternal nation
as it navigates turbulent centuries of its existence —
is dedicated to the emerging generation of a family
that exemplifies Jewish determination
to remain true to its Torah heritage:

**Joseph Aaron, Jonathan Richard, and Jeffrey Adam
    Schottenstein**

**Elie Michael, David Scott, Dara Lauren, and Daniel Matthew
    Deshe**

**Jillian Leigh, Joshua Louis, and Jacob Meyer
    Diamond**

*A*s the grandchildren of

Jerome Schottenstein ע״ה **and Geraldine** תחי׳

and the children of
    Jay and Jeanie Schottenstein,
    Ann and Ari Deshe, and
    Susan and Jon Diamond,

they are heirs to a family tradition of dedication to Torah
and incredible generosity.

Their grandfather was always accessible and kind.
His vision that Jewish education is essential to Jewish survival
found expression in countless institutions and,
most prominently, in the

Schottenstein Edition of the Talmud

which will be his enduring monument for generations to come,
wherever there are Jews.

With the help of Hashem, may the growing generation
of this royal family of Torah philanthropy
carry on its noble legacy,
in good health and success.

❧ Contents

Acknowledgments

Sand and Stars has been a work of love, but the love - and the work — have been shared. They have been given shape and form by many hands and minds. I am grateful and indebted to all of the people who helped turn my manuscript into a book.

To the publishers — and to SHMUEL BLITZ, who represents Shaar Press in Jerusalem — whose combined efforts have enriched the world of English Judaica; to the hard working Shaar Press staff — especially ELI KROEN, who transformed the manuscript into a graphic work of art; to my highly competent editor PESSY BUSELL NOVICK; and of course to RABBI BERL WEIN whose unique gift of viewing the world through a clear, wide angle lens, enables us to better perceive God's guiding Hand in the complex pathways of history.

V'acharon, acharon, an endearing, heartfelt thank you to my wise and patient husband who was often served a course of history instead of dinner.

In sum, I am privileged and grateful for having had the opportunity to retell part of the story of the Jewish people. I pray that the reading of it will be as enlightening and inspiring as was the writing.

Yaffa Ganz
Rosh Chodesh Elul 5755

Author's Dedication

In memory of my father
Gershon ben Shaul Halevi Siegal z"l

*A Lithuanian Jew from Shirvint,
a student of Remailles and Dvinsk,
he reached the New World,
but carefully guarded and passed down
the treasures of old.*

*An avid student of Jewish history,
his love and concern for Am Yisrael and Eretz Yisrael
filled our home and fueled our dreams.*

May his deeds be an example and his memory a blessing.

יהי זכרו ברוך

❧ *Introduction*

Sand and Stars — a Jewish Journey Through Time tells the story of the long Jewish Galus — the Diaspora. The first volume covered approximately one thousand four hundred years of Jewish history. It began with the destruction of the Second Temple in the year 68 C.E. and ended with the Expulsion of the Jews from Spain in 1492. It dealt with Roman, Byzantine and Medieval times. This second volume tells the story of the Jewish people in the modern era. It describes the past five hundred years from 1500 C.E. until today.

The modern era brought great changes to the Jewish world. New freedoms existed side by side with old hatreds. Although the Jewish people helped create and enrich modern civilization out of all proportion to their small numbers, they remained a people different and apart. When they thought they had finally found freedom, equality and acceptance, they were engulfed by a tidal wave of destruction.

Yet even with the sorrows and tribulations and indescribable suffering, wondrous things have occurred in the past five hundred years. After the catastrophic Expulsion from Spain, Am Yisrael found refuge and opened new doors of understanding in the world of Kabbalah. In Eastern Europe, the study of Torah spread to the masses and reached new heights. After almost nineteen centuries of Exile, an incredible return and ingathering to the Land of Israel gathered strength and speed. After the horrors of the Holocaust, the Tree of Torah is spreading its branches and blossoming anew. Three thousand, eight hundred years after the appearance of Avraham Avinu, Am Yisrael Chai — the Jewish people is still alive.

We are still in the midst of writing our remarkable story. Each week, each month, each year brings exciting new accomplishments, but also new problems and unexpected challenges. Many of these problems and challenges will one day be solved by readers like yourself, young people who are still studying in school today. But in order to step forward and help shape the Jewish future, you must first look back and try to understand the Jewish past. You must know who we are in order to know where we want to go and what is the best way to get there.

God promised Abraham that his children would be like ``the stars of the heavens and the sand on the seashore." Though they are scattered far and wide by roaring waves and endless tides, countless grains of sand nonetheless form the shore which shapes and contains the mighty waters of the sea. And high above our heads, spread across the dark, nighttime sky, tiny pinpoints of light emanate from immeasurable stars to guide mankind across the world.

Like the sand and the stars, we, the Children of Abraham, shape and guide the world. The story of our long and difficult journey through the Diaspora is in these two volumes; the story of our complete, future Redemption is waiting to be written. As the descendants of Abraham, Isaac and Jacob, of Sarah, Rivka, Rachel and Leah, you will undoubtedly play an important part in the writing. May you prosper and may your work be blessed.

Yaffa Ganz
Rosh Chodesh Elul 5755

PROLOGUE:

A Bird's-Eye View
From 1500 Until Modern Times

TIMELINE

1492	*Expulsion from Spain & Discovery of New World*
1517	*The Protestant Revolution*
1626-1676	*Shabtai Tzvi*
1648	*The Massacres of Tach V'Tat*
1698-1760	*Baal Shem Tov and Chassidus*
1720-1779	*Vilna Gaon and Misnagdim*
1776	*The American Declaration of Independence*
1789	*The French Revolution*
1795	*Establishment of Pale of Settlement in Poland*
1799-1815	*Napoleon Bonaparte*
1800	*Founding of Volozhin Yeshivah*
1820-1883	*Rabbi Yisrael Salanter and the Mussar Movement*
1848	*Karl Marx and the Communist Manifesto*
1880-1920	*Age of Pogroms in Russia and Period of Jewish Emigration*
1894	*Dreyfus Trial and Theodore Herzl*
1914-1918	*First World War*
1917	*Russian Revolution*
1917	*Balfour Declaration*
1929	*The Great Depression*
1933	*Death of Chafetz Chaim*
1939-1945	*Second World War*
1948	*Declaration of the State of Israel*
1967	*Six Day War*
1973	*Yom Kippur War*

THE MIDDLE AGES

The sixteenth century marked the end of the Middle Ages. The Jewish people had been in exile for almost 1500 years. They had passed through Babylonia, North Africa, Spain and the French-German lands of Ashkenaz. In each place they had created great centers of Torah, but Asia and Europe never became their real home. No matter how settled, how successful, how satisfied the Jews were, the lands of the Diaspora were always *Galus* — Exile — and Jewish settlement always came to an abrupt, usually violent, end. Nonetheless, each resting place provided an opportunity to reorganize and grow, to develop and live lives that were filled with holiness.

The Jews were always a nation apart, yet in the early Middle Ages they were a crucial, creative part of society. Through their contacts with Jews in other countries, they kept lines of communication and trade open. They served as an international banking community and introduced modern commerical transactions. They supported kings and produced scholars, developed towns, invented instruments, doctored the sick and contributed greatly to the expansion and exploration of the New World. Without them, Western civilization would have been immeasurably poorer.

Nevertheless, the Middle Ages were filled with Jewish suffering. Accused of killing the Christian god, the Jews were separated from Christian society and sorely discriminated against. Anti-Jewish laws kept them dependent upon the mercy of the Church and their neighbors. Bloody Crusades, the Black Plague, the inhuman Catholic Inquisition, vicious pogroms and expulsions from country after country made Jewish life difficult indeed.

Yet the Jews did more than survive. They created a vibrant, holy society which was more loving, more merciful, more educated and much more civilized than the Christian society they lived in. Firm in

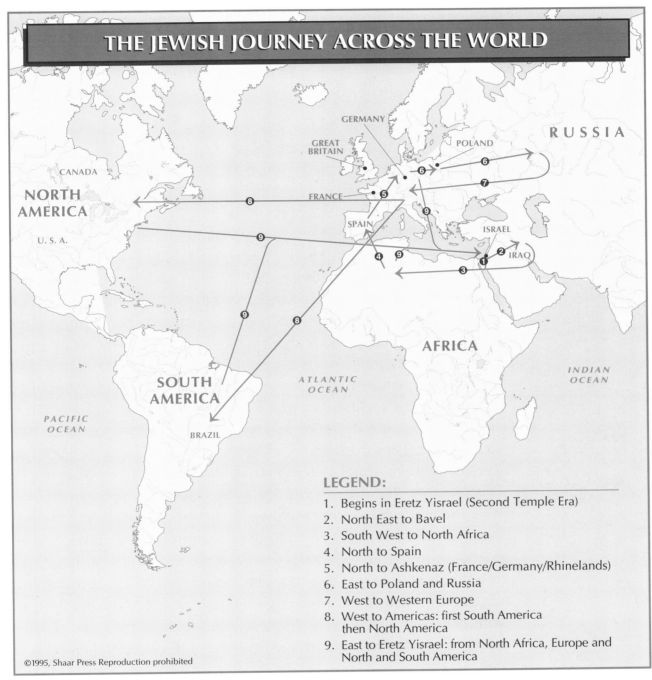

THE JEWISH JOURNEY ACROSS THE WORLD

LEGEND:
1. Begins in Eretz Yisrael (Second Temple Era)
2. North East to Bavel
3. South West to North Africa
4. North to Spain
5. North to Ashkenaz (France/Germany/Rhinelands)
6. East to Poland and Russia
7. West to Western Europe
8. West to Americas: first South America then North America
9. East to Eretz Yisrael: from North Africa, Europe and North and South America

their belief that they were a special, chosen nation, they always found the strength to go on.

There had been a constant eastward movement of Jewish refugees during the Middle Ages. For approximately four hundred years (from the eleventh to the fifteenth century), Jews emigrated from the anti-Semitic lands of France, Germany and Spain to the friendlier borders of Poland and Turkey. For the next two centuries, the Jewish population of Europe remained more or less stable. But after the horrendous pogroms in Poland in 1648, the Jews turned back towards the West where the gates to the ghetto were opening and new freedoms beckoned. Jewish immigration would now flow to the liberal, emancipated countries of Western Europe. It would then move further west across the ocean to the New World.

CHANGING TIMES

The sixteenth and seventeenth centuries saw the beginning of modern times. The world was teeming with change. The Pope and the Catholic Church were no longer all-powerful; new Protestant religions appeared throughout Europe; kings were no longer considered Divine. Nations grew strong, established their power and shaped the lives and loyalties of their citizens. A new spirit of rational inquiry urged people to question the old values and ways. The scientific revolution led to improved technology, industry and medicine; the discovery of the Americas caused a flurry of international finance and trade; and the French Revolution spread the idea of liberty and equality for all men.

There was room for everyone to contribute to this growing world, and here and there the lot of the Jews began to improve. Borders were opened and Jews were allowed to reenter countries from which they had been expelled in years past. Powerful court Jews, Jewish financiers and international Jewish traders rose to positions of prominence. The Jews played an important part in the development of the Americas. But then the age-old anti-Semitism would flare up with renewed vigor and the Jew in Europe would be forced once again to snatch his children and his belongings and flee in search of new safety.

THE MODERN ERA

As pogroms, terror and fiery anti-Semitism engulfed the East, the Jewish people longed for relief and the coming of the Messiah. A false Messiah by the name of Shabtai Tzvi appeared, but instead of Redemption, he left a trail of destruction and despair throughout the Jewish world.

During the eighteenth and nineteenth centuries, the world changed almost beyond recognition. Reform, revolution, emancipation, new economic opportunities, industrialization, emigration — each new development affected the Jews and gave rise to a Jewish response. As the Jewish people entered the modern stage on a free and equal basis for the first time since the destruction of the Second Temple, it seemed as though the nation had lost its sense of direction. The Torah came under attack, not from gentiles, but from Jews who were anxious to break loose from the old laws and restrictions. Split into countless factions and tempted to assimilate into the surrounding gentile world, entire Jewish communities stood on the verge of assimilation. It would take periodic outbursts of anti-Semitism and finally the horrors of the Holocaust to remind them that they were still a nation apart.

THE REBIRTH OF ZION AND TORAH

Two great world wars would shake the planet. Amidst all of the seeming equality and liberation of an emancipated world, the German sons of Esav rose like some cursed monster of old, bringing horrendous suffering and destruction to European Jewry. Yet even they could not destroy God's Eternal People. At the end of the nineteenth century, a small but steady stream of Jews began to return to Eretz Yisrael. The nations of the world recognized the Jews' right to their ancient homeland, and after the Holocaust, this small stream turned into a mighty wave. In 1948 the State of Israel was proclaimed and a new Jewish state took its first tottering steps towards a sovereign existence.

The study of Torah was being nurtured as well. After the war, Jews began to replant the life-giving seeds. Carefully and lovingly, they cultivated their crop. Jewish education took root and began to blossom. The voice of Torah would be heard again wherever Jews lived — in the New World and the Old — and especially in the Land of Israel.

SECTION I

Grievous Times
(From 1600 to 1800)

1
Jewish Poland
(From 1300 to 1600)

*D*uring the Middle Ages, the center of Jewish history had been in Spain and Ashkenaz (France/ Germany). But as the sufferings of the Jews increased, God provided new havens for His people. Far across the seas to the west, many Spanish and Marrano Jews found refuge in the Americas. In the east, a sprawling, primitive country called Poland opened its gates to the Jewish people. Invited to enter as privileged guests, the Jews would play a vital role in Poland's development. For several hundred years, Jewish life in Poland would thrive as Poland became the next great stopping place in the Jewish journey through the Exile.

POLISH BEGINNINGS

Jewish beginnings in Eastern Europe went back many centuries. Greek-speaking Jews had lived in the Crimea as far back as the first century C.E. In the eighth century, the semi-barbaric Khazar tribe in the Ukraine converted to Judaism. For two hundred years the Khazar Kingdom was an important, independent state in the Byzantine Empire.

In the year 965, the Khazar kingdom was attacked. Its territory was divided between Russian tribes and the Byzantine Empire. Many Khazar Jews were killed; many others assimilated into the surrounding non-Jewish culture. But some remained true to Judaism and their descendants survived in small Jewish communities throughout the Caucasus Mountains.

In the 13th century, wild Tartar tribes conquered Russia and destroyed much of Poland. When the king of Poland invited German merchants and craftsmen to help rebuild his country, many Jews arrived. Most of them were killed in pogroms during the time of the Black Death, but in 1334, Casimir the Great ("King of the Serfs and the Jews") guaranteed Jewish safety and promised certain basic rights to Jewish immigrants. The 1300's were a time of great hardship

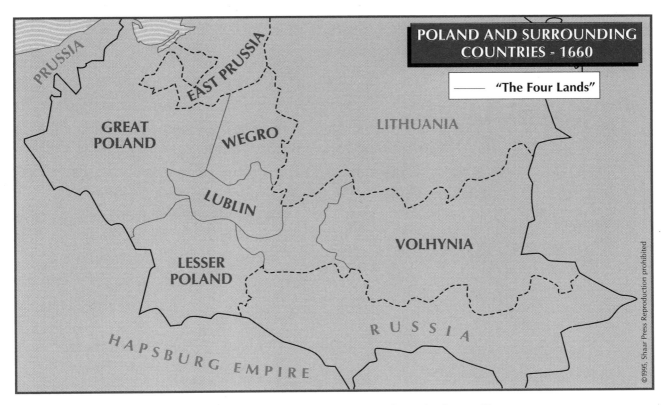

POLAND AND SURROUNDING COUNTRIES - 1660

——— "The Four Lands"

PRUSSIA

EAST PRUSSIA

GREAT POLAND

WEGRO

LITHUANIA

LUBLIN

VOLHYNIA

LESSER POLAND

RUSSIA

HAPSBURG EMPIRE

for the Jews of Europe and many took advantage of Casimir's offer. A constant stream of immigrants arrived in Poland.

The Jews were merchants and craftsmen. They worked as tailors, shoemakers, carpenters and lumberjacks; they were cattle dealers and river bargemen. They ran the Polish salt mines and flour mills, traded timber and furs, and exported wheat. They set up inns and were awarded the right to produce alcoholic drinks which they sold to the Poles. And they were the financial agents for the absentee Polish landlords, leasing lands to the serfs, administering the great estates, and collecting the endless taxes for the nobles and the kings.

Most Polish Jews lived on farms or in small Jewish towns — the *shtetl* — in rural areas. They spoke their own language, Yiddish. Yiddish was a form of early Medieval German enriched with countless Hebrew words and written in Hebrew letters. The Jews were governed by the *Vaad Arba Aratzos* — the Council of Four Lands (Little Poland in the area of Cracow, Great Poland of Silesia, Polish Russia and Volhynia). The Council was an official, independent body which dealt with legal, administrative and spiritual matters. It represented the entire Jewish community and its decisions were recognized by the Polish king.

THE STUDY OF TORAH

If the city of Tzefas in Eretz Yisrael was known for the study of Kabbalah, the communities of Poland became famous for their study of Talmud. In addition to its other responsibilities — helping the poor, visiting the sick, burying the dead — each community paid for its own schools and supported its own scholars. Every child went to *cheder*. Every able young man continued to study. Every adult studied in the evenings and on the Sabbath. In 1663 Rabbi Nathan Hanover wrote in his book, *Yevein Metzullah*: "That which is known to all needs no further proof. In all the far-flung settlements of Israel, nowhere was there as much Torah as in the land of Poland."

From the very beginning of its history, Poland was blessed with great rabbis. The saintly and beloved Rema (Rabbi Moshe Isserles) of Cracow wrote basic additions to the *Shulchan Aruch* which included the rulings and customs of Ashkenazic Jews. Rabbi Yaakov Pollak of

The Rema Synagogue in Cracow, Poland

Cracow and Lublin developed a complex method of studying Talmud called *pilpul*. His student, Rabbi Shalom Shachna, headed a yeshivah in Lublin where most of the great rabbis of Poland had studied. The Maharshal (Rabbi Shlomo Luria) founded a second great yeshivah in Lublin.

Rabbis Isserles and Luria were accomplished Kabbalists whose halachic decisions were often based on the teachings of the Zohar. Polish Jewry did not always differentiate between Kabbalah and Halachah, between the mystical world and the logical world. Everything was created by God; everything had its place in God's great scheme of things. Much of the Chassidic movement in the 18th century was based on the teachings of Kabbalah. Because Kabbalah was already so accepted and widespread among Polish Jews, Chassidus was able to spread quickly and easily throughout Poland.

A steady stream of scholars visited Poland in the sixteenth and seventeenth centuries. Both Ashkenazic and Sefardic Jewry were amazed at the great scholarship of the Polish Jewish community. The

*17th century synagogue
in Zabludow, Poland*

list of famous Polish rabbis from the years 1450-1650 is long and impressive. Their classic works are still studied today; their halachic decisions still influence or determine our behavior.

HERE WE SHALL RESIDE

Poland was a land rich in natural resources. Water, timber, animals and wheat were found in abundance. During the Thirty Years War, when the powerful Catholic German Hapsburgs battled the Protestant countries of Europe, armies on both sides were in constant need of supplies. Poland became an important source of timber and wheat and Polish Jews became Poland's main financial agents and exporters.

With its varied possibilities of earning a livelihood, the protection of its kings, its independent Jewish courts and towns and its widespread study of Torah, Poland was a haven and a refuge for the Jewish people from the fourteenth to the seventeenth centuries. In

1500, it is estimated that 50,000 Jews lived in Poland; by 1650, the number increased tenfold to half a million. Despite the ever present anti-Semitism of the peasants and the Church, life in Poland was good for the Jew. In a play on the Hebrew words, the Jews declared *"Po-lin — Here we shall reside!"*

POLISH RABBIS FROM THE 16th & 17th CENTURIES	
Rabbi Yaakov Pollak	1455-1530
Rabbi Moshe Isserles (*Rema*)	1530-1572
Rabbi Shalom Shachna	c. 1490-1558
Rabbi Shlomo Luria (*Maharshal*)	1520-1573
Rabbi Mordechai Yafeh (*Levush*)	1535-1612
Rabbi Yehoshua Falk	1545-1614
Rabbi Meir of Lublin (*Maharam*)	1558-1616
Rabbi Shmuel Edels (*Maharsha*)	1555-1632
Rabbi Yoel Sirkis (*Bach*)	1561-1640
Rabbi David HaLevi (*Taz*)	1586-1667
Rabbi Shimshon of Ostropolle	c. 1578-1648
Rabbi Yom Tov Lipman Heller (*Tosafos Yom Tov*)	1579-1664
Rabbi Yehoshua Heschel of Cracow	c. 1590-1663

2
The Massacres of Tach V'Tat
(From 1600 to 1650)

TIMELINE

_I_n 1618 war broke out across Europe between the Protestant countries and the powerful Catholic Hapsburgs, heirs to the Holy Roman Empire. Germany, Austria, Bohemia, Spain, Italy, France, Belgium, the Netherlands — all were pulled into the long and bloody battle known as the Thirty Years War.

The war devastated Europe. Huge numbers of people were killed by the sword or died from disease. Farms and fields were abandoned. Enemy troops swarmed across entire countries, destroying everything in their path. It was the largest, most widespread, most destructive war the world had ever known till then. At the end, the German Hapsburgs fell from power and France emerged as the leader of Europe.

THE THIRTY YEARS WAR

The job of supplying the huge armies during the war fell mostly to the Jews. Jewish connections were trustworthy, and they crisscrossed all geographical borders. International Jewish networks supplied food for soldiers, fodder for horses, arms and ammunition. By the end of the war, Jews were supplying armies on both sides of the conflict. The Jews in the West were the contractors and the financiers; the Jews of Poland, in the East, produced or delivered much of the wood, wheat and liquor for the soldiers. The Catholic Polish peasants, however, deeply resented the activities of the Jews. They were bitterly anti-Semitic and very poor. They had not benefited from the war. And the feudal system in Poland guaranteed that no matter how hard they worked, or how much money others earned, the peasants would not share in any of the profits.

In 1635, the peasants and Cossacks in the Ukraine revolted against their absentee Polish landlords. Landlords lived far away, but the Jews, who acted as their overseers and representatives, were nearby. Within a week, 2,000 Jews were killed by the Cossacks. Thousands of others fled from the Ukraine into Poland. The rebellion was put down, but the peasants' hatred simmered on. In 1648 a Greek Orthodox Cossack by the name of Bogdan Chmielnicki appeared. Strong and fearless, he hated both Catholics and Jews. Chmielnicki organized the Cossacks into a strong fighting force. He allied himself with the Asiatic Tatars from Crimea, and with widespread support from the peasants, he invaded Poland. Nuns and priests were tortured and beheaded and Polish noblemen were kidnaped and killed. But the Cossack's true fury was saved for the Jews. The Jews were almost destroyed.

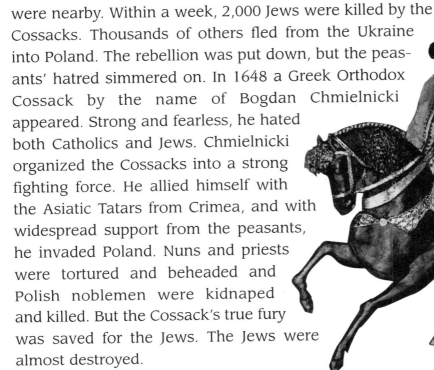

*Bogdan
Chmielnicki*

Between 1648 and 1653, nearly 100,000 Jews died by the sword and from the resulting chaos, sickness, famine and disease. Three hundred Polish-Jewish communities were destroyed. Even the thick-walled, fortress-like synagogues, fortified with cannons on the roofs, could not save the Jews from the hatred and fury of the Cossack mobs and their Polish neighbors.

Chmielnicki's massacres took place in the Hebrew years *Tach V'Tat* — 5408 and 5409 (corresponding to 1648 and 1649). Poles, Cossacks and Tatars — all were vicious in their treatment of the Jews, but the horrible cruelty of the Cossacks still burns in Jewish memory. Jews were skinned, ripped apart, burned and buried alive; children were tortured and killed; Torah scrolls were torn and made into boots. Jews gave themselves up to the Tatars who were more "merciful." Realizing that a live Jew was more valuable than a dead one (he would always be redeemed by his Jewish brethren), the Tatars did not kill their prisoners. Instead, they held them for ransom or sold

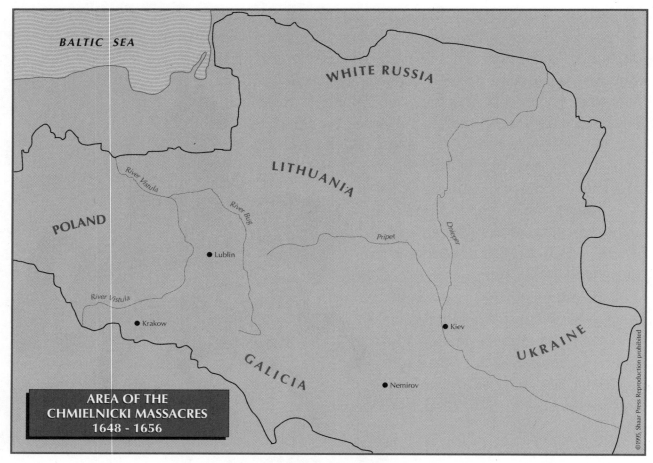

AREA OF THE CHMIELNICKI MASSACRES 1648 - 1656

them as slaves. Thousands of Polish Jews were eventually purchased and freed by Jewish communities in Italy, Morocco, Greece, Turkey and Palestine.

The Cossacks had originally offered to spare any Jew who would convert to Christianity. Out of hundreds of thousands of Polish Jews, only a tiny fraction agreed to convert. After one particular battle, the traitorous Polish nobles handed their Jewish allies over to the enemy Cossacks. Rather than accept baptism, all the Jews — a total of one hundred and fifty — went willingly to their deaths. The Cossacks, infuriated, went on yet another killing rampage. Realizing that forced conversions were worthless, the Polish king later allowed the surviving converts to return to Judaism.

During the Destruction of the Second Temple and the wars with the Romans, the Jews had been fierce fighters. Now, however, there was no chance to fight, no possibility of defending themselves, no hope of assistance. Yet the Jews did not surrender; they went to their death as brave martyrs. They believed that the suffering and death of the innocent and the righteous would atone for the sins of others and would be regarded as a merit for the Jewish people.

On the 20th of Sivan, 1649, 6,000 Jews were massacred in the city of Nemirov. The river outside Nemirov ran red with their blood. The Council of Four Lands proclaimed that date a public fast day. Meanwhile, the revolt continued amidst growing confusion as Cossacks and Tatars changed alliances, killing everyone at random. One thousand Jews were tortured and killed on the 4th of Tammuz; 10,000 on the 3rd of Av; 3,000 on Tisha B'Av; 4,000 on the 15th of Tishrei; and 12,000 on the 17th of Cheshvan. An epidemic of cholera swept through Poland, and in Cracow alone thousands of Jews perished. Jews fled en masse to Russia, Lithuania and Germany. One of Poland's largest yeshivos was disbanded in Lublin. Three hundred Jewish communities were destroyed and well over 100,000 Jews killed. Europe was swamped with Jewish refugees.

Chmielnicki continued his fight for Ukrainian independence. He turned to Russia and then to Sweden for help, but in 1657, after fifteen years of rebellion, he died. He had been responsible for hundreds of thousands of deaths and had achieved nothing. Today, a heroic statue stands in the Ukrainian city of Kiev commemorating the vicious butcher of *Tach V'Tat* as a national Ukrainian hero.

FINDING MEANING

Since 1492, the Jews of the world had tried to understand why the double catastrophe of the Inquisition and the Expulsion had befallen the Jews of Spain. Was it perhaps because they had studied science, medicine, music and philosophy? Was it because they had dressed and acted and lived like Spaniards? Perhaps they had not been observant enough, or had not learned enough Torah? Whatever the reason, Ashkenazic Jewry felt secure; surely their lifestyle was more in keeping with the law and spirit of the Torah.

Then the massacres of *Tach V'Tat* descended like bolts of lightning. There had not been such a mass slaughter of Jews since the

Jewish Quarter, Lublin

end of the Second Temple. What had Polish Jewry done to deserve such destruction? They had clung faithfully to the Torah; they dressed differently from the Poles; they spoke their own language; they studied only Torah, and they did so with love and devotion. What had they done wrong?

There was no answer except to accept God's will. After the Inquisition and Expulsion, Spanish Jews had turned to the Kabbalah in an effort to find comfort in their time of suffering. Now, too, Polish Jews despaired of finding solutions in the frightening and dangerous world they lived in. This could not possibly be the true world. The true world was a place of the spirit, a Godly place, full of love and mercy, truth, justice and righteousness. And so they, too, turned to the mystical world of Kabbalah, seeking answers to their questions and finding comfort in its teachings.

Even in the midst of the horrors of Chmielnicki, Torah was safeguarded. During the terrible years of *Tach V'Tat* when yeshivos and Jewish courts were closed and the study of Torah almost ground to a halt, the Shulchan Aruch, together with the comments of Rabbi Moshe Isserles of Cracow, guaranteed the observance of Jewish law. The invention of the printing press had brought the Shulchan Aruch into every Jewish household. It was almost as if each family had its own private rabbi. With the Shulchan Aruch in his possession, a Jew always knew what the Halachah required him to do.

Rabbi Yehoshua Heschel of Cracow was one of the leading rabbis in Poland in the 1660's. Two of his students, Rabbi David HaLevi (the Taz) and Rabbi Shabsai Cohen (the Shach), wrote additional notes on the Shulchan Aruch. Rabbi David fled from the Cossacks and lived out his life in dire poverty and with much suffering. Rabbi Shabsai left Poland and died a young man, far from home. The commentaries of the Taz and the Shach were written under terrible circumstances, yet they were so important that they became an inseparable part of the Shulchan Aruch.

3

The False Messiah — Shabtai Tzvi

(From 1650 to 1700)

After the Thirty Years War, Europe was in a state of chaos. Germany, Spain and the Catholic Church were in turmoil; England was in the midst of a civil war. New rulers vied for power all over the continent while the common people tried to reorganize their disrupted lives and recuperate from the terrible wounds of the war.

CHAOS The Jews had not yet forgotten the double nightmare of the Expulsion from Spain and the Inquisition which had destroyed so much of Jewish life one hundred and fifty years before. Now the monstrous massacres of *Tach V'Tat* further weighed them down. News of Chmielnicki had spread throughout Europe and to the Sefardic Jewish communities around the Mediterranean. Although far away from Poland, they too were filled with despair for their Jewish brethren.

Yet the Children of Abraham continued to believe. They were sure that God's help was forthcoming and they waited faithfully for it to appear. There were constant rumors and Kabbalistic calculations that great miracles would occur in the year 1648.

After the horrors of the Thirty Years War, Europe was full of wandering mystics — gentiles as well as Jews — who claimed to be prophets and holy men. Rumors of the Messiah were common. In 1655, the English Commonwealth considered readmitting the Jews to England in order to fulfill a Biblical prophecy and hasten the coming of the Messiah (see chapter on Menasseh ben Israel, Sand and Stars, Vol. I, p. 222). The stage was set for something out of the ordinary to happen.

SHABTAI TZVI

Shabtai Tzvi was born in Smyrna, Turkey in 1626. His father was a prosperous merchant from Greece, a descendant of Jewish exiles from Spain. Shabtai was a gifted, charismatic child. Highly intelligent, he had a photographic memory and he excelled in his studies. He was soon considered a scholar and a serious student of Kabbalah, and by the time he was twenty, he was ordained as a *chacham* (a Sefardic rabbi).

Shabtai Tzvi

Shabtai Tzvi's behavior, however, was often strange. In 1648, perhaps after hearing of the horrors of Chmielnicki, he began to have visions of himself as the savior of Israel. He married twice and immediately divorced both his wives. He fasted, lived alone for long periods, afflicted his body and meditated. He claimed to have fought wolves and serpents and to have been miraculously saved from death. Today we know that his behavior and visions were a clear sign of mental disease, but in his lifetime they were viewed by many as signs of holiness and proof of Divine prophecy.

In 1651, as a result of his odd behavior and his blatant disregard of Jewish law, the rabbis of Smyrna banished Shabtai from the community. He spent the next seven years wandering through Greece, Albania and Turkey. Although he was driven out of several communities because of his bizarre behavior and his violations of Halachah, his great charm and his impressive scholarship won him many friends and followers.

THE "MESSIAH"

Shabtai made his way to the Holy Land. In 1663 he met Nathan of Gaza. Nathan was known as a Talmudic scholar and a kabbalist. He had come to the conclusion that Shabtai Tzvi was the Messiah and that he, Nathan, was chosen to be Shabtai's prophet. The enthusiastic Nathan convinced Shabtai that the time had come to reveal himself to the Jewish people, and amidst great fervor and rejoicing, Shabtai Zvi was proclaimed the Messiah in Gaza. He entered Jerusalem in triumph, adopting the role of Jewish savior and king and promising the people that the long-awaited Redemption was now at hand.

Thanks to Nathan's many letters and pronouncements, stories of

Shabtai's supposed miracles and cures spread throughout the Jewish world. In less than two years, news of the "Messiah" had reached Europe, Asia, North Africa and the New World. The rabbis were powerless to subdue the masses of Jews who went wild with adoration and joy. Those living around the Mediterranean were first to accept Shabtai's leadership. In Greece, Italy, Syria, Egypt and Turkey, Jews began selling their homes and businesses in preparation for their trip to Eretz Yisrael. Next, Jews in Western Europe — including many wealthy Marrano communities in Amsterdam, Hamburg and Frankfurt am Main — were caught up in the Messianic fervor. Entire communities chartered boats and packed their possessions. Even

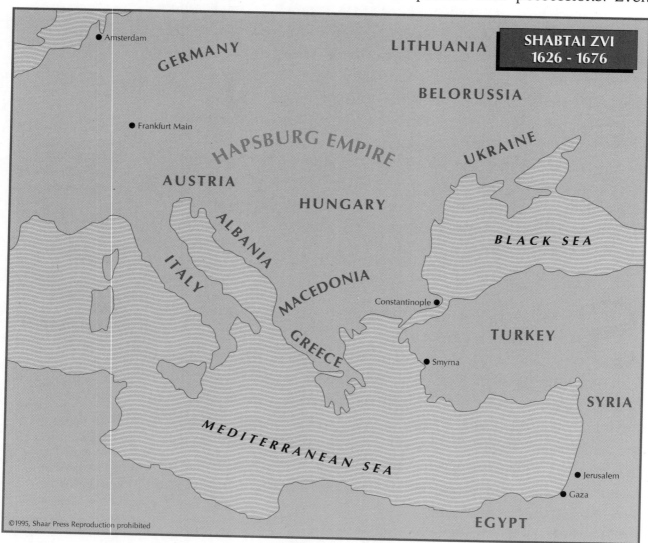

©1995, Shaar Press Reproduction prohibited

Jews in Russia and Poland fell victim to the fever. English ambassadors wrote home to describe the effect that the "Messiah" was having on the European economy. Jewish trading stopped, property values fell, and most of the Dutch fleet was monopolized by Jews waiting to sail to Palestine. All of Europe watched and waited.

Even many rabbis and scholars were swept along by the wave of enthusiasm and belief in Shabtai Tzvi. Those who tried to oppose him were shouted down and often threatened. Some rabbis felt that even if Shabtai were not the Messiah, he was nonetheless strengthening Jewish pride and stopping Jewish assimilation in a difficult and trying time.

One lone figure stood out from the rest. Rabbi Yaakov Sasportas of Amsterdam stubbornly fought the overwhelmingly popular belief in Shabtai Tzvi. He wrote letters to all the rabbis of Europe and warned the people of the tragedy they were preparing for themselves. Unfortunately, no one listened and Rabbi Sasportas was forced to leave Amsterdam.

Shabtai ruled like an emperor, holding court in Constantinople,

Shabtai Tzvi in prison

receiving visitors and gifts, and making promises. He abolished the fast days of the Ninth of Av and the Seventeenth of Tammuz. He permitted various forbidden activities — including the eating of non-kosher foods — with a new blessing, "Who has permitted that which was previously forbidden." At that point, all of the rabbis protested, for even the Messiah has no right to change the laws of the Torah. But it was too late to stem the tide of belief and enthusiasm.

The Sultan, however, did what the rabbis could not do. When Shabtai announced that he would march on Jerusalem and liberate the Holy City, the Sultan of Turkey decided that events had gone far enough. Shabtai was placed under house arrest. He still enjoyed a large measure of freedom, dressing like an emperor and receiving guests and gifts, but in 1666 his story drew to its bitter end. The Sultan, worried perhaps about the possibility of Jewish revolt, offered Shabtai the choice of conversion to Islam or death. To the shock and horror of the entire Jewish world, the supposed Jewish Messiah converted to Islam. He took the name Aziz Mehmed Effendi and was made an officer at the Sultan's court.

SHOCK AND SHAME

The hoax was over, but the trauma, the shock and the shame were just beginning. For another ten years, great numbers of Jews continued to hope that Shabtai Tzvi was deceiving the Turks. But they were the ones who had been deceived. Now they were frightened and ashamed. For many, their homes and businesses were gone; for many more, their hearts were broken and their faith badly shaken. How could God have let such a thing happen? The people had believed so ardently! How could they ever trust themselves to believe in Mashiach again? Even their rabbis and teachers had been fooled. How many disappointments could the Jewish nation endure? Would the Redeemer of *Am Yisrael* never come? Never again would the Jewish people hurry to accept someone as the Messiah. The real Messiah would have to prove himself beyond all doubt before he could open the doors to Jewish hearts.

Loss of innocence was not the only result of the Shabtai Tzvi episode. There was a feeling that the Jews must get on with their lives, leaving Redemption and the Messiah, mystical calculations and Kabbalah aside. Most turned with renewed vigor towards the time-tested study of Talmud and Halachah (Jewish law) to safeguard them. Some followed different paths which would eventually lead them away from Torah. Still others would seek Jewish redemption by redeeming the Land of Israel.

Shabtai Tzvi had swept through the Jewish world in a few short years, but the shock waves he set in motion would continue to reverberate for generations to come.

4
Guarding The Future
(From 1650 to 1800)

*I*n their desire to protect the Jews from further damage, the rabbis found themselves in a difficult position. Belief in Shabtai Tzvi had spread all through Europe and the Middle East. Even after his death, this false Messiah remained a great source of danger. New "messiahs" appeared and disappeared, each concocting strange, new practices and beliefs which further confused the people.

HERESIES

As a result of so much suffering, many Jews became easy prey for these impostors, their miracles and magic. The Marrano Jews seemed particularly naive and vulnerable. Heresy was therefore considered a very real danger and the rabbis felt they had to be constantly on guard. Every new idea or custom was carefully examined. Belief in the false messiahs had to be wiped out, once and for all. Unfortunately, in the process many good, pious and innocent men were also suspected and accused of wrongdoing.

THE YAVETZ (RABBI YAAKOV EMDEN)

*Rabbi Tzvi Ashkenazi —
The Chacham Tzvi*

*R*abbi Tzvi Ashkenazi of Amsterdam (the Chacham Tzvi) and his son Rabbi Yaakov ben Tzvi of Emden (the Yavetz) were two of the most dedicated and zealous Torah guardians of their time. The Chacham Tzvi had bravely stood his ground against the Sabbateans (the followers of Shabtai Tzvi), and his son, the Yavetz, followed faithfully in his footsteps.

The Yavetz lived in A'HU, the great Jewish community composed of the three cities of Altona, Hamburg and Wandsbeck on the border between northern Germany and Denmark. He was a recognized scholar and the author of many books. Although he was also a student of Kabbalah, he firmly believed that Kabbalah should only be studied privately and by mature scholars. Quick of temper, fearless and thorough, the Yavetz was a formidable foe. He was determined to stamp out any lingering traces of Shabtai Tzvi. In order to do so, he was convinced that the use of Kabbalah to perform mystical ceremonies and rituals must be stopped. In a sad twist of events, one of his first battles was against a holy scholar — the Ramchal.

Rabbi Moshe Chaim Luzzato — the Ramchal — was a quiet, serious, young scholar from Padua, Italy. His wide knowledge of Torah had earned him students and followers while he was still an adolescent. But the Ramchal was a nonconformist who dressed differently from other scholars and who studied and practiced Kabbalah despite the fact that the rabbis did not approve. By the time he was twenty, he revealed that he communicated with a spirit from Heaven who taught him mystical secrets. In those anti-mystical times after Shabtai Tzvi, such a declaration was sure to make the Ramchal an object of immediate suspicion.

As word of his teachings began to reach other countries, his books were banned in Italy. Eventually, he was forced to leave. He went to Frankfurt but the rabbis of Germany, Holland, Denmark and Poland insisted that he stop teaching Kabbalah. He then moved to Amsterdam where he earned his living as a lens grinder and diamond polisher.

When he was attacked by the Yavetz for his continued study and practice of Kabbalah, the Ramchal did not defend himself. He chose instead to remain silent and faithful to his own inner truths. In 1743 he moved with his family to the Land of Israel. Three years later, at the age of forty, he died in a plague. He was buried next to the grave of the famous *tanna* Rabbi Akiva, on a hill outside the city of Tiberias.

Despite a difficult life filled with much humiliation, the Ramchal earned an eternal place in Jewish history. He wrote books on Hebrew grammar, poetry, Kabbalah and philosophy. All that he wrote was deep, honest and fresh. Even his language was different. The Hebrew was beautiful, simple and clear, and it was full of new words and modern concepts. The great Gaon of Vilna said that if the Ramchal were still alive, he, the Gaon, would have traveled to learn from him.

The Ramchal's three best known books — *Mesillas Yesharim* (The Path of the Righteous), *Daas Tevunos* (The Knowing Heart) and

Derech Hashem (The Way of God) — have become Torah classics. *Mesillas Yesharim* defined the course of study for the ethical Mussar movement in the 1850's. All three books are studied wherever Jews search for a way to come closer to God.

RABBI YONASAN EYBESCHITZ

Rabbi Yonasan Eybeschitz was Chief Rabbi of Prague (in Bohemia). One of the leading rabbinic personalities of his time, he wrote important commentaries on the Talmud and Jewish law. In 1740 he became rabbi of A'HU.

Rabbi Yonasan was world famous for his wisdom. He was also a practicing kabbalist who distributed amulets (a parchment with kabbalistic blessings; amulets are often worn to bring blessing or to protect against injury or evil) which were in great demand. Convinced that Rabbi Yonasan's amulets contained references to Shabtai Tzvi, the Yavetz called for a ban against Rabbi Yonasan. Rabbis were asked for their support; their response was divided. The Gaon of Vilna defended Rabbi Yonasan, but other rabbis sided with the Yavetz. The Emperor of Denmark became involved (A'HU was then under Danish control). He decided in favor of the Yavetz and he removed Rabbi Yonasan from his rabbinical post in A'HU. Then the matter was appealed and the Emperor changed his mind. From 1751 until 1756 a bitter battle raged throughout the entire European Jewish community, splitting it into two camps — those who sided with Rabbi Yonasan and those who supported the Yavetz.

It is difficult for us today to understand how two such great men, each a tower of Torah scholarship and an important leader, became involved in such a fiery dispute. Each tried, in his own way, to protect the Jewish people from danger, but their points of view were so far apart that they were unable to work together for a compromise.

Rabbi Yonasan died in 1764. The Yavetz died in 1776, on a Friday. In the rush to complete the funeral before Shabbos, he was buried in an already opened grave which happened to be close to the grave of Rabbi Yonasan. The two Torah champions who did such furious battle during their lives came together, at last, in death.

W hile Shabtai Tzvi was wandering through Asia Minor and developing his delusion of grandeur, a different type of heresy was developing in the midst of Western Europe.

A large Sefardic population lived in the Dutch city of Amsterdam. Spanish exiles and Marrano Jews had turned the little city into a great trading center, the crown of the Dutch Empire. Amsterdam was also a hub of messianic hopes and intriguing, new ideas, many of which flew in the face of Jewish tradition.

Baruch Spinoza was born in Amsterdam of Spanish Jewish parents. He received a traditional Jewish education but rebelled against many central Jewish beliefs. He did not believe the Torah was given by God; he wrote that the Bible should be analyzed and dealt with just like any ordinary piece of literature. Furthermore, he said, God was just another name for the forces of nature. When Spinoza published his works, his books were banned both by Jewish and Christian authorities. Nonetheless, Spinoza's philosophy became popular in the Western world. It fit in well with the growing Western belief in scientific inquiry and rationalism, the idea that through careful reasoning man could eventually understand all the mysteries of the world.

BARUCH SPINOZA

Baruch Spinoza

Shabbos in a 17th century Dutch home

Spinoza's philosophy was popular among many people, but it was not Judaism. In 1656 he was officially excommunicated from the Jewish people and his name was struck out of the register in the Portuguese synagogue in Amsterdam. He gained a reputation as a famous philosopher, but lost his place among Am Yisrael.

JACOB FRANK

The last pages in the unbelievable story of Shabtai Tzvi tell the story of a Polish Jew by the name of Jacob Frank. While traveling in the Middle East, Frank somehow decided that he was a rebirth of Shabtai Tzvi. He gathered a group of followers who proceeded to desecrate the entire Torah. When the rabbis of Poland excommunicated them, the Frankists turned to the Catholic Church for help. In 1757, the Church forced the rabbis to debate the Frankists. As a result of the debate, many copies of the Talmud were publicly burned. The Frankists' behavior shocked the Jews, and the involvement of the Church put them in great danger. The Church later forced the Frankists to convert, and the movement faded away. This was the closing chapter of a sorrowful era of dire poverty and severe persecution, dashed hopes and dreadful internal dissension. It left the Jews poorly prepared to deal with the challenges they would soon face as they entered the modern world.

GLUCKEL OF HAMELN

Gluckel of Hameln

History tells about rulers and kings, but it is always difficult to imagine what daily life must have been like long ago. Fortunately, a wonderful description of seventeenth century Jewish life in Western Europe has survived in a colorful, detailed diary written by Gluckel of Hameln (1645-1724). Gluckel was the wife of a wealthy merchant in A'HU, the mother of twelve children, and a businesswoman who worked at her husband's side. She traveled to the great spring and autumn fairs where she sold jewels and other wares. At the age of forty-six, after her husband's death, she wrote her memoirs. Copies of her manuscript were passed down in the family by her descendants.

Gluckel wrote in an old form of Yiddish. Her diary describes everyday life, the social events in her family and community, the fire in her synagogue on Shavuos, the careful matchmaking and marriages of her children (all of whom were married to well-known families across Europe). She explains the complications of being Jewish in Hamburg, Altona, Hameln, Hanover, Berlin and Amsterdam. She tells how the Jews helped the Polish refugees who poured into A'HU after Chmielnicki's massacres, and she informs us how the community reacted to news of Shabtai Tzvi. She draws a vivid picture of the lives of 17th century Jews. Harassed by hundreds of anti-Jewish laws, taxed for every conceivable activity (crossing borders, entering and leaving towns, sleeping away from home, selling at the fairs, dealing in business, renting a house), she nevertheless captures the faith and joy which gave the Jews the strength to go on.

Gluckel was blessed with a sharp memory, a good education and a wonderful ability to tell a story. A deeply pious woman, she was well versed in Jewish tradition and in the popular Yiddish books of her times. Her diary is full of parables and stories from the Midrash as well as faith in God and His Torah. She is constantly concerned about her children — their education, their marriages, their livelihood — and about her husband's study of Torah. She prayed desperately for the coming of the Mashiach and a return to Eretz Yisrael. She is the eternal *Eshes Chayil* and Jewish mother, and she makes A'HU of the 1700's as real as Jerusalem or New York of today.

SECTION II

Winds of Change
(From 1700 to 1900)

5
Emancipation and Enlightenment
(From 1700 to 1800)

*T*he 18th century marks the beginning of modern Jewish history. For the first time, the Jews entered the stream of Western civilization as citizens of equal standing who possessed full rights and freedoms guaranteed and protected by the law. The results were often disastrous to Jewish life. The rapid complex changes of the eighteenth and nineteenth centuries cannot be told in a smooth, flowing story. Too much happened all at once. We will try, therefore, to describe the important ideas and events one by one, and to travel from country to country to see how they affected the Jews in the East and in the West.

THE HUMANIST ENLIGHTEN- MENT

*A*s the 18th century dawned, Christianity still ruled the hearts of men, but the Church no longer commanded kings and nations. While society searched for new answers to old problems, a movement called the Enlightenment spread throughout Europe and America. The Enlightenment was based on an older Renaissance idea called Humanism which was, in turn, based on very old, pre-Christian ideas from Classical Greece and Rome. Humanism and the Enlightenment declared that Man does not need God. In the Humanist

Printing press, Holland, 1828

TWO CENTURIES OF CHANGE & RESPONSE

FROM 1700-1850

- Humanism and the Enlightenment
- Equality and Civil Rights for All
- The Reform Movement and Assimilation in Western Europe
- The Orthodox Response to Reform in the West
- The Rise of Chassidus in the East
- The Opposition to Chassidus

FROM 1850-1900

- The Yeshivah Movement
- The Industrial Revolution, Capitalism and Urbanization
- The Haskalah and Secularization
- The Mussar Movement
- The Return to Eretz Yisrael
- The Development of Political Zionism
- Emigration to the New World

dream, reason, not religion, was the sole source of human knowledge and good. Logical reasoning would lead humanity to scientific knowledge, to progress, to justice and to world peace. Reason would solve all of Man's problems. In the Humanist dream, Man was king and Reason was his crown.

O ne of the most dramatic turning points in history was undoubtedly the discovery of the New World. When Christopher Columbus landed on the shores of the Americas, he turned a new page in the story of civilization. The New World meant new hopes, new ideas, new possibilities. It signaled the end of medieval serfdom, the Divine rights of kings, the unchal-

THE INFLUENCE OF THE NEW WORLD

New Sefardic Synagogue, Amsterdam

lenged rule of the Church. It would also hasten the collapse of the Jewish ghetto and promote Jewish assimilation and reform.

The earliest Jewish immigrants to the New World were, by and large, Sefardim of Spanish or Portuese origin. Many were Marranos who returned to their Judaism as soon as they had escaped the long arm of the Spanish Inquisition. But the Ashkenazi Jews of Europe, whether they were living in the wretched ghettos of Eastern Poland and Russia, or in the more liberal Western cities of London and Amsterdam, followed the exploits of their Jewish brethren in the Americas. Jewish interest and imagination were captivated by stories of the unbelievable New World where Jews could live as free and equal citizens.

Although America had been founded by people seeking freedom from religious domination, settlers found both freedom *of* and freedom *from* religion. Many of the Founding Fathers — Benjamin Franklin, Thomas Jefferson, Thomas Paine and others — were Humanists who did not believe in the traditional ideas of God and the Church; they viewed religion as the enemy of progress. In America, a man could choose to live without God, and Jews, if they wished, could choose to live without Torah.

M ost of the confusing wars and politics in the 1700's revolved around two main struggles. In Eastern Europe, Prussia, Russia and Austria rose to power while Sweden, Poland and Turkey declined. Poland was conquered, divided up and wiped off the map; Russia took the largest slice. She also took the rich Crimea from Turkey.

THE BALANCE OF POWER IN EUROPE

In Western Europe, France and England struggled for control of colonial empires in India and North America. England would eventually win control of North America, but Napoleon Bonaparte would make France a great European empire.

T he Hohenzollern dynasty had turned Prussia, a small territory around the city of Berlin, into a strong German empire. Frederick the Great, grandson of the founder, was an educated, liberal leader. Anxious to improve German society according to Enlightenment ideas, he decided to experiment with Jewish emancipation. Of all the people in his empire, the Jews were the most problematic and the least productive.

PRUSSIA AND FREDERICK THE GREAT

The "problems" were the result of Germany's laws. All the old medieval laws were still in force. Jews were not permitted to work in most professions; they could not marry before they were twenty-five; they were not permitted to own their homes. They were limited in travel and forced to pay a special "body-tax." Viewed by the population as suspicious and dangerous, they were barely protected by the government. Frederick granted certain new rights and canceled some of the old laws. He permitted the Jews to study in the universities and to earn their livelihood in a variety of professions.

Frederick's Edicts of Toleration had a far-reaching effect upon German Jewry, allowing them, for the first time, to enter the mainstream of German society. Eventually, they would invent a new form of "enlightened" Judaism which would, in turn, lead to mass assimilation and conversion of German Jews. Frederick's plan to "modernize" the Jews succeeded beyond his wildest dreams. It is indeed ironic that of all the countries in Europe, Germany — home of the Nazis — was the first to grant modern rights and freedom to its Jews.

NAPOLEON AND THE ENLIGHTENMENT

Napoleon

At the end of the 18th century, the French Revolution burst onto the European stage with promises of liberty, equality and fraternity for all men. But the promises quickly degenerated into a reign of terror, chaos and destruction. Then Napoleon Bonaparte rose to power. He brought law, liberty and order to France and began to build a mighty French empire. His armies reached as far eastward as the Holy Land. Wherever Napoleon went, the Jews were granted civil rights and the walls of the ghetto were torn down. French Jewry, drunk with their newfound freedoms, rushed to assimilate into French society. The gentile citizens of France, Prussia, Austria and other countries were not happy with the Jewish advances; centuries of anti-Semitism could not be erased by signing new laws. But the Jews marched naively forward into the Age of Emancipation and Enlightenment.

NAPOLEON'S SANHEDRIN

Napoleon turned his attention to the Jews. In 1807 he convened a Great Sanhedrin. He invited seventy-one rabbis, leaders and laymen (Orthodox and Reform) to participate. He hoped to finally solve the Jewish "problem" through rational planning. Equal rights and new opportunities would turn the Jews of the Empire into loyal, modern citizens; assimilation, intermarriage and conversion would do the rest. He gave the Sanhedrin a list of twelve questions defining "correct" Jewish belief and behavior. It was understood that the answers must be acceptable to Napoleon.

The questions were highly sensitive. Are non-Jewish Frenchmen

Napoleon's Sanhedrin

considered brethren or strangers? Is a Jewish divorce valid since French law does not recognize divorce? The questions dealt with the basic question of whether Jews are bound to obey civil or religious law in matters of marriage and divorce, financial dealings, civic responsibility, and relationships with non-Jews. Under the leadership of the great scholar Rabbi David Sinzheim, the Sanhedrin carefully formulated nine general answers which would satisfy Napoleon without negating Halachah. Napoleon accepted the answers and made them legally binding. He hoped they would enable the Jews in France to become, at long last, "normal," upstanding, assimilated French citizens.

The Sanhedrin was a major, impressive, historic event. It captured the interest of the entire world. The ceremonies were regal and elaborate. Participants were dressed in judges' robes; proceedings were conducted in Hebrew; participants' expenses were paid. Jews in every country followed the deliberations carefully. Traditional Jews were

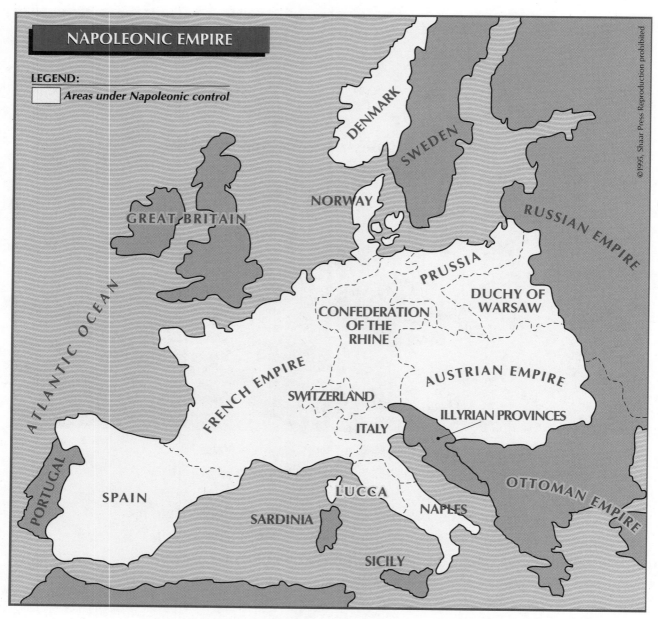

NAPOLEONIC EMPIRE

LEGEND:
☐ *Areas under Napoleonic control*

fearful and troubled. How could one trust a gentile king? Who knew what the outcome of Napoleon's plans would be? Reform Jews were ecstatic, positive that Jewish redemption was on its way. Non-Jews viewed the proceedings with suspicion. They were convinced that Napoleon's interest in the Jews was proof of the great power and influence Jews wielded.

Napoleon's grand scheme for the Jewish people did not produce any changes in the Jewish religion, but the mere fact that a

"Sanhedrin" had met had a great effect on the Jewish world. Many viewed it as a royal invitation, welcoming Jews to the secular world. French Jewry was ecstatic. Other communities were less enthusiastic, realizing that this was merely a political maneuver.

In 1799 Napoleon invaded Palestine, then under Turkish rule. The Jews of the Holy Land were united in their opposition to him. His siege of the port city of Acre was unsuccessful and he was forced to retreat from the Middle East. Then, in 1812, he marched on Russia with an army of half a million soldiers. Many Jews in Russia, especially among the Chassidim, opposed him. The Czar was a rabid anti-Semite and a vicious dictator, but many rabbis feared that Napoleon's liberal rule posed an even greater threat to Jewish existence than the physical cruelty of the Czar.

The French army brought the beginnings of modernity and enlightenment into backward Russia. Although forced to retreat, the French left their language and culture behind. French influence on Russian society was strong; it affected the Jews as well as the Russian gentiles. French ideas would later surface in the Haskalah — the Jewish Enlightenment movement — and would leave their mark on East European Jewry.

For all his liberal, enlightened intentions, Napoleon dealt a blow to the traditional world of Torah. He represented another attempt to make Judaism and Jews more acceptable to the gentile world. Western Humanism and Enlightenment were locked in a great battle against the traditional Torah way of life.

Bronze medallions commemorating Napoleon's Sanhedrin

NAPOLEON BONAPARTE	
1789	French Revolution
1799	Napoleon Comes to Power
1804-1814	Napoleonic Empire
1807	The Sanhedrin
1812	Invasion of Russia
1815	Battle of Waterloo and Napoleon's Abdication

6

The Challenge of Reform

(From 1750 to 1850)

MOSES MENDELSSOHN — FATHER OF REFORM

Moses Mendelssohn

One of the first Jews to benefit from Frederick's liberal, new edicts in Prussia was Moses Mendelssohn. Born Moses ben Menachem Mendel, he was a wonder child, highly intelligent and diligent in his studies. He received a good, traditional education in Talmud and the Bible and at the age of fourteen went to Berlin to begin his secular education.

Mendelssohn worked as a bookkeeper, a tutor and a silk merchant, but he was not destined to be a businessman. He wrote scholarly works of philosophy in beautiful, classical German and won a distinguished prize. He became one of the most honored and famous men in Germany. Mendelssohn was often invited to the king's court where he was easily recognized by his hunched back and his long Jewish nose. But even his Jewish appearance did not lower his status. He was the first German Jew to attain such imperial honor and enjoy such high privileges.

Mendelssohn was a Jewish activist. He corresponded with many rabbis. He translated the Bible into such poetic and powerful German that his translation was considered superior to that of Martin Luther. Mendelssohn also wrote a German commentary on the Bible. He fought for Jewish equality and civil rights as part of the reforms of the Emancipation. He considered himself a defender of Torah and the Jewish people.

But despite all of his good intentions, Mendelssohn's ideas were faulty. They seemed to imply that the detailed laws of the Torah were no longer necessary, that in a time of Enlightenment, when all men were supposedly searching for truth and justice, perhaps it was enough to be guided by the great moral truths and the lofty ideas the Torah contains, but not by its commandments.

In his eager desire for equality, Mendelssohn felt that Western culture and the Enlightenment would improve Judaism and the Jews.

He wanted the approval of the gentile world, believing that one should be a German — like everyone else — in public, and a Jew in the privacy of one's home. History would prove that such a division was impossible. When the rabbis objected to his ideas, Mendelssohn refused to listen.

Although he himself remained an observant Jew throughout his life, Mendelssohn's ideas helped pave the way for the development of Reform Judaism. Halachah was left behind as Mendelssohn's fine-sounding philosophy opened the gates to widespread assimilation and intermarriage. Most of Mendelssohn's own children and grandchildren converted to Christianity.

After Mendelssohn's death, Reform leaders continued to adjust Judaism to conform to the gentile world. The first Reform temple was opened in Germany in 1820. The reform rabbis declared: This city is our Jerusalem and this synagogue is our Temple. It included an organ, a mixed choir, German sermons and songs, prayers and robes. And it had separate seating for men and women since the churches of the time also had separate seating! Reform continued to grow, and despite great rabbinical opposition, it gained control over most of the Jewish communities in Germany.

THE REFORM MOVEMENT

Reform leaders argued against accepting the Talmud, circumcision, covering one's head during prayers, wearing a tallis, blowing the shofar, using Hebrew, believing in a Messiah, the return to the Land of Israel and even keeping Saturday as the Sabbath. The moving spirit of Reform was not religious, but secular. It wished to make Judaism more acceptable in the eyes of society, not in the eyes of God.

In its early stages, Reform swept through German Jewry. But as time went on, realizing how cut off they were from the rest of the Jewish people, Reform leaders retreated from their extreme, anti-Jewish positions on many of the issues mentioned above. They attempted to regain some of the color and flavor — if not the essence — of a more traditional Judaism.

In 1819 a group of German Jews organized a movement called the Science of Judaism. They set up a society whose aim was to investigate the nature of Judaism by modern scientific methods and to show the universal value of Jewish knowledge. It was neither religion nor science and it faded away. Unfortunately, the religious ties of many of the Jews who had participated in the project faded away as well.

Reform never represented the majority of Jews in the world; it was never mainstream Jewish history; it never made the Jews welcome in gentile society. It served mainly as a road towards assimilation and conversion. One hundred years later, Germany, the home of liberal freedom and of Jewish Reform, would go to insane lengths to identify the descendants of Jewish converts and return them to the ranks of their fellow Jews. Traditional Jews, assimilated Jews and converts to Christianity would all march to the Nazi gas chambers together. Reform had not provided the answer to Jewish suffering.

JEWISH APOSTATES

In the 1780's, Frederick's Edicts of Toleration were decreed in Prussia, the Austro-Hungarian Empire and even in Italy and the Papal States. These liberal laws removed many restrictions on Jews and allowed them to attend the universities and work in more occupations and professions. It was hoped that these new rights would "improve and civilize" the Jews and turn them into "normal, productive citizens."

But the greatest freedoms of all were introduced by the French Revolution. Although the French, like the Germans, enjoyed a long history of anti-Semitism, there seemed to be no legal way of denying the Jews the "Liberty, Equality and Fraternity" which the Revolution was supposed to bring to all men.

These new freedoms exerted a tremendous pull on Jews to enter the newly opened doors to the non-Jewish world. Many people, anxious to take advantage of the new opportunities, came too feel that Judaism was a great hindrance. The rabbinate and the Jewish community were unable to overcome the challenge of freedom and equality. Jews began to convert in ever increasing numbers. It is estimated that perhaps 250,000 Jews converted to Christianity in the nineteenth century in Central Europe alone. It was the highest number of Jewish conversions since the days of the Spanish Inquisition.

These apostates did not necessarily view Christianity as the true religion; in fact, many of them did not view it as a religion at all. For them, it was a ticket to success, a way of gaining membership in the international club of Western civilization. The German poet Heinrich Heine called his baptism an "entrance ticket to European society."

Heinrich Heine

Many of the converts were brilliant men who attained great fame and made important contributions to Western civilization. Unfortunately, many of them also suffered from severe pangs of guilt and self-hatred. They found no respite from their Jewishness, even after their baptism. Benjamin Disraeli, the great British Prime Minister whose father had converted to Christianity, was an unusual exception. As the child of a Christian mother, he himself was Christian, but he was proud of his Jewish ancestry and believed that the Jews were a unique and valuable nation. He remained a warm and loyal friend of the Jews and he helped to create a positive environment for them to live in.

Benjamin Disraeli

7
Fortifying the Old
(From 1750 to 1900)

When large numbers of Western European Jews left the ghetto, they also left traditional Jewish life behind. Orthodox Jewry in Western Europe was unprepared and overwhelmed by the unexpected success of the Reform movement — first in Germany and then in France. The Reform movement denied the Divine origin of the Torah and commandments. By 1850 Reform had spread to other communities in Western and Central Europe. German law required that the Jews in each town or city belong to the single, central Jewish communal body and pay communal taxes. In most German cities, this central body was affiliated with the Reform movement. This meant that Orthodox Jews were forced to be a part of and pay taxes to a leadership that was opposed to its beliefs. It took time until the Orthodox rabbis and leaders in the West found ways of dealing with this new challenge to Torah.

THE CHALLENGE FROM THE WEST

Rabbi Isaac (Seligman Baer) Bamberger, the Rav of Wurzburg, (a city in Bavaria, Germany), was a recognized scholar and author. Although he never attended university, he acquired a broad secular education. He formed a strong traditional community in Wurzburg with a large synagogue, a yeshivah, a rabbinical training program and a Jewish school system. The congregation was open to everyone, traditional or not. Rabbi Bamberger attempted to influence through education, not force. Although he opposed Reform control of communities, whenever the Reform leaders were willing to accommodate and work with the Orthodox members and accept their authority, he was willing to work together with them.

RABBI ISAAC BAMBERGER — GERMAN ORTHODOX LEADER

RABBI
SAMSON
RAPHAEL
HIRSCH —
TORAH IM
DERECH
ERETZ

Rabbi Samson Raphael Hirsch, another major leader of German Orthodoxy, refused to work — or even associate — with the Reform movement. Insisting that Orthodox Jews could not in good conscience be represented by people who did not believe in the Torah, Rabbi Hirsch insisted on *Ausstritt*, or secession from non-Orthodox communities. He began a movement called *Torah im Derech Eretz* — "Torah combined with the ways of the world." He resigned as the Chief Rabbi of Moravia and as a member of the Austro-Hungarian Parliament and became, instead, the rabbi to a small group of Orthodox families in Frankfurt am Main, in Germany. Although the government recognized the Frankfurt Reform community as the representative of all Jews, Rabbi Hirsch fought for and eventually won the legal right to organize an independent *kehillah* (community), Khal Adath Jeshurun. He established an elementary and high school where thorough religious training was combined with secular studies.

Rabbi Hirsch borrowed the outer, Western, cultural veneer of German society — education, style of dress, manners, language — but shaped them into an integral part of Orthodox Judaism. His students went on to study in German universities. They dressed, studied, looked like everyone else, but they were loyal, observant, uncompromising Torah Jews.

Rabbi Samson Raphael Hirsch

In Rabbi Hirsch's view, Western culture was the "handmaiden" of the Torah; it was only a means to an end. The end was to live a full Torah life, based on Torah values, and uncompromising observance of all the commandments, while utilizing the tools of contemporary culture. His system put the Torah first. It decreed "Torah *im* Derech Eretz — Torah *with* the ways of the world." The Torah — not the ways of the world — was the essence of Jewish life.

Khal Adath Jeshurun became one of the leading Jewish congregations in Europe. Rabbi Hirsch's successful blend of Torah and *derech eretz* has proved to be a strong, healthy model even in our own times. His popular book, *The Nineteen Letters of Ben Uziel*, answered basic questions about Judaism. He wrote *Horeb*, as exposition on the 613 mitzvos, as well as extensive commentaries on the Bible, the Psalms and the prayer book, and many articles and letters. All were written in perfect, elegant German and they provided relevant answers to timeless Jewish questions.

RABBI MOSES SCHREIBER SOFER — THE CHASAM SOFER

Rabbi Moses Schreiber-Sofer was born and raised in the German city, Frankfurt am Main. He was a child genius who studied Torah under great scholars and later became familiar with anatomy, astronomy, biology, botany, mathematics and history. He was known as the *Chasam Sofer* — the name he gave to his written works and rabbinic responsa.

The Chasam Sofer watched as Reform began to invade the Jewish communities in the Austrian-Hapsburg Empire. He understood clearly the dangers posed by the new freedoms of Enlightenment and Emancipation. When he was offered the position of rabbi in the imperial city of Pressburg (today called Bratislavia, in Slovakia), he accepted the challenge.

The great yeshivah he built in Pressburg became the main bastion of Orthodoxy in Central Europe for the next hundred years. His disciples became the rabbis and communal leaders of Austria, Rumania and Hungary. His motto against Reform was *Chadash asur min haTorah* — anything "new" is forbidden by the Torah. By this the Chasam Sofer meant anything new which was not sanctioned by the rabbis and Jewish tradition. His yeshivah in Pressburg was considered a modern institution, with an ordered curriculum of study, regular examinations, training in public speaking, and communal projects. But the studies, the spirit, and the governing laws were as old as Sinai itself.

The Chasam Sofer believed in complete separation from Reform. He used his influence at the Hapsburg court and opposed granting

The Chasam Sofer

The Pressburg Shul, destroyed by the Nazis during World War II

the Reform communities any further rights or recognition. He exposed Aron Horin, the influential leader of Reform in Austro-Hungary, as being completely unlearned in Jewish law. (Horin's own children converted to Christianity.) The Chasam Sofer's strict standards of loyalty to Torah strengthened European Jewry and kept Reform from advancing in Austro-Hungary for the next hundred years.

LEADING TORAH SCHOLARS
OF THE 18TH AND 19TH CENTURIES

	Died
Rabbi Chaim ibn Attar (*Or HaChayim*)	1743
Rabbi Moshe Chaim Luzzato (*Ramchal*)	1747
Rabbi Yehoshua Falk (*Pnei Yehoshua*)	1756
Baal Shem Tov	1760
Rabbi Yonasan Eybeschitz	1764
Rabbi Yaakov Emden (*Yavetz*)	1776
Rabbi Aryeh Leib Gunzberg (*Sha'agas Aryeh*)	1785
Rabbi Yosef Teomim (*Pri Megadim*)	1792
Rabbi Yechezkel Landau (*Noda B'Yehudah*)	1793
Rabbi Eliyahu of Vilna (*Vilna Gaon*)	1797
Rabbi Pinchas Horowitz	1805
Rabbi Chaim Yosef David Azulai (*Chida*)	1806
Rabbi Levi Yitzchak of Berditchev	1810
Rabbi Aryeh Leib HaCohen Heller	1813
Rabbi Yaakov Yitzchak Horowitz (*Chozeh of Lublin*)	1815
Rabbi Chaim of Volozhin	1821
Rabbi Akiva Eiger	1837
Rabbi Moses Schreiber-Sofer (*Chasam Sofer*)	1839
Rabbi Moshe Teitelbaum (*Yismach Moshe*)	1841
Rabbi Yisrael of Rozhin	1850
Rabbi Mendel of Kotzk	1859
Rabbi Yitzchak Meir Alter (*Chidushei HaRim* of Ger)	1866
Rabbi Samson Raphael Hirsch	1888
Rabbi Yisrael Salanter	1883

Pogroms, false messiahs, Reform and Enlightenment took a terrible toll in the seventeenth, eighteenth and nineteenth centuries. Yet, incredibly, it was at the same time a golden age of Torah scholarship. Many of the scholars did not leave written works; others left only unpublished manuscripts (many of which were destroyed during the Holocaust). But even the incomplete list of Torah works which have survived is very impressive. Sefardic as well as Ashkenazic rabbis contributed to the growing wealth of Torah knowledge. Except for the period of Rashi and the Tosafists in the eleventh and twelfth centuries, the amount of Torah scholarship produced during these three hundred years was almost unmatched in Jewish history. As always, it was the Torah which guaranteed the continued survival of the Jewish people. As always, the study of Torah did not cease, even when times were difficult.

It is impossible to list all of the hundreds of great scholars of the 18th and 19th centuries, but the chart on the opposite page contains some of the most famous and outstanding.

THE STUDY OF TORAH

8

Rothschild and Montefiore — Heroes of the Age

(From 1750 - 1900)

THE HOUSE OF ROTHSCHILD

The Jew of the New Era was personified by the House of Rothschild. The name "Rothschild" came from the identifying sign of a "red shield" which hung on the family home in Frankfurt am Main. It came to signify boundless wealth, worldwide power and the epitome of success.

Mayer Amschel Rothschild, founder of the House of Rothschild, was an observant Jew who had studied for the rabbinate. He went, however, into banking, becoming a financial agent for the German royal court. His success, his fortune, and his reputation grew.

Mayer had five sons. Each was sent to a different city to direct the family's financial dealings — Salomon to Vienna, Nathan to London, Amschel to Frankfurt, Karl to Naples and Jacob to Paris. The era of international private banking was born.

The Rothschilds lent money to all of the armies in the Napoleonic wars. They advanced the funds for reconstruction after the wars and they financed the building of the Austrian railway. They even developed their own exclusive communications system of coded messages sent by carrier pigeons, couriers and then, by telegraph. They gave prodigiously to charity and entertained lavishly. By scribbling a few short lines, they could bring down kings or alter the course of European history. At the time, there were five major powers — France, England, Austria, Prussia and Russia. Rothschild was called "the sixth great power of Europe."

The Rothschilds became a legend, heroes of the nineteenth century emancipated Jew. Citizens with full rights, equal to all, second to none; free of persecution and fear, accepted by the gentile world; unimaginably wealthy, powerful, and proudly Jewish, the Rothschilds had succeeded beyond anyone's wildest expectations. They were a dream come true.

Mayer Amshel, founder of the family, remained an observant Jew

Meyer Amshel Rothschild

throughout his life. Many of his descendants, however, did not. The outstanding success of the Rothschilds helped propel many Jews into the Western world and sadly, towards eventual assimilation. The achievements of the Rothschilds were a mixed blessing.

The Rothschild family residence in Frankfurt am Main. It was destroyed by the Nazis during World War II.

The Rothschilds are the most famous of the newly wealthy Jews, but the nineteenth century saw the rise of many influential Jewish financiers. The Goldsmids of England, the brothers Pereire of France (descended from a Marrano family), the Sterns, Oppenheims, Wertheims, Seligmans, and the Sassoons of India were all international bankers with enormous influence.

The Jews made money mobile. They were able to transfer capital from country to country and make it available wherever it was needed. The world was on the brink of the Industrial Revolution. The newly organized, centralized states required huge sums for their large armies, their wars, their industries and development. Without money, society and progress would grind to a halt.

Banking was not the only activity in which Jews distinguished themselves. The Jews were good businessmen with a gift for organization. They made connections and enabled business to develop. They became merchants, wholesalers and stockbrokers. It was they who introduced the methods of mass-production into the clothing industry. Thanks to their efforts, the working classes could, for the first time, afford to purchase good quality, ready-made clothing.

There was no area which the Jews did not enter. They contributed to every sphere of society out of all proportion to their small numbers. In industry, science, literature, entertainment, journalism,

JEWS IN INDUSTRY AND FINANCE

sports, political life — they left their distinctive mark everywhere. To our great misfortune, the more they succeeded in the world at large, the more they assimilated.

The old Europe was rapidly disappearing. Ghetto walls were coming down, radical new ideas were developing and the Industrial Revolution was about to change the face of the West. The Jews were sometimes dragged along, sometimes pushed from behind, and sometimes they ran ahead, leading society along new paths. They helped change the world, and the world changed them in return.

MOSES MONTEFIORE

Another — and different — Jewish folk hero was the English nobleman Sir Moses Montefiore. Sir Moses was born in Italy, descended from an ancient and respected Sefardic family. He became a successful businessman whose firm acted as brokers for Nathan Rothschild in the London stock market. By the time he was forty, Sir Moses had amassed a large fortune and retired from business. He devoted the rest of his life to the service of the Jewish people.

Sir Moses Montefiore

Despite his great wealth and many opportunities to assimilate, Montefiore remained a loyal, observant Jew. He maintained his own synagogue, traveled with his own *shochet* (ritual slaughterer), and attempted to restrict the growth of Reform Judaism in England. Though a patron of scholars, he made no pretensions to scholarship himself. He was humble and kind, and despite his vast wealth, influence and honors, he never forgot that he was only a simple human being who would one day be required to give an accounting of his life to his Creator.

In 1840, the head of a Franciscan convent in Damascus, Syria disappeared with his servant. The Church accused the local Jews of murdering the priest in order to obtain Christian blood for baking matzos. The French consul in Syria did his utmost to incriminate the Jews. Several Jews were arrested and barbarously tortured. One died, one converted and others supposedly admitted their guilt. More were arrested, including sixty children who were starved in order to force their parents to admit their participation in this affair. Massacres and pogroms were in the air. The Jews of Western Europe and America were aghast that such things could still happen in the modern, enlightened, emancipated world of 1840. They banded together to pressure the Turkish-Ottoman Empire.

Sir Moses, who had been knighted by Queen Victoria, organized an official Jewish delegation from England and France with the blessings and backing of the Queen. He obtained an audience with the Ottoman ruler in Syria and succeeded in releasing the Jewish captives. He even extracted a promise from the Sultan to ban further blood libels in his empire.

Montefiore's return was a triumphant celebration. Never before had the Jews achieved such an outstanding, far-reaching public success. Montefiore was a hero. He continued his travels around the world on behalf of the Jewish people. In 1846 he visited the Czar Nicholas I to attempt to ease the conditions for the Jews of Russia. He made seven trips to Eretz Yisrael where he supported the process of Jewish colonization in Palestine. He helped found agricultural colonies and attempted to bring industry, a printing press, and a textile factory to the Holy Land. In 1855, he was appointed to administer a large sum of money from the estate of the wealthy American Jew, Judah Touro, on behalf of the Jews of Eretz Yisrael.

His most famous project was Yemin Moshe, the first neighborhood built outside the walls of Jerusalem. Yemin Moshe and its dramatic windmill have been renovated and are one of the historic landmarks of Jerusalem today.

Sir Moses' wife Judith accompanied her husband, supported his ventures and shared his accomplishments. She also made valuable contributions of her own. She wrote a fascinating diary of her trips to Palestine and was the author of the first Jewish cookbook written in English.

On his hundredth birthday, Montefiore was presented with a book

Early lithograph of Mishkenot Shaananim, settlement established by Sir Moses Montefiore, the first outside the walls of Jerusalem

of letters from great rabbinic leaders and Jewish communities around the world, together with honors from governments and leaders of state. The Montefiores had no children, but after Sir Moses' death, Jewish institutions throughout Eretz Yisrael and the Diaspora were named in his memory. Welcomed, loved and respected by Jews and non-Jews alike, Moses Montefiore was indeed a modern Jewish hero.

SECTION III

Challenges and Responses
(From 1700 to 1900)

9
The Baal Shem Tov
(From 1700 to 1760)

The modern era began during the turbulent 1700's, when the world was caught up in the throes of revolution and vast political, economic and social changes. As modern man turned towards the secular Enlightenment and away from religion, the Jews of Central and Western Europe were strongly affected. Even in faraway, isolated Eastern Europe, the Jews were eventually challenged by the Haskalah. In the West the trend was to become less Jewish and more like the Christians. In the East, however, Enlightenment caused Jews to search for new ways of being Jewish. Some turned to the Torah for added strength and understanding; others looked outside traditional Judaism. But whether they became more or less observant, the Jews of the East generally chose to remain Jewish.

The different reactions to the ideas of Enlightenment lay in the fact that the West offered the Jews civil rights, new freedoms and opportunity, while the more primitive East continued with its pogroms and oppression. Still ruled by tyrannical kings and under the strong anti-Semitic influence of the Church, Eastern Europe did not encourage the Jews to assimilate. Liberty and opportunity, even for gentiles, were limited.

The Jewish world of Poland had declined sharply from the privileged and elite status it enjoyed in the fourteenth and fifteenth centuries. Anti-Semitism flourished. Slanderous, anti-Semitic writings were published, Jews were accused of ritual murder, and vicious pogroms were allowed to take place.

By the middle of the seventeenth century, new decrees limited Jewish rights, professions and profits. Taxes increased by leaps and bounds. Jews were forced to pay a community head tax, individual body taxes, annual taxes to protect their schools, taxes to the Crown, and were required to donate large "gifts" to the Church.

Most Jews lived in small villages and rural areas on the great Polish estates. In addition to the endless taxes, the enormous rents demanded by the Polish nobility left them thoroughly impoverished. Unable to pay their debts, they became poor peasants, not very different from medieval serfs.

In the villages, there were often not even ten Jewish families to make a *minyan*. Once or twice a year, the inhabitants traveled to larger communities for the holidays. The great scholars of Poland rarely reached these little villages spread throughout the country. Poland had once been a stronghold of Torah study, but now, ignorance of Jewish law was widespread and Polish Jews were in a state of deep spiritual depression. It was in the midst of this situation that a new and promising light appeared.

THE BAAL SHEM TOV

On the 18th of Elul in 1700 (some say 1698), a child was born to an elderly couple in the Polish province of Podolia. Yisrael ben Eliezer was an unusual boy. He was orphaned at an early age and left to grow up by himself. The synagogue became his home; he slept on a bench in the daytime and awoke at night to learn and pray alone. He fetched the children to *cheder* in the mornings and brought them home in the afternoons. He assisted the *gabbai* and did other odd jobs.

The Baal Shem Tov

Upon reaching adulthood, Rabbi Yisrael married the sister of a scholar, even though he was not yet known to be a learned man. He and his wife moved to the Carpathian mountains where he worked as a laborer, digging lime for cement. For a while, he lived by himself. When he returned home, he became a *shochet* and a holy man who wandered from village to village, preaching to the people. In those times, the arrival of a "holy man" was a great event. Usually learned in Kabbalah, they acted as rabbis and teachers, comforting and encouraging the Jewish peasants. They were warmly welcomed.

By the age of thirty-six, Rabbi Yisrael was widely

The Baal Shem Tov's shul in Mezibuzh

known as a healer and a holy man. A group of disciples gathered around him, collecting his remarks and teachings. He visited the Jewish towns in the Polish provinces of Podolia, Volhynia and Galicia and attracted many followers. He was called the Baal Shem Tov — the Master of the Good Name (or, as it is commonly abbreviated, the Besht) as a result of the many miracles he performed.

BEGINNINGS OF CHASSIDUS

The Besht began to preach certain basic ideas which are the foundation of the movement we call Chassidus. *Chessed* means righteousness and loving-kindness; a *chassid* is a person who is pious and faithful, and tries to do more than the minimum required by the Torah. Chassidus was an old-new way of relating to God. The Besht taught that God is not far away in the heavens; He is everywhere, right here, with you. Nothing is too small or unimportant for His attention. Is your cow sick? Has your hen stopped laying eggs? Did you break your axe? Even though God created the universe with its suns and stars, its mighty mountains and wondrous oceans, you, your family, your farm and animals — anything

The Baal Shem Tov's signature

important to you — is important to God, too. Every single person — together with all of his concerns — has great significance in creation.

Chassidus asked a basic kabbalistic question: If God is everywhere, how can there be evil in the world? Like the Arizal (see Sand and Stars, Volume I, Chapter 25), the Besht gave the kabbalistic answer that even evil has its place in the world. It contains Divine Sparks which Man can redeem and turn into good.

Prayer was a basic tenet in Chassidus. Prayer is the way man speaks to God; it is the direct connection to Him. Chassidim prepared for prayer with great concentration, and they prayed long and fervently. They viewed prayer as a central activity of their day, competing even with the study of Torah.

Chassidim also emphasized the importance of joy. One cannot stand in God's presence without *simchah* — joy. Sadness and depression lead man away from God and towards sin. If prayer is the key to communication with God, then joy is the key to God's presence.

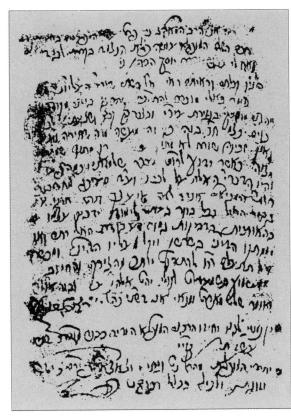

Document in the Baal Shem Tov's handwriting

Lastly, the person who is able to tie all of these links together is the *tzaddik*, or Rebbi. The Rebbi acts as combined rabbi, teacher, father, adviser and source of holiness to his followers.

These ideas were always part of Judaism, but the Baal Shem Tov changed their emphasis and put them together in a new way. It was as if he had turned a kaleidoscope and created a new pattern with old pieces of stone. His "pattern" was a perfect program for the large masses of poor, unlearned, but faithful Jews who needed a simple, direct connection with God and the Torah. The rabbis had frowned upon widespread study of Kabbalah after the harm caused by Shabtai Tzvi and Yaakov Frank, but Chassidus now turned to the Kabbalah as a main source of Torah wisdom.

Hundreds of miraculous stories about the Baal Shem Tov circulated through Poland and Galicia. They made the Jews feel that God

*The Baal Shem Tov's
Chanukah Menorah*

was close by, always ready to help; they made simple people feel loved and important, even if they were not great Torah scholars. They offered hope and faith and joy so that the people had strength to go on, despite the poverty, the danger and the terrible conditions in which they lived.

The Baal Shem Tov died on Shavuos 1760, but by then Chassidus had become a whirlwind of spiritual renewal and activity. It would sweep up the masses of East European Jews in its embrace and change the face of the Jewish people.

10
The Growth of Chassidus
(From 1750 to 1800)

THE MAGGID OF MEZERITCH

The main disciple and spiritual heir to the Baal Shem Tov was Rabbi Dov Ber of Mezeritch. He was known as the Maggid of Mezeritch (a *maggid* was a preacher who traveled from place to place, teaching the people by telling stories and parables).

The Maggid did more than tell stories. He was a brilliant scholar of both Talmud and Kabbalah, and he founded a center of Chassidic study in Mezeritch which produced the next leaders of the Chassidic movement. Gifted, extraordinary people came to study with him. He molded them into great, far-seeing leaders who, nevertheless, remained humble, holy men. The stories of these men fill encyclopedias; their strength and fire and inspiration breathed new life into the downtrodden Jews of Eastern Europe.

Although it was the students of the Maggid who became the main leaders of Chassidus, the actual descendants of the Baal Shem Tov were also great and holy people. The Baal Shem Tov's daughter Aidel and her daughter Feige were both considered holy women and miracle workers. Rabbi Boruch of Mezibuzh, grandson of the Baal Shem Tov, was a major figure, and the famous Rav Nachman of Breslov, a great-grandson, became the rebbe of the Breslover Chassidim. Eventually, Chassidus reached all parts of Poland, the Ukraine, Hungary and even Lithuania.

The Chassidim developed their own way of life. Their customs, food, dress, music, way of praying — all had their own distinct style. They also made changes in the standard Ashkenazic order of prayer

Left: Signature of R' Levi Yitzchak of Berditchev
Right: Signature of R' Shneur Zalman of Liadi

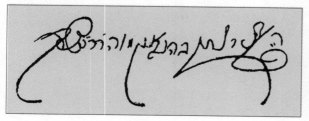

STUDENTS OF THE MAGGID OF MEZERITCH — EARLY FOUNDERS OF CHASSIDISM

- The brothers Rabbi Pinchas HaLevi Horowitz and Rabbi Shmelke of Nicholsburg

- Rabbi Aharon Perlow of Karlin

- The brothers Rabbi Elimelech of Lizhensk and Rabbi Zusia of Hanipoli

- Rabbi Nachum Twersky of Chernobyl

- Rabbi Abraham of Kalisk

- Rabbi Levi Yitzchak of Berditchev

- Rabbi Shneur Zalman of Liadi, founder of Chabad Chassidus

- Rabbi Yisrael of Kozhnitz

- Rabbi Avraham Yehoshua Heschel of Apt

and introduced features from the Kabbalistic Nusach Ari. (Nowadays, this prayer order is called Nusach Sfard, although it is not the one used by Sefardic-Oriental Jews.) On the Sabbath, and especially on holidays, the Chassidim came to the rebbe's court to hear, see and bask in the glow of the tzaddik's holiness.

Left: Tombstone of R' Elimelech of Lizhensk Right: Handwriting of his brother, R' Zusia of Hanipoli

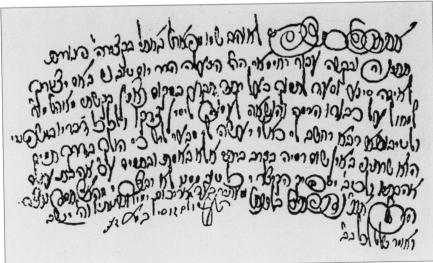

After the death of the Maggid, his disciples continued his work in almost every part of Eastern Europe. Chassidism struck strong roots. It is impossible to discuss each Chassidic group in the length it deserves, but we will follow the development of the movement in Poland as an example. Later, we will briefly mention other movements that survived the Holocaust.

Rabbi Yaakov Yitzchak Horowitz — the famous Chozeh (Seer) of Lublin — eventually became the leader of Polish Chassidus. He infused the Chassidic movement with new vigor. Feeling that the study of Torah may not have been sufficiently emphasized in Chassidus, the Chozeh called for renewed Torah study, searching for new meanings and the deep truths in the old texts. Like the Maggid before him, the Chozeh attracted many great men as his disciples.

His primary student was Yaakov Yitzchak Rabinowitz of Peshis'cha. Known as the *Yid HaKadosh* — the Holy Jew, Rabbi Yaakov established his own Chassidic court and continued to pursue the inner truths of Chassidus. In Peshis'cha, the Chassidim abhorred ignorance. They demanded honesty in thought and in action. They turned away from comfort and quiet, searching only for truth. It was a difficult road to travel. When the Yid HaKadosh died, his successor was Rabbi Simchah Bunam of Peshis'cha.

Rabbi Simchah Bunam was a brilliant, worldly man with a magnetic personality. He had been a lumber dealer and a pharmacist who played chess and loved music. He became a fiery rebbe whose vision and criticism were infused with guidance and hope. Yet he understood that not every Jew was able to walk the diffi-

Tombstone of the Chozeh of Lublin

cult path of Peshis'cha Chassidim. He chose several towering students to continue his teachings — one would become the famous Kotzker Rebbe, another the founder of the Ger dynasty, and the third the Rebbe of Vorki.

THE SCHOOL OF PESHIS'CHA AND THE FOUNDING OF THE GERRER DYNASTY

	died
Baal Shem Tov	1760
Maggid of Mezeritch	1772
The Chozeh of Lublin	1815
The Yid HaKadosh	1814
Rabbi Simchah Bunam of Peshis'cha	1816
The Kotzker Rebbe	1859
The Chidushei HaRim	1866
The Sfas Emes	1905

THE FIRE IN KOTZK

Upon Reb Simchah Bunam's death in 1827, Rabbi Menachem Mendel Morgenstern — the Kotzker Rebbe — took his place as head of Peshis'cha. The Kotzker Rebbe was a genius with an awesome knowledge of Torah. But his Torah was not merely intellectual knowledge; it was a search for perfect *Emes* — distilled Divine truth. The Kotzker could not tolerate falsehood, laziness, imperfection or injustice.

For twenty years he locked himself in a small room, away from his students and his family, and studied Torah. He viewed Torah study as the way to search for truth. But the Kotzker warned that even study had its dangers; even a student of Torah can become conceited or self-satisfied. Such prideful feelings are akin to idol-worship; they push man further than ever away from God and truth. The

SOME SAYINGS OF THE KOTZKER REBBE

🍃 Where can God be found? Wherever man allows him to enter.

🍃 I prefer an evil person who knows he is evil to a pious person who believes he is pious.

🍃 Not all that is thought should be said; not all that is said should be written; not all that is written should be published; not all that is published should be read.

Kotzker Rebbe's unending search for truth, his standards of honesty and his strict self-discipline were so fierce and demanding that his disciples trembled in his presence. Where the Baal Shem Tov had brought joy and warmth and light, the Kotzker Rebbe now brought scorching fire.

Before his death, the Kotzker burned all of his writings, but hundreds of his piercing stories, sayings and teachings were preserved by his students.

The followers of Kotzk developed several new dynasties — Aleksander, Amshinov, Ger, Izhbitza, Radzin, Sochatchov and Vorki. Ger, founded by Rabbi Yitzchak Meir Rothenberg-Alter, author of the *Chidushei HaRim,* became the largest Chassidic group in Poland.

During the Holocaust, nearly all of Polish Jewry was wiped out,

The Kotzker Rebbe's Mezuzah

Left: R' Avraham Mordechai Alter of Ger

Right: Document in the handwriting of his great-grandfather, the Chidushei HaRim, founder of the dynasty of Ger

and with it the rebbes and their followers. One of the main exceptions was the Gerrer Rebbe, Rabbi Avraham Mordechai Alter. In 1940 he miraculously escaped from the Nazis and settled in Jerusalem. Today Ger is the largest Chassidic dynasty in Israel. It has a large community in New York as well. Thus did the school of Peshis'cha leave its stamp on the world of Chassidus, even outside of Poland.

GROWTH OF CHASSIDUS

Lubavitch
Liadi
Vilna
Kalisk
PRUSSIA
LITHUANIA
BELORUSSIA
River Bug
Pripet River
Dnieper River
Sochatchov
Warsaw
Amshinov
Ger
Karlin
POLAND
Kotzk
Peshischa
Lublin
VOLHYNIA
Chernobyl
Apta
Mezritch
Vistula River
Crakow
Belz
UKRAINE
Bobov
Berdichev
Sanz
Ruzhin
GALICIA
Skver
PODOLIA
Breslov
AUSTRO-HUNGARIAN
EMPIRE
Vizhnitz
BESARBIA
Dniester River
Satmar
MOLDAVIA
BUKOVINA
Klausenberg

MORE MAJOR DYNASTIES

We have used the development of Peshis'cha Chassidus as an example, but there were dozens of other famous and important Chassidic courts. Each began with one leader who was so saintly, learned and magnetic that followers and disciples flocked to him. After his death, his teachings were carried on by his sons or disciples.

Not all Chassidic movements were the same. Even the Maggid's own great students had different approaches on how best to serve God. But wherever they lived, they taught and inspired people to become better Jews. As time went on, the Chassidim dominated Jewish life in most of Eastern Europe.

The Holocaust destroyed many Chassidic movements, but some great rebbes survived and rebuilt their communities in Israel or America. Their attitude was well expressed by Rabbi Yochanan Perlow, the only survivor of the Karlin-Stolin rebbes in Russia. He

Chassidim in front of the Old Synagogue in Crakow, Poland, c. 1939

said, "We did not want to lead, but if we are called upon to lead, we will do it to the last drop of blood."

During the fruitful history of Chassidus, there were scores of great leaders and large "courts," too many to be detailed here. The following is a short summary, in alphabetical order, of the most well-known groups which survived the Holocaust:

BELZ — Founded in the Galician part of Poland by Rabbi Shalom Rokeach (1779-1855). By the time of the Holocaust, Belz had tens of thousands of adherents and was active in education and community welfare. Its leader, Rabbi Aharon, who was revered for his exceptional piety, escaped miraculously to Israel. Although his sons were murdered by the Nazis, he reestablished the movement in Jerusalem and Tel Aviv. Several years after his death, he was succeeded by his nephew, Rabbi Yissachar Dov.

LUBAVITCH/CHABAD — Established in Liadi by Rabbi Shneur Zalman (1744-1813), a disciple of the Maggid of Mezeritch and of Rabbi Mendel of Vitebsk. He was the leading spokesman of Chassidus in Russia, and was jailed twice because of false accusations by his opponents. His approach to Chassidic thought is given in his classic work, *Tanya,* and is known as Chabad — Chochmah, Binah, Daas (Wisdom, Understanding, Knowledge). The sixth rebbe in the dynasty, Rabbi Yosef Yitzchak (1880-1950), came to the United States, where he began the development of Lubavitch activities throughout the world. This work was continued and greatly expanded by his son-in-law and successor, Rabbi Menachem Mendel Schneerson (1902-1994).

Left: R' Aharon of Belz Middle: Handwriting of R' Dov Ber of Lubavitch. Right: R' Menachem Mendel Schneerson of Lubavitch

MUNKATCH — Established by Rabbi Shlomo Spira (1831-1893), a grandson of Rabbi Tzvi Elimelech of Dinov (1783-1841). He was also the progenitor of the dynasty of Blozhev, which was reestablished in Brooklyn after the war by Rabbi Yisrael Spira, and continued by his son, Rabbi Tzvi. Rabbi Shlomo's grandson, Rabbi Chaim Elazar (1871-1937), was a prolific author and fiery leader of Munkatch Chassidus. The present leader of the movement, in Brooklyn, is Rabbi Moshe Leib Rabinowitz.

RUZHIN — Rabbi Yisrael (1797-1851) was one of the most prominent and respected rebbes of his time. His children formed the dynasties of Bohush, Boyan, Chortkov, Husyatin, Kopitchinitz and Sadigura. Rabbi Mordechai Shlomo Friedman became the Boyaner Rebbe. He lived on the Lower East Side of Manhattan from World War I until after World War II. Many years after his passing he was succeeded by his grandson Rabbi Nachum Dov Brayer, who settled in Jerusalem.

Top:
Document in the handwriting of R' Tzvi Elimelech of Dinov, author of B'nei Yissoschor and other works.
Bottom, l. to r.: R' Yisrael Spira of Blozhev, R' Mordechai Shlomo Friedman of Boyan, R' Chaim Elazar Spira of Munkatch

SANZ — Rabbi Chaim of Sanz (1793-1876) was raised as a misnaged, but as a youngster he became a disciple of the Chozeh of Lublin and later of Rabbi Naftali of Ropshitz. He was a noted Talmudic scholar, and many dynasties stemmed from him. The most prominent among them are Bobov and Klausenburg.

• **Bobov** was founded by Rabbi Chaim's grandson, Rabbi Shlomo Halberstam (1847-1906). Before the War, Rabbi Shlomo's son and successor, Rabbi Ben Zion, led a large movement in Galicia and founded many yeshivos. His grandson Rabbi Shlomo survived the War and recreated the movement in Israel and Brooklyn.

• **Klausenburg,** Rumania was the home of Rabbi Yekusiel Yehudah Halberstam (1904-1994). During the Holocaust, he lost his wife and eleven children, but not his spirit. He rejuvenated hundreds of survivors and established thriving communities. His sons, Rabbi Tzvi Elimelech in Bnei Brak and Rabbi Shmuel David in New York, continued his work.

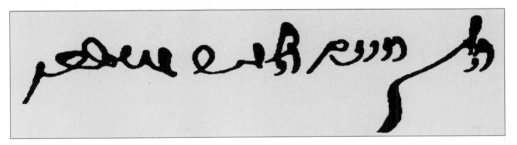

*Top: Signature of R' Chaim Halberstam of Sanz, author of the classic halachic responsa Divrei Chaim, and other works
Bottom:
left.: R' Ben Zion Halberstam of Bobov, and his son, R' Shlomo, the present Bobover Rebbe
right: R' Yekusiel Yehudah Halberstam of Klausenberg*

SATMAR — Rabbi Yoel Teitelbaum (1888-1979), who settled in Satmar, Rumania, was a great-grandson of Rabbi Moshe Teitelbaum of Uhel (1769-1841). After the War, Rabbi Yoel established a very large movement with tens of thousands of Chassidim in the United States and Israel, including communities in Brooklyn, and Upstate Monroe, New York and Jerusalem. Upon his passing, he was succeeded by his nephew, Rabbi Moshe Teitelbaum of Sighet.

SKVER — Founded in Ukraine by Rabbi Yitzchak Twerski (1812-1885), a grandson of Rabbi Nachum of Chernobyl (1730-1798). The Chassidus was reestablished in Brooklyn after the War by Rabbi Yoseph Yitzchak Twersky. Later he established the town of New Square, in Upstate New York, the first incorporated Chassidic community in the country. He was succeeded by his son Rabbi David in 1968.

SPINKA — Founded by Rabbi Yosef Meir Weiss (1838-1876), a disciple of the rebbes of Belz, Sanz and Ziditchov. His successor was murdered in the Holocaust, but several of his sons and nephews reestablished the movement in the United States and Israel.

STOLIN — Founded by Rabbi Aharon of Karlin (1736-1772), a disciple of the Maggid of Mezeritch. He attracted tens of thousands

left: R' Yitzchok Isaac of Spinka, son of R' Yosef Meir Weiss. Center: R' Yochanan of Rachimstrivk, brother of R' Yitzchok of Skver. Right: R' Yoel Teitelbaum of Satmar

of people in Lithuania before he died at the very young age of thirty-six. The only European scion of the Karlin-Stolin rebbes who survived the Holocaust was Rabbi Yochanan Perlow (1900-1956). He revived the movement in both America and Israel. Several years after his passing, he was succeeded by his grandson, Rabbi Baruch Meir Yaakov Shochet, who led a period of vigorous growth in Brooklyn and Israel, as well as many programs in the former Soviet Union.

*Handwriting of R'
Aharon of Karlin*

⬦VIZHNITZ — Founded in Rumania by Rabbi Menachem Mendel Hager (1830-1885), a grandson of Rabbi Yisrael of Ruzhin. His grandson Rabbi Yisrael (1860-1936) moved to Grossverdein, Hungary during World War I. His son, Rabbi Chaim Meir (1888-1972) reestablished the movement in the United States and Bnai Brak, Israel. He was succeeded by his two sons, Rabbi Moshe Yehoshua (1916-) in Bnai Brak, and Rabbi Mordechai (1922-) in Monsey, New York.

*R' Chaim Meir Hager
of Vizhnitz*

❖   ❖   ❖

The first generation of Chassidic leaders were chosen because of their own personal greatness, but as time went on, leadership was passed down in families and the great dynasties were born. Names of many small towns in Eastern Europe which would probably have disappeared from history are still familiar to us today as the names of the Chassidic dynasties which were founded there. By 1820 Chassidus had made such gains and was so well established that it became, in effect, the dominant Jewish force in Poland and Russia. It also spread to Hungary and Rumania. But this would not happen quietly. First the Chassidim would do battle with their ideological opponents — the Misnagdim.

11
The Gaon of Vilna and the Misnagdim
(From 1750 to1800)

In the year 1720, a star was born in the Lithuanian city of Vilna. Eliyahu, the son of Shlomo Zalman, was a child prodigy, gifted with a phenomenal mind and a photographic memory. Although he rarely left the confines of his study and never held any public, rabbinical or community post, his fame spread across the entire Jewish world. He was called the Gaon of Vilna — the Genius of Vilna. (The name is often abbreviated to the *Gra* — the first Hebrew letters of Gaon Rabbeinu Eliyhau.) It is said that the Gra never slept for more than two hours a day or for more than half an hour at a time! His time — every moment, day and night — was spent in the study of Torah. The combination of such rare natural genius with such diligence and endless study produced a star so bright that other great rabbis of his time — and there were many — paled in his overpowering light.

BIRTH OF A STAR

The Gaon wrote sharp, illuminating commentaries on the Tanach (the Bible), the Talmud and the Shulchan Aruch. In order to understand parts of the Torah, the Gaon mastered mathematics, music, medicine, biology and philosophy. He found the entire world inside the Chumash — the Five Books of Moses — and he revealed many secrets of the Torah by closely examining every word. His student, Rav Chaim of Volozhin, said he could recite the entire Torah backwards from the "lamed" of the last word *Yisrael* to the "beis" of the first word *Bereishis*. Just as Rabbi Yisrael ben Eliezer became *the* Baal Shem Tov — the Master of the Good Name, so did Rabbi Eliyahu, son of Shlomo Zalman, become *the* Gaon — the genius of the Jewish people.

The Gaon was a younger contemporary of the Baal Shem Tov and the leading opponent of Chassidus. Each of these two great men illuminated different facets of Torah and

The Vilna Gaon

man's relationship to God. The Gaon opposed many concepts and customs in Chassidus, but his main objection stemmed from his belief in the importance of the study of Torah. For the Gaon, the scholar — not the miracle worker — was the Jewish hero.

Although he himself was a master of Kabbalah, the Gaon severely criticized the Chassidic teachers for emphasizing Kabbalah and mysticism, especially when this was done at the expense of Torah study. Joy, prayer and deep belief in God were necessary. God's Presence was everywhere and He was available to everyone, but only intense Torah scholarship would reveal His Divine Will. Nothing else would do.

The Gaon's absolute refusal to recognize Chassidus forced the Chassidim to re-examine their philosophy and helped assure that they remain in the mainstream of Jewish life.

TWO JOURNEYS

Only twice did the Gaon leave his house of study. When he was a young man of thirty, he "went into exile." He spent five years wandering alone across Europe as a poor, unknown wayfarer. During this time he searched for, examined, compared and studied rare manuscripts scattered throughout the Jewish communities of Eastern Europe. He also discovered great but unknown scholars who were living in far-flung, isolated villages. When he was finally recognized, he ended his exile and returned home.

After his exile, the Gaon began a mind-boggling project. Singlehandedly, he edited the entire Talmud, Midrash and other holy books, correcting the numerous printers' errors which had crept into the texts throughout the centuries. The task was enormous, and it was done without staff, assistants or modern technology. His student, Rabbi Chaim of Volozhin, said that the Gaon fasted and prayed for days before making any changes in a text. His changes have passed the test of time and have been universally accepted as true and faithful to the original versions. In recent years, many ancient texts have been found in *genizos* and libraries around the world and the Gaon's editing has always been found to be correct.

The second and last time the Gaon left his studies was when he attempted to *leave* the Exile and settle in the Land of Israel. He made all the necessary arrangements and began the difficult journey, but he was inexplicably forced to turn back. He said that "the hand of Heaven restrained him." Instead, he sent delegations of his students to Eretz Yisrael. (See Chapter 18.)

THE DEATH OF THE GAON

The Gaon died on the fifth day of Succos in 1797 and was buried in the old cemetery in Vilna. After World War II, the cemetery was turned into a soccer field. Only three Jewish graves remained, one of which was the Gaon's. Only one portrait of the Gaon survives. It was painted by a non-Jewish artist, and we do not know how accurate it is. Yet the Gaon is still vividly alive for the Jewish people. His descendants and disciples collected his work and published his writings, and his teachings spread throughout all of Eastern Europe. They would become the basis for two important

The tomb of the Vilna Gaon

movements — the Yeshivah movement and the Mussar movement — which would soon evolve.

It was said that only once in a thousand years does a star like the Gaon of Vilna rise in the sky, illuminating the Torah for centuries to come.

MISNAGDIM OPPOSE CHASSIDUS

Chassidus intended to infuse Judaism with new spirit and strength, but the established Jewish communities in Eastern Europe were not searching for "new spirit," especially when it came with so many drastic changes. The opposition to Chassidus was strong, especially in Lithuania and White Russia; the opponents, called *Misnagdim*, were well organized and determined to protect Judaism from any suspicious "new" changes.

There was a bitter debate between the two camps and in April 1772, the first ban on Chassidus was issued in Vilna and signed by many rabbis including the Gaon himself. Among other things, it charged that the Chassidim had separated themselves from the community, changed the form of prayer, and did not conduct themselves respectfully during prayer. But the real underlying reason for the ban was the fear that the Chassidim no longer considered the study of Torah, especially the Talmud, to be the central pillar of Judaism. It was charged that the Chassidim believed that prayer and joy were all a Jew needed to live a life of Torah. The Misnagdim considered this heresy.

In the heated battles between the Chassidim and the Misnagdim, both sides turned to the Russian government with accusations against the other. In 1798 Rabbi Shneur Zalman was charged with having sent money illegally to Turkey (i.e., to the Jews in Palestine, a crime almost *all* Jews were guilty of!). He was eventually cleared of all charges, but the mutual accusations continued. In time, the Chassidim and Misnagdim understood that more united than divided them, and that their real ene-

Rabbi Shneur Zalman of Liadi, the Baal HaTanya

mies were the anti-Semitic Russian government and the secular Haskalah (the Hebrew name for the Enlightenment in Eastern Europe).

Although they continued to disagree on many points, both Chassidim and Misnagdim came to realize that there are "seventy faces" to the Torah — and that so long as a Jew believes the Torah was divinely given at Sinai and lives by the laws of the Shulchan Aruch, he is a faithful Son of the Commandments. The fiery struggle between the Chassidim and the Misnagdim began to dim. The darkness of dissension gave way to welcome glimmers of peace.

12
The Yeshivah Movement
(From 1800 to 1900)

We usually think of the East European *shtetl* — the small, Jewish village — as a happy, peaceful, thoroughly religious place. But this is not an accurate picture. Life in the shtetl was often poor, often dangerous, and always difficult, especially under the Romanov Czars in Russia. Traditional Jewish life was the norm, but the level of Jewish knowledge was often low. When the Haskalah — the Enlightenment — reached Eastern Europe with its promises of progress and a better life, it found many followers, not only among the Jews in the cities, but among the Jews in the villages as well.

TORAH STUDY IN EUROPE

The Jewish people had always learned Torah in houses of study called yeshivos (singular: yeshivah). But since the majority of the people in East Europe were so poor, most boys went out to work either before or shortly after their Bar Mitzvah. Gifted students who continued to learn until age sixteen or seventeen were considered scholars. Only the brightest, most promising scholars continued to study full-time after that. Jewish communities valued their scholars. They paid great respect to their *talmidei chachamim* and took pride in their achievements.

The yeshivos in Europe were unlike the yeshivos of today. Students met in a synagogue or in the rabbi's house. There were no classes, no organized curricula, no examinations. Each student learned individually, at his own pace, under the guidance of a rabbi or teacher. Each yeshivah was small and private. This system could only function in an atmosphere of peace and security. War always meant the disruption of the study of Torah.

Between the years 1772 and 1794, Poland was conquered, divided up and parceled out to its neighbors — Russia, Prussia and Austria. The partition of Poland wreaked havoc on Jewish life in Eastern Europe. New borders, new governments, new laws, together with the poverty and centuries old anti-Semitism caused untold suffering. In addition, the Haskalah sowed much confusion, preaching that Torah was no longer the salvation of the Jewish people. These interacting forces led to a sharp decline in Torah study and in the respect accorded to Torah scholars. Young men no longer felt that Torah was a vital and honorable calling. The Jewish world was in danger of drowning in a sea of ignorance. Chassidus had proved itself to be an anchor for the Jews of Poland; now the Misnagdic Jews in Russia and Lithuania were in need of help.

VOLOZHIN — 1803

Every serious Jewish history book describes the movements of the nineteenth century — the Enlightenment, the Reform movement, Zionism, the Industrial Revolution, Communism, and the various other cultural, social and political movements which affected the Jewish people in this frenetic hundred years. Few, however, bother to discuss or describe one vital movement which strengthened and guarded the very essence of the Jewish people and guaranteed its continued existence. At a time when the secular world threatened to destroy the traditional world of Torah, an old institution in modern dress appeared on the scene.

In 1803 a new type of yeshivah was founded by Rabbi Chaim Itzkowitz of Volozhin, the famous student of the Gaon of Vilna. This yeshivah would be the first in a chain of yeshivos that would cover Europe and move on from there to Eretz Yisrael and the United States. Rav Chaim wished to establish a large, central house of learning for Lithuanian Jewry, a place which would provide a proper physical and spiritual environment for intensive Torah study. Hundreds of Lithuanian communities contributed to building the yeshivah and students from all over Lithuania flocked to Volozhin. The finest young minds competed to enter its beis midrash.

Volozhin was based on communal, rather than private, study. Determined to end the highly complicated (and often exaggerated) method of Talmudic study called *pilpul*, Rabbi Chaim demanded that his students learn all of the basic Torah commentaries; use straightforward, logical reasoning and clear analysis; be tolerant of other

The Volozhiner Yeshivah

The Netziv

people's opinions, and retain their humility even while advancing their own opinions. This, he said, would bring joy and satisfaction in the study of Torah. His formula succeeded. Not only did he produce lucid scholars, but he strengthened and revitalized Lithuanian Jewry as well.

Volozhin eventually grew to four hundred and fifty students. It became the center of Torah in Lithuania. But in 1827, the Russian authorities began to interfere in Jewish educational institutions. Volozhin was spied upon and harassed; the head of the yeshivah was arrested and questioned for "illegal" activities; the yeshivah was kept under inspection. Several fires swept through the yeshivah (a constant hazard in the thatched-roof houses of the shtetl), but the end of Volozhin came as a result of governmental, not natural, forces. In 1892, the Czar made a set of impossible, anti-Semitic demands. He insisted that the yeshivah include secular studies in its curriculum; that it hire only teachers with diplomas from Russian institutions (which none of the Rabbis had); and that nighttime study of Torah be drastically limited. The Netziv (Rabbi Naftali Zvi Yehudah Berlin, Rosh Yeshivah of Volozhin

Yeshivah) refused to meet the demands of the Russian government and the government closed the doors of Volozhin.

The Jews of Europe mourned the closure of the "Mother of the Yeshivos," but its seeds had been sown and other yeshivos established. The yeshivah movement continued to grow and many of Volozhin's students became its teachers and rabbis.

MIR — 1815

In 1815 a yeshivah was founded in Mir, a small town in Poland/Lithuania. By 1840 it numbered one hundred students. Between the world wars, the Mirrer Yeshivah became the leading yeshivah in Europe, under the leadership of Rabbi Eliezer Yehudah Finkel and Rabbi Yerucham Levovitz. Students came from the United States, South Africa, England, and even from faraway Australia. Mir became the first international yeshivah of modern times. During World War II, the student body escaped from the Nazis and spent the war years in Shanghai, China. After the War, the yeshivah was reestablished in Jerusalem and New York and is one of the world's great yeshivos today.

R' Eliezer Yehudah Finkel

R' Yerucham Levovitz

The Yeshivah in Mir

SLOBODKA — 1863

In 1863 a yeshivah was founded in Slobodka, a suburb of Kovno, the capital of Lithuania. It became an outstanding "Mussar yeshivah" (see Chapter 16) and a major producer of rabbis, teachers and leaders. In 1924, Rabbi Nosson Tzvi Finkel and Rabbi Moshe Mordechai Epstein left Slobodka and founded a new yeshivah in Chevron in Palestine. The Chevron Yeshivah was destroyed by an Arab pogrom in 1929, but it reopened in Jerusalem where it still exists as one of Jewry's major yeshivos. Many of the great rabbis who came to America before and during World War II were from Slobodka — Rabbis Aharon Kotler, Reuven Grozovsky, Yaakov Kaminetzky, Yitzchak Yaakov Ruderman, and Yitzchak Hutner. They were the ones who established higher yeshivah education in the United States.

Top row, l. to r.: R' Moshe Mordechai Epstein, R' Nosson Tzvi Finkel, R' Reuven Grozovsky. Bottom row, l. to r.: R' Yitzchak Hutner, R' Yaakov Kaminetzky, R' Yitzchak Yaakov Ruderman.

Radin was the home of the yeshivah of Rabbi Yisrael Meir HaCohen Kagan — the Chafetz Chaim. The Chafetz Chaim was a rare man — a tzaddik who never spoke a forbidden word, a creative genius, yet a humble Jew. He died at age ninety-five, beloved and respected by all of world Jewry. Some of the great students of Radin were Rabbi Elchanan Wasserman, head of the great yeshivah in Baranovitch before World War II; Rabbi Yosef Kahaneman, founder of the Ponivezher Yeshivah in Israel; and Rabbi David Leibowitz, founder of the Yeshivah R' Yisrael Meir HaCohen (Chafetz Chaim) in New York.

The Chafetz Chaim   *R' Elchonon Wasserman*   *R' Yosef Kahaneman*

Telshe, founded by Rabbi Eliezer Gordon, was the most progressive and one of the most popular of all the Lithuanian yeshivos. Its organized educational system, curriculum and institutions made it a formidable foe of the Haskalah movement. Telshe founded a secondary school, a kollel, teachers seminaries for men and for women, and a girls school. After World War II, the yeshivah was reestablished in Cleveland, by Rabbi Eliyahu Meir Bloch and Rabbi Chaim Mordechai Katz, who were succeded by Rabbi Mordechai Gifter and Rabbi Boruch Sorotzkin. In later years, affiliated institutions were founded in Chicago, Riverdale, New York, and Telshe-Stone in Israel.

R' Eliezer Gordon

R' Chaim Mordechai Katz.

R' Eliyahu Meir Bloch

**SLUTZK/
LAKEWOOD**
Under the guidance of its founder, Rabbi Yaakov David Willowski, and Rabbi Isser Zalman Meltzer, Slutzk grew into a major educational force. But the First World War and the Russian Revolution disrupted Jewish life and caused the yeshivah to move. Under Rabbi Aharon Kotler, it was reestablished in Kletzk, Poland. In 1943 Rabbi Kotler reestablished it in the United States as Beis Medrash Govoha in Lakewood, New Jersey, Under his inspiring leadership, continued by his son, Rabbi Shneur Kotler, it became one of the largest and most influential yeshivos in the world.

R' Aharon Kotler

R' Yaakov David Willowski

R' Isser Zalman Meltzer

Top: laying of the
cornerstone for the
Kletzker Yeshivah
Bottom: R' Isser Zalman
Meltzer giving a shiur in
Yeshiva Eitz Chaim,
Jerusalem

Novardok, a famous Mussar yeshivah, was founded in 1896. It grew and prospered despite the opposition to the Mussar movement (see chapter 16). It founded twenty other yeshivos

**NOVARDOK/
BEIS YOSEF
— 1896**

YESHIVOS OF EUROPE AND THEIR FOUNDERS
(1800-1900)

VOLOZHIN: 1800-1892	Rabbi Chaim Itzkowitz of Volozhin Rabbi Naftali Zvi Yehudah Berlin (*Netziv*)
MIR: Founded 1815	Rabbi Shmuel Tikitinsky, founder Rabbi Eliezer Yehudah Finkel, Rosh Yeshivah Rabbi Yerucham Levovitz, Mashgiach
SLOBODKA: Founded 1863	Rabbi Tzvi Levitan Rabbi Nosson Tzvi Finkel, Rosh Yeshivah
RADIN: Founded 1869	Rabbi Yisrael Meir HaCohen Kagan, the Chafetz Chaim Rabbi Naftali Trop, Rosh Yeshivah
TELSHE: Founded 1875	Rabbi Eliezer Gordon Rabbi Yosef Leib Bloch Rabbi Eliyahu Meir Bloch
SLUTZK/KLETZK (LAKEWOOD): Founded 1897	Rabbi Yaakov David Willowski Rabbi Isser Zalman Meltzer Rabbi Aharon Kotler
NOVARDOK: 1896 (Mussar Yeshiva)	Rabbi Yosef Yoiz'l Horowitz Rabbi Avrohom Yaffen Gave rise to twenty yeshivos
PRESSBURG: Founded 1807 (Austria-Hungary)	Rabbi Moshe Sofer (*Chasam Sofer*) Rabbi Avraham Shmuel Binyamin Sofer (*K'sav Sofer*)
BARANOVITCH	Rabbi Elchanan Wasserman
GRODNO	Rabbi Shimon Yehudah Shkop
CHACHMEI LUBLIN	Rabbi Meir Shapiro

under one unified school system known as Beis Yosef. These yeshivos were characterized by intense Torah study combined with the practice of mussar, humility, and the pursuit of truth. The students suffered greatly under the Communists, but managed to reestablish themselves in Poland. Beis Yosef institutions had over four thousand students. They published books, pamphlets, periodicals and newspapers. During World War II, the yeshivah was destroyed and the survivors exiled to Siberia. After the war, Novardok yeshivos were reopened in France, Israel and New York.

GRODNO/ KEW GARDENS

The yeshivah Shaar HaTorah in Grodno, Lithuania, became a major Torah center when the eminent Rosh Yeshivah Rabbi Shimon Yehudah Shkop assumed its leadership in 1920. He was famous for his analytical approach to the Talmud. His works were published after the war by his grandson-in-law, Rabbi Zelik Epstein, who re-established the Yeshivah in Kew Gardens, New York.

PRESSBURG — 1807

The largest and most influential yeshivah in Central Europe was in Pressburg (now called Bratislava, in Slovakia). Established by the Chasam Sofer (Rabbi Moshe Sofer) in 1807, it educated generations of leaders, stopped the tide of Reform in Central Europe, and became the main institution in Jewish life in the Austro-Hungarian Empire. It has been said that Lithuanian yeshivos produced great scholars while the Hungarian yeshivos produced strong Torah communities. The graduates of Pressburg were pious observant Jews, meticulous in the performance of mitzvos even while they followed their careers. They participated in commerce, spoke fluent German and were familiar with Western culture. When Hitler invaded Czechoslovakia in 1938, Rabbi Akiva Sofer, great-grandson of Rabbi Moshe, moved to Eretz Yisrael and opened the Pressburg Yeshivah in Jerusalem.

R' Akiva Schreiber-Sofer of Pressburg

THE LIST GOES ON Only the most well-known yeshivos have been mentioned here. There were many other great institutions of Jewish learning in Europe: Lomza, Slomin, Kobrin, Baranovitch, Warsaw, Lublin, Dvinsk and Rameiles (Vilna). There was a network of Lubavitch yeshivos, and Vizhnitz and Satmar had their own schools. Ger operated a large system throughout Poland. Each school had its own style and its own method and outlook, but all shared a common purpose. Each was another link in the great chain of Torah which began at Sinai and stretches down to our own times, today.

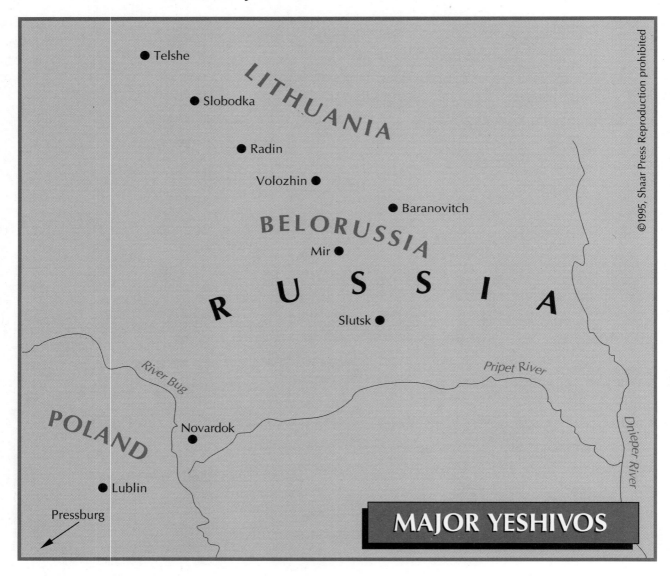

MAJOR YESHIVOS

Learning in the beis midrash of the Lomza Yeshivah in Poland

R' Yechiel Gordon of Lomza

R' Baruch Ber Leibowitz of Kamenitz

R' Naftali Trop of Radin

All of the old European yeshivos were destroyed during the Second World War, but many reopened in Israel or the United States. Scores of new yeshivos have opened in the Diaspora since the War, and hundreds more have blossomed in the Land of Israel. The "new" Yeshivah movement, which began in Volozhin in 1803, has continued for almost two hundred years, guaranteeing the survival of Torah and the Jewish people in the modern world. The yeshivos have been rightly called the "national, creative workshop of the Jewish people."

13
The Haskalah
(From c. 1850 to 1900)

As we have mentioned before, not everyone agreed that the answer to Jewish problems was to be found in the study of Torah. The ideas of Emancipation and Reform made their way eastward, eventually reaching the great Jewish centers in Poland, Lithuania, Galicia, Russia and Hungary.

DIFFERING FORMS — EAST AND WEST

The Haskalah was the Eastern version of the secular, humanistic Enlightenment of the West. (Haskalah came from the Hebrew word *sechel* — intelligence; followers of the Haskalah were called *Maskilim*.) The movement, however, took on a different form in the more backward, autocratic countries of the East. French and German Jews might enjoy equal rights but Russian Jews never experienced that luxury. Assimilation might open the door to opportunity to Jews in the cultured West; in the primitive East, not only was there less to offer, but the door remained tightly closed. Therefore, there was less pressure to convert, or even to assimilate, in the East.

Nonetheless, the Maskilim believed that if the Jews were sufficiently cultured, if they became more Russified, if they viewed Judaism as a culture rather than a religion, then the reasons for anti-Semitism would fade away and Jews would finally be allowed to live in peace.

The Haskalah took many forms. The Yiddish Haskalah was determined to create secular literature in Yiddish; its most famous writer was Shalom Rabinowitz, known by his pen name, Shalom Aleichem. The Hebrew Haskalah used the old Holy Tongue as a new and modern vehicle for secular ideas and literature. The Russian Haskalah advocated the importance of the Russian language and literature. The socialist, or labor, branch of Haskalah tied Jewish culture to the ideas of justice for the worker, and eventually, to labor unions and even to the Communist Revolution.

Shalom Aleichem, famous Yiddish author

There were also religious, scholarly, "modern" Jews who were considered Maskilim. However, they had no intentions of changing the laws of the Torah or abandoning traditional Jewish faith. What they did do, just as the followers of Rabbi Samson Raphael Hirsch had done in Germany and some of the newer yeshivos and Mussar schools had done in Eastern Europe, was to adopt certain outward changes such as Western dress, and to make certain adjustments in the curriculum of the schools. This allowed them to fight the Haskalah with its own weapons.

Various educational institutions were established by the Haskalah itself, but they were unpopular and short-lived. Except for the city of Odessa, which became the center of Haskalah, the movement never turned into a strong, active, mass movement for East European Jewry. Nonetheless, its ideas were well-known and discussed.

THE BATTLE FOR MINDS

The Maskilim used their pens to popularize their ideas. They published many books, newspapers and magazines. The new secular Haskalah literature ridiculed and criticized the rabbis, Jewish tradition and Torah life. These publications were widely read, even in many of the yeshivos. They were, after all, "Jewish" publications. They discussed Jewish problems of identity, religion and anti-Semitism, and they were usually written in the Holy Tongue or in Yiddish. Haskalah ideas thus led to the destruction of many Torah values, especially in the eyes of the young.

There had always been individual non-observant Jews, but now, for the first time in the history of the Jewish people, there was a philosophy of a secular, cultural "Judaism." The Reform movement removed the Law from the Torah; the Haskalah removed God.

JEWISH EDUCATION

The Jews were fighting a terrible battle for survival in Czarist Russia. Body and soul were in mortal danger. Between the grinding physical poverty and the barbaric anti-Semitism on the one hand, and the onslaught of the Haskalah on the other, traditional Jewish life was being constantly whittled away.

The Maskilim approached the Russian authorities, offering their services to help Russify the Jews if the Czar would curb the activities of the yeshivos. The Czar was only too happy to help. He issued strict new decrees interfering with the yeshivos. The Russian government even tried to establish its own rabbinical academies under the auspices of the Maskilim to produce official "Russian" rabbis. They were not successful; their schools were closed by the government twenty-five years later.

One of the collaborating Maskilim was the German Jew, Dr. Max Lilienthal. In 1842 Lilienthal was appointed by the Russian government to "revise" Jewish education in Russia and to set up a "modern" school system for Jewish students. The head of the Volozhin Yeshivah and Rabbi Menachem Mendel Schneerson, the Rebbe of Chabad (Lubavitch), joined forces, vigorously opposed Lilienthal and prevented him from closing the traditional Jewish schools. Within ten years, Lilienthal's own schools were closed for lack of students. Lilienthal emigrated to America where he became a leading Reform rabbi.

Meanwhile, in Galicia, Hungary, Lithuania and Russia, the battle for and against Haskalah raged. Jewish Poland, with its huge population of Chassidim, also proved to be a battleground. The Maskilim ridiculed and persecuted the Chassidim shamelessly, yet the Chassidim held their own. The Chassidim were so opposed to all forms of Haskalah that they even fought traditional Torah scholars who were in favor of more modern educational methods. Although the Chassidim were the main targets of the Maskilim, it was, on the whole, the Misnagdim who fell victim to the Haskalah.

SECTION IV

The Russian Front
(From 1800 to 1900)

14
A Bird's-Eye View
(From 1800 to 1900)

Between the French Revolution in 1789 and the beginning of World War I in 1914, Europe developed at a furious dizzying pace. The Scientific Revolution brought about vast technological development; the Industrial Revolution brought men from the villages to the cities and transformed the way they lived; the French Revolution gave birth to great social and political changes. Its famous slogan "Liberty, Equality, Fraternity," became the rallying cry of a newly emancipated Europe.

THE INDUSTRIAL REVOLUTION

For the first time in history, abstract scientific theories were systematically applied to technology. The new technologies led to the development of industry; industry led to urbanization. As more and more people moved to the cities, the masses of people became a force to be reckoned with. They used their new-found political power to demand civil rights; they used their economic power to demand better working conditions and a higher standard of living.

The world was on the move. Medical advances and the discovery of vaccinations would soon eliminate deadly diseases like smallpox, typhus and diphtheria. Better agricultural methods produced more food. As a result of the increased food supply and higher standards of health, the population increased rapidly. From the twelfth to the seventeenth centuries, there were approximately two million Jews in Europe. In the eighteenth century, there were two-and-one-half million Jews. By the end of the ninettenth century there were ten-and-one-half million Jews — a rise of five hundred percent in one hundred years!

The Industrial Revolution: The new steam locomotive arrives in a town

A new invention for faster mass printing turned newspapers into inexpensive everyday items. News and information spread quickly. In 1875 an international public postal agreement was signed. Steady communication between countries and people was assured.

Lastly, the building of the railroads had a revolutionary effect on all of civilization. Transport and communication became rapid, orderly and economical. Trains made it easier to move goods and people. Crops, chemical fertilizers, machinery — everything could be cheaply transported. By 1870, Western Europe was crisscrossed with railroads. The world was suddenly smaller and more interdependent. These developments would have great consequences for modern warfare, making it possible to wage wars on a scale the world had never seen before.

NATIONALISM

The French Revolution marked the beginning of modern European nationalism. Germany, Spain, Italy and Austria soon followed the French example and consolidated their territories, their political policies and their national, cultural ideologies. After Napoleon's downfall, the rulers of Europe tried to erase the new freedoms and reinstall their old powers. But the July Revolution in France in 1830, and then a series of revolutions across Europe in 1848, proved beyond a doubt that the old order had passed. Nationalism, democracy and progress were now the goals of all nations. In Western Europe, the most important development was the creation of a strong, new, united Germany. In the East, the giant, sleeping Russian bear began to awake.

THE SEARCH FOR A BETTER WORLD

Just as the French Revolution ignited the spark of nationalism, it also lit the fire of liberalism in Europe. Freedom, civil rights and equality were now supposed to be the inheritance of all men, not only of the rich and powerful. Yet at first, the Industrial Revolution often made men's lives worse, not better. The working class suffered. Crowded into miserable quarters, working twelve hours a day, they slaved while the rich enjoyed the fruits of progress. The world thrived, but many people suffered. The seeds of revolt were being planted.

RUSSIA

The effect of all these developments in agriculture, industry, health, science, communications and transport was tremendous. Most of the improvements, however, began in the West while Eastern Europe remained primitive and poor.

At the time of the Industrial Revolution, Russia was a vast, backward country with endless natural resources. Only a tiny fraction of its population was affected by the new ideas from the West; the vast majority of people were poor, ignorant peasants. Industrialization, emancipation and new technologies had not yet reached the shores of the Baltic and Black Seas. The Romanov Czars were powerful, tyrannical leaders who ruled with an iron hand and isolated Russia from the West. But the Crimean War forced the Czar to reconsider his plans.

Russia had carefully watched the Turkish Ottoman Empire on its southwestern border. The Ottoman Empire was huge, corrupt and weak, but it controlled important areas, including Palestine. In 1854 an argument over the holy places in Palestine served as the excuse for Russia to attack Turkey. But France and England, anxious to keep Russia from expanding, sent their armies to fight the Czar in Turkish Crimea. Backward and incompetent, Russia lost the war and was forced to sign a humiliating peace treaty.

The Czar Alexander II was convinced that in order to defend itself against the West, Russia must now reform, Westernize and develop. In 1861, he freed the serfs and made certain democratic changes, but they were short-lived. Suffering from their own poverty and primitiveness, hoping to catch up with the West yet fearing and hating everything Western, Russia was caught in a trap of its own making. The Russians looked for someone to blame. They found a time-honored scapegoat: the Jews. As it entered the 19th century and began a rapid process of modernization, Russia turned into a living nightmare for the Jewish people.

POLITICAL TURMOIL

By the end of the 19th century, Europe was entangled in a web of conflicting interests. The French and British Empires were rivals in Africa and Asia; Russia, Austria and Great Britain were competing for power in the Ottoman Empire when Germany entered the scene and displaced them. The Balkan states — Greece, Serbia, Rumania, Bulgaria, Albania and Turkey — seethed with conflicting national interests. In 1890 the German Emperor Kaiser William decided to turn Germany into a great sea power, a rival to the British navy. His policies threatened France, Russia and Great Britain, causing them to ally themselves against Germany, Austria and Turkey. The stage would be set for a horrendous World War.

But first we must turn back and accompany the Jewish people in Russia and Eastern Europe during the difficult, tumultuous years of the nineteenth century. The waves of change which rocked the Jews of Western Europe had now reached the East.

15
The Pale of Settlement
(From 1800 to 1900)

TIMELINE

1772, 1793, 1795	*Partitions of Poland*
1795	*Pale of Settlement established*
1796-1801	*Czar Paul I*
1789	*The French Revolution*
1801-1825	*Czar Alexander I*
1800-1814	*Napoleon Bonaparte*
1803	*Founding of Volozhin Yeshivah*
1808-1888	*Rabbi Samson Raphael Hirsch in Germany*
1825-1855	*Czar Nicholas I*
1827	*Nicholas passes the Cantonist Decrees*
1838-1933	*The Chafetz Chaim*
1841	*Death of Rabbi Moshe Teitelbaum of Satmar*
1846	*Sir Moses Montefiore visits the Czar*
1848	*Karl Marx and the Communist Manifesto*
1848	*Liberal Revolutions across Europe*
1854	*Crimean War*
1855-1881	*Czar Alexander II*
1855	*Alexander II revokes Cantonist Decrees*
1871	*Pogrom in Odessa*
1881-1894	*Czar Alexander III*
1885	*Death of Sir Moses Montefiore in England*
1894	*Dreyfus Trial*
1894-1918	*Czar Nicholas II*
1892	*Rabbi Chaim Soloveitchik becomes Rav in Brisk*
1897	*Theodore Herzl and the First Zionist Congress*
1900	*Kishinev Pogrom*
1905	*Death of Sfas Emes (Ger)*
1905	*Pogrom in Odessa*
1911	*Beilis Trial*
1914-1918	*World War I*
1917	*Russian Revolution*

Unlike Poland, Russia had never welcomed Jews. In 1550, Czar Ivan IV had said, "It is not convenient to allow Jews to come into Russia ... many evils result from them." By the beginning of the eighteenth century, few Jews lived in the country, but the partitions of Poland (1772, 1793 and 1795) and the territorial adjustments after Napoleon's wars added over one million Jewish inhabitants to Russia's population. By 1815 there were 1,500,000 Jews living under Russian rule, most of them in the western provinces of Poland and Lithuania. The Czar was convinced that his Jewish subjects were disloyal, dangerous and useless. He immediately began to search for ways to solve the "Jewish problem."

In 1795 Czar Paul I established the Pale of Settlement. Twenty-

THE PALE OF SETTLE-MENT

Shoemakers' Shul, Lithuania

five western provinces, including most of Eastern Poland, Lithuania, White Russia, the Ukraine, the Crimea and Bessarabia, were declared a limited area for Jewish settlement. Jews could not live anywhere else; they could not work or travel outside the Pale without special permits. They were trapped in the towns and shtetls of the Pale, just as they had been trapped in the medieval ghettos four hundred years before.

Alexander I issued further decrees against the Jews. They could not remain in the villages in the Pale but had to move to the cities; they could no longer sell liquor (which had

*Top:
A Russian shtetl
Bottom:
Jewish water carriers*

Marketplace on Market Day in a typical pre-World War II Eastern European town

been the traditional trade of one-third of the Jewish population); they could not study in the universities. He claimed he was trying to move the Jews into "productive labor," but in reality, he severely limited them in all areas.

His successor, Nicholas I, was determined to turn Russia into a great military power. Instead, he created a tyrannical government, full of spies and secret police, a corrupt bureaucracy and a poor, ignorant population. He brought Russia to the verge of ruin.

Nicholas was a fiery anti-Semite. In 1827 he issued the infamous Cantonist decrees drafting Jewish children into the Russian army. Until then, Russians could legally purchase their release from army service. Now every Jewish community was forced to provide a certain number of children for the draft; there was no way for a community to avoid its quota. Boys were conscripted at age twelve (and often younger) and sent to military preparatory schools. At eighteen they entered the army for an additional twenty-five years!

A large percentage of these Jewish children died from malnutrition, beatings, misery and disease. Some could not withstand the pressure and converted to Christianity. Stories of the Cantonists have survived. They are as shocking today as they were one hundred years ago.

The Jewish communities were in an impossible situation. Which children were to be turned over to the Russian authorities? Kidnapers stalked the streets in search of young prey. Orphans or the children of the poor were often sent to fill the quotas. Unable to solve or deal with the problem, many rabbis were silent; others left their positions in protest.

In 1840 new decrees were issued. The Pale was made smaller; traditional Jewish clothing was prohibited; Jews were not allowed to marry before the age of eighteen (marriages had normally been performed at younger ages). Thousands were exiled to different towns and cities; the quota for the army was tripled; Jewish books were censored; and the government insisted that approved "Russian" rabbis keep official records of births, deaths and marriages. Jews were divided into groups — "useful" Jews and "useless" Jews — with varying new decrees for each type. There were twelve hundred anti-Jewish laws extant in Russia; half of them had been passed during Nicholas' regime. The only way the Jews could survive was by constantly bribing the corrupt Russian officials in an attempt to avoid the cruel, impossible, unjust laws. Even that did not always help.

CZAR ALEXANDER II

When Nicholas died in 1855, his son Alexander II seemed to offer a ray of hope. On the day of his coronation, Alexander revoked the hated decrees of Cantonism. He enlarged the Pale and eased some of the anti-Jewish laws. He abolished serfdom and emancipated the peasants. The Jews were filled with joy. They hoped the bad times were over. But Alexander had given too little, too late. Russia was seething with discontent and violence and secret plans for reform. Afraid of the future, Alexander abandoned his liberal policies and returned to the heavy-handed

THE ROMANOV CZARS	
1796-1801	Paul I
1801-1825	Alexander I
1825-1855	Nicholas I
1855-1881	Alexander II
1881-1894	Alexander III
1894-1918	Nicholas II
1917	Russian Revolution

policies of his father.

Poland revolted against Russia in 1863. The Polish revolution was brutally crushed, but it sparked intense Russian patriotism and great anti-Semitism. All the Jewish government schools, run by the Maskilim, were closed, and in 1871 a major pogrom took place in Odessa, the center of the Haskalah movement. The Maskilim had preached that anti-Semitism would disappear if the Jews would leave their Jewish ways and replace them with Russian culture. Unfortunately, the anti-Semites had not read the publications of the Maskilim. For the Russians, a "dirty-Zhid" remained a "dirty-Zhid," whether he was a Maskil or not.

CZAR ALEXANDER III

Alexander II had good reason to fear the liberals; he was assassinated in 1881. He was succeeded by his son, Alexander III. The new Czar's ideal was a Russia containing one nation, one language and one religion, despite the fact that he ruled Jewish, German, Polish, Finnish and Swedish subjects who believed in a host of religions. For the Jews of Eastern Europe, this turned into a time of great tragedy.

In 1881 a series of pogroms, lasting over a year, destroyed Jewish communities in one hundred different towns throughout Russia. In 1891, ten thousand Jews were expelled from Moscow. In 1893 there were huge expulsions from areas outside the Pale where Jews had managed to reside. Deportations, arrests and beatings left the Jews no respite. In 1894 the great synagogue in Moscow was closed.

NICHOLAS II — THE LAST CZAR

In 1894 Alexander died and his son Nicholas II came to power. Nicholas would be the last of the Romanov Czars. A timid, shy man, Nicholas was married to Alexandra, granddaughter of Queen Victoria of England. Their only son, the Czarevich, was a hemophiliac. In their unending search for a cure for his disease, they came under the influence of Grigori Rasputin, a vicious and insane monk.

Pogroms raged throughout Russia, many organized by the government itself. Expulsions, quotas limiting the number of Jewish students in schools, restrictions on Jewish observance — all made Jewish life in Russia intolerable. Out of desperation, many young Jews joined the revolutionary movements of the times: anarchy, socialism, communism. These movements shared the belief that only by destroying the old traditional life could a new and just world be

Czar Nicholas II and his family

created. It made no difference what they destroyed, Torah or Czar; if it was "old," it was evil.

During Passover, 1900, a vicious four-day pogrom took place in Kishinev. Forty-five Jews were killed, six hundred were injured and

Top: Kishinev after the pogrom
Bottom: Funeral for Torah scrolls after the Kishinev pogrom

THE AGE OF POGROMS

1871	Pogrom at Odessa
1881	Assassination of Alexander II followed by wave of pogroms in Kiev, Odessa, and 200 other places
1882	May Laws expelling Jews from all Pale villages
1891	20,000 Jews expelled from Moscow
1893-1895	Wide expulsion of Jews from outside Pale areas
1898	7,000 Jews expelled from Kiev
1903	Savage four-day Easter Pogrom in Kishinev
1903-1907	Pogroms in 284 towns; 50,000 casualties
1905	Police join pogrom in Bialystok
1905	Riots of Black Hundreds at fifty localities
1910	1,200 Jewish families expelled from Kiev
1911-1913	Anti-Semitic campaign during Beilis Trial

thirteen hundred homes were destroyed. Beatings, torture and atrocities raged while the authorities encouraged the mob. This time, the world protested. The Russian response was, "The Jews are at fault."

Russia had other problems to deal with besides its Jews. In 1905 strikes, civil war and peasant riots hit the country. The Czar was forced to make democratic concessions. He granted all Russians civil rights and agreed to a limited parliament. But he also had to appease the reactionaries who were angry about reform. One of the "concessions" was to allow the reactionaries to vent their anger on the hapless Jews. An organization called the Black Hundreds launched a wave of pogroms that swept through Southern Russia. In Odessa the killings and unspeakable acts of horror lasted for four terror-filled days. Nicholas congratulated the Black Hundreds on their work. Again, he blamed the Jews for the uprising. He called them "trouble-

The Black Hundreds

makers" who had angered the Russian people and brought the riots on themselves.

The unrelenting anti-Semitism in Russia caused large numbers of despairing Jews to join radical movements, but the more revolutionary the Jews became, the worse the anti-Semitism was. In 1911 an unbelieving world watched and protested

THE
BEILIS
TRIAL

Mendel Beilis

as Mendel Beilis, a Jew from Kiev, was accused of killing a Christian child to use his blood for baking matzos. The ancient blood libel was still alive. Two years later Beilis was released for lack of evidence although the charges against him were never officially withdrawn. The Beilis trial was the last incident in a long bloody period. It was the final act which proved that Russia held no hope for the Jewish people. A tidal wave of emigration began to surge. Flight from Mother Russia seemed to be the only escape.

The Czar's government held no hope for the Russian people either. In 1917 the reign of the Romanovs came to a violent end. The long-awaited Russian Revolution had arrived.

16
Ethics and Mussar
(From 1850 to 1900)

*T*he nineteenth century presented two different types of problems to the Jewish people. Enlightenment and liberalism were spiritual challenges; repression and tyranny were physical dangers. Both of these forces damaged traditional Jewish life. The Jews had faced many spiritual challenges in their long history, but these usually came from outside the ranks of Judaism. Now, for the first time since the rise of the Karaites in the seventh century, Torah Jewry had to defend itself and prove its significance in the eyes of its own people.

BREAK-DOWN

For centuries, kings, governments and the Church had always dealt with the *kehillah* — the Jewish community — which was represented by its rabbis and leaders. But the policies of the Czar destroyed the kehillah's authority. The Czar dealt with "approved" rabbis, with various Jewish informers, and with the Maskilim who fought traditional Jewish authority relentlessly. The Maskilim were especially ferocious towards the Chassidim whom they constantly ridiculed. With the help of the Russian government, they did everything in their power to dismantle the traditional community. Unfortunately, the traditional community was engaged in its own internal struggles. Rivalries between different Chassidic courts, strife between Chassidim and Misnagdim, and the struggle against the new Mussar movement were constant and often fierce.

Torah leaders were overburdened. Reeling from pogroms, trying to keep the community intact, aiding the refugees who were forced to leave the villages and who came streaming into the larger cities of the Pale, protecting the schools and yeshivos, battling the government and the Maskilim — the rabbis were unable to do everything all at once. Traditional family and community life began to weaken.

In Poland, Chassidus proved to be a strong religious support against the evils of the times, but outside Poland, the vast majority of people were not Chassidim. The young, Lithuanian Yeshivah movement would eventually produce great rabbis and leaders who would keep the spark of Torah burning for future generations. At the moment, however, only a small percentage of young men were studying in the yeshivos. Most people were out working, trying to keep body and soul together in the villages and cities of Czarist Russia.

Yet help was on its way. During their worst periods — the Dark Ages, the Crusades, the Inquisition — the Jewish people had always found the strength to rejuvenate themselves. Now, too, in the midst of the dark Russian night, the unquenchable spark inside the Jewish soul began to burn more brightly.

A new movement, programmed to answer some of the Jews' most pressing problems, began in Lithuania in the 1850's. It was never a mass movement, but it would spread throughout Eastern Europe and mold Jewish leadership for generations to come.

RABBI YISRAEL SALANTER

Rabbi Yisrael Lipkin was known as Rabbi Yisrael Salanter, after the Lithuanian town of Salant where he studied for fifteen years. Rabbi Yisrael was a genius with a phenomenal memory. Like the Gaon of Vilna and Rabbi Chaim of Volozhin, he rejected the complicated system of studying Talmud with *pilpul*, and searched instead for simplicity and accuracy in understanding the Talmud. The great Rabbi Zundel of Salant, a disciple of Rabbi Chaim of Volozhin, became his role model. Rabbi Zundel directed Rabbi Yisrael to the path of Mussar — a method of constant self-examination and improvement — as a way to greatness and service of God.

Rabbi Zundel had never occupied any official position; Rabbi Yisrael never accepted any rabbinic post either. Rabbi Zundel studied *Mesillas Yesharim* — the Path of the Righteous — (written by the kabbalist Rabbi Moshe Chaim Luzzato in the 1700's); Rabbi Yisrael made Mesillas Yesharim the basic book of Mussar study. Shortly after Rabbi Zundel moved to Jerusalem in 1838, Rabbi Yisrael moved to Vilna where he founded the first Mussar yeshivah.

Rabbi Yisrael was a charismatic, holy personality. He conducted classes in synagogues and study houses in Vilna, and his fame spread

The town of Salant

as one of the leading Talmudic scholars of the age. He outlined a program for the recovery of traditional Judaism. He established special "Mussar houses" where Mussar would be taught and studied, and he developed a group of disciples to do the teaching. Mussar books were printed; lectures and speeches were given regularly.

The goal of Mussar was to strengthen Jewish thought and belief. By combining the spirit and ethics of the Torah with the performance of the mitzvos, Jewish life would be elevated. Mussar taught its adherents to observe the spirit, as well as the letter, of the law, and to do so in a refined, esthetic manner. It would correct failings which had developed as a result of the terrible conditions of their long exile. Poor manners, discourteous behavior, lack of cleanliness, lack of complete honesty in their dealings with Jews and gentiles — all had to be removed in order to properly observe the Torah.

Mussar was psychology, sociology, philosophy and religion all rolled into one. Rabbi Yisrael believed that Mussar would improve general society as well as Jewish society, and that it was the answer to Enlightenment and Reform. It would bring a new dimension of holiness to Judaism; it would infuse the Jews with internal pride and self-worth in an age when the Torah was subjected to harsh criticism and ridicule. A century after the Chassidic revolution changed the life of its people. Mussar would be the parallel revolution that would change the life of the Misnagdim.

Hundreds of students came to study Torah and Mussar with Rabbi Yisrael. In Vilna and Kovna and scores of cities and towns throughout Lithuania, the movement grew. The Mussar yeshivos of Lithuania influenced the Yeshivah movement and became the model for many of our modern yeshivos today. Telshe, Slobodka, Radin, Mir, Kelm, Novardok — all were products of the Mussar movement. Although Mussar was less drastic a change than the Chassidic revolution had been, its effects were as permanent, as positive, and as important.

New movements arise because of the need for change or improvement. But not everyone agreed with all of the changes Rabbi Yisrael made. Some rabbis were concerned that the study of Mussar would come at the expense of the study of Talmud; they felt that good character traits could and should be achieved through the old methods of study without any additional, new programs. But the younger, idealistic Mussar students were not daunted by criticism. Convinced of the superiority of the Mussar school, they worked enthusiastically to win new believers. As a result, they often came into conflict with established rabbis and heads of yeshivos. Much as the Vilna Gaon had forced the early Chassidim to reexamine their actions and ideals, now too the rabbis forced the Mussar movement to control their fervor and moderate their methods in order to live peacefully with the Misnagdim. In turn, the Mussar movement forced the Misnagdim to reexamine their own weaknesses and look for ways to improve, not only their religious observance, but their attitudes and spirit as well.

TORAH OPPOSITION TO MUSSAR

A different source of opposition to the Mussar movement came from the Haskalah. At first, the Maskilim thought that the Mussar movement would be a natural ally of Haskalah. After all, Rabbi Yisrael was objecting to the very same Jewish traits and deficiencies which the Haskalah objected to. Both camps wished to lift the Jew out of his degrading position and make him an honorable, proud member of society.

HASKALAH OPPOSITION TO MUSSAR

But the Maskilim soon discovered that Rabbi Yisrael's agenda differed greatly from their own. Meticulously observant and utterly dedicated to the study of Torah, Rabbi Yisrael was not trying to impress the gentiles or "normalize" the Jews. Just the opposite. He wanted to raise the Jews up so that they could perform their job as God's Chosen People in a holier, more dignified manner. One cannot be a "Light unto the nations" if one has no sense of pride and self-value. God's Children are the sons and daughters of the King of the Universe. Rabbi Yisrael wanted to teach them how a royal family acts and feels.

It was not an easy job. Even children of rabbis and scholarly Jews were led astray by the temptations of the Haskalah and secular life. Rabbi Yisrael's own son, Yom Tov Lipman Lipkin, was a tragic example. A genius (not unlike his father) he received a doctorate at the University of Vienna and won a prestigious prize (the first Jew in Russia to do so) for an important discovery in applied mathematics. He was showered with honors. Sadly, he had left much of his Judaism behind, but to the Maskilim, he was a hero. They hurried to publicly congratulate Rabbi Yisrael on his son's good fortune in the Haskalah newspaper Hamaggid. Compelled to announce that he was not honored by a son who had abandoned the Torah, Rabbi Yisrael answered with a heartbreaking letter to the editor:

"... I am compelled to publicly announce that my son is not a "crown" for me as your editor indicated, but rather the opposite is true. He is a source of disappointment and sadness and

FAMOUS TORAH SCHOLARS FROM 1850-1900	
Rabbi Menachem Mendel of Kotzk	*d.* 1859
Tzemach Tzedek of Lubavitch	*d.* 1866
Rabbi Yitzchak Meir Alter of Ger (Chidushei HaRim)	*d.* 1866
Rabbi Chaim Halberstam of Sanz (Divrei Chaim)	*d.* 1876
Malbim (Rabbi Meir Leibush)	*d.* 1879
Rabbi Yisrael Salanter	*d.* 1883
Rabbi Shlomo Ganzfried	*d.* 1886
Rabbi Samson Raphael Hirsch	*d.* 1888
Rabbi Yehuda Aryeh Leib Alter of Ger (Sfas Emes)	*d.* 1905
Rabbi Yechiel Epstein (Aruch HaShulchan)	*d.* 1908
Rabbi Yosef Chaim of Baghdad (Ben Ish Chai)	*d.* 1909
Rabbi Chaim Soloveitchik of Brisk	*d.* 1918
Chafetz Chaim (Rav Yisrael Meir Kagan)	*d.* 1933
Rabbi Yosef Rozin (Rogatchover Gaon)	*d.* 1942

my heart weeps over his way of life. Anyone who loves him and can influence him to change his way ... will be doing me a great favor ..."

As the Mussar movement grew, the opposition of the Haskalah increased. The elite young men who joined the Mussar yeshivos were the very same people whom the Haskalah hoped to attract. Haskalah, together with the other forces of the nineteenth century, would cause great damage to the traditional life and beliefs of the Jewish people. Many Jews, and their children, would be lost to Torah. Chassidus, the Yeshivah movement and Rabbi Yisrael Salanter's Mussar movement would save and heal and lay the foundations for the future.

17
Turmoil and Ferment
(From 1850 to 1900)

CHANGES

As a result of the Czars' policies, more and more Jews left the villages to move to the big cities. The process of urbanization caused many social and religious problems. Crowded living conditions, poverty and the frantic pace of city life all contributed to the breakdown of traditional family and community life. Many Jews felt that observance was becoming too difficult and they drifted away from religious practice. New ideas and possibilities were in the air, times had changed; this was reason enough to change with them.

The railroads and steamships also stirred physical movement. The Jews of Russia were in a gigantic jail. Wherever they went, they were confronted with the same Czar, the same government, the same intolerable decrees and the same anti-Semitic gentiles. But the railroads seemed to signal a possibility of escape. They led out of Russia to the ports, where far away, across the ocean, was a new and free land. Emigration was in the air.

NEW IDEALS

The modern era throbbed and churned with new ideas, social revolution, shifting alliances and economic change. Many of the new movements were based on ancient Jewish ideals. Human equality, civil rights, education, the rights of the working man, an end to economic exploitation — all were part and parcel of the Torah. The longing for social justice led to the establishment of a large Jewish labor movement. Hundreds of thousands of members joined. Other Jewish movements emerged — idealistic, radical, sometimes violent. They were filled with Jews dreaming of a better world. They believed that the old order must first be erased; in its place they would create a brave new world of justice and equality.

The Jewish Left, the Bund, Communists, Socialists, Labor Zionists and Anarchists flooded the scene. They created a new stereotype of the Jew: not the cowardly moneylender, but the revolutionary radical. This frightening, fighting, "new" Jew represented anarchy, violence and danger. He would set off a fresh wave of anti-Semitism and would cost the Jewish people dearly.

Jews — both apostates and assimilated Jews — were in the forefront of social change, of scientific advance and of modern, Western culture. Jewish names suddenly adorned all the arts — in music, painting, literature and the theater. Jewish financiers were active in the world of finance; Jewish industrialists were among the new rising class of capitalists. It was as if the moment the Jews were allowed to leave the gates of the ghetto they exploded onto the European scene. Three Jews in particular — Karl Marx, Sigmund Freud and, towards the end of the century, Albert Einstein — stand out. Together with the gentile biologist, Charles Darwin, they would leave an indelible mark on Western civilization.

DARWIN, MARX, FREUD AND EINSTEIN

Charles Darwin had developed a theory of evolution based on natural selection and survival of the fittest. It was a speculative idea as to how life might have evolved; it was based on limited, observed phenomena and cannot be proven. In accordance with his theory, Darwin traced the descent of man from the apes. He caused a furor. His theory seemed to contradict the literal account of Creation and dealt a great blow to belief in the Bible.

Karl Marx, father of communism, was a pessimistic, anti-Semitic, apostate Jew. He harbored a deep hatred for much of mankind, but had a special hatred for Jews and Judaism. Marx viewed society purely through the economy. He claimed that evil and injustice began, not in man's soul, but in his pocketbook — in the private ownership of property. True justice could only be attained when the working classes of the world rose in revolt against their capitalistic masters and regained the wealth which they had created and which, therefore, belonged to them. Then a new and just era would begin.

Sigmund Freud, father of psychoanalysis, worked with the indi-

Tombstone of Karl Marx

Albert Einstein

vidual rather than with society. He probed the human personality and explored the human subconscious. He believed that man is governed by strong, instinctive physical forces which he is usually unaware of but which shape his behavior. Understanding this subconscious would free man and allow him a greater measure of success, satisfaction and happiness.

Albert Einstein, a brilliant scientist, searched for order in the universe. He formulated his famous Theory of Relativity which unified the concepts of time and energy, of matter and space, connecting the tiniest atom to the vast galaxies and beyond.

The single individual, society at large and the universe in all its grandeur — all were probed, analyzed and defined in the nineteenth century. Landmarks and anchors which had supported civilization for thousands of years were uprooted and discarded. However, nineteenth century conclusions were not always correct, even when reached by great, creative minds.

Darwin's ideas were later used to support the Nazi theory that a "superior" race of human beings — which Hitler called the "Aryan" race — had evolved in the Germanic countries. Marxism gave birth to seventy-five years of horror in Communist Russia. Freud's theories led to a completely distorted view of the human personality and to a crisis in human values and behavior.

Today, the work of Darwin, Marx and Freud has been largely discredited. Unfortunately, they did much to destroy religious values and beliefs, both Jewish and Christian. Even the brilliant work of the peaceful and gentle genius, Albert Einstein, produced bitter fruit — the development of the atom bomb. By the twentieth century, man stood confused, alienated and alone.

SECTION V

Old-New Horizons
(From 70 to 1800)

18
Zion — A Bird's-Eye View
(From 70-1800)

THE JEWS IN ERETZ YISRAEL

1738 B.C.E.-1523 B.C.E.	**ABRAHAM, ISAAC AND JACOB IN ERETZ YISRAEL**

1273 B.C.E.-423 B.C.E.	**ENTERING THE PROMISED LAND UNTIL END OF FIRST TEMPLE**

353 B.C.E.-68 C.E.	**SECOND TEMPLE PERIOD**

68-476	**ROMAN RULE — THE TANNAIM AND THE MISHNAH IN ERETZ YISRAEL**

	68-85	Rabban Gamliel and Yavneh
	132	Bar Kochba and the Revolt at Beitar
	c.150-250	Rabbi Yehudah HaNasi and the Mishnah
	c.250-500	The Rise of Christianity and the Fall of Rome

476-638	**CHRISTIAN/BYZANTINE RULE**

Time of severe persecution. No Jews allowed in Jerusalem. Jewish communities living in Northern Galil.

614	Persian Conquest of Eretz Yisrael

638-1099	**MOSLEM RULE**

Situation improves. New towns, more trade. Visitors and pilgrims arrive.

638	Arab Conquest of Eretz Yisrael

1099-1291	**THE CHRISTIAN CRUSADER KINGDOMS**

Terrible conditions under Crusaders. Jews again evicted from Jerusalem. Conquest of Saladin greatly improves situation.

1099-1291	The Christian Crusaders
1141	Yehudah HaLevi
1170	Benjamin of Tudela
1187	Saladin conquers Eretz Yisrael
1210	Aliyah of 300 Rabbis from England and France
1270	Aliyah of the Ramban to Jerusalem

FROM ABRAHAM TO OUR TIMES

1291-1516

THE MAMLUKS OF EGYPT
Growing Spanish and European Jewish settlement.

1315	Ashtori HaParchi
1488	Ovadyah of Bartinoro
1492	Expulsion from Spain
1492	Renewed Immigration to Eretz Yisrael

1516-1917

TURKISH OTTOMAN RULE
At first, blossoming Jewish settlement. Height of Tiberias, Safed communities. Decline of Ottoman Empire brings poverty, problems. Beginning of Modern Period.

1516-1917	Ottoman Turks rule Palestine
1536	Rabbi Yosef Caro in Safed (Tzefas)
1537	Suleiman the Magnificent rebuilds walls of Jerusalem
1560's	Don Yosef Nasi in Tiberias (Teveryah)
1700	Rabbi Yehudah Chassid
1740	Rabbi Chaim Abulafia in Tiberias
1746	Rabbi Gershon Kitover
1770's	Aliyot of Chassidim, students of Baal Shem Tov
1800's	Aliyot of Perushim, students of the Vilna Gaon
1841-1909	Rabbi Shmuel of Salant as Rav of Jerusalem
1855	Moses Montefiore builds Mishkenot Shaananim
1880's	Edmond de Rothschild's colonies
1881	First Aliyah

1917-1948

THE BRITISH MANDATE
Growth of Jewish Yishuv. Struggles with the British and the Arabs leading to proclamation of the State of Israel.

1904	Second Aliyah
1917	General Allenby enters Jerusalem
1921	The Third Aliyah
1921	First Partition of Palestine
1929	Pogrom in Chevron
1939	British White Paper limiting immigration to Palestine
1947-48	Struggle for Israeli Independence

1948

THE STATE OF ISRAEL

Because the mainstream of Jewish history flowed across the lands of the Exile, the history of the Jews who remained in Eretz Yisrael after the Churban is not always well known. Palestine came under the rule of many nations — Rome, Byzantine Empire, Persia, Moslem invaders, Christian Crusaders, Egyptian Mamluks, the Turkish Ottomans and finally, the British. Borders changed, the population decreased and the countryside became desolate. (For an explanation of the many names given to Eretz Yisrael — Canaan, Judea, Palestine, Israel — see *Sand and Stars*, Volume 1, pages 4-5.) The once vibrant Land seemed to be asleep. Yet never, in the long saga of our people, was there a time when a remnant of Jews was not living in the Land of Israel. In every age, despite hardships and suffering, faithful, dedicated Jews remained in Zion.

THE CHILDREN OF ISRAEL IN THE LAND OF ISRAEL

UNDER ROMAN, BYZANTIUM AND MOSLEM RULE

Large Jewish communities continued to exist in Eretz Yisrael even after the Destruction of the Temple. Jews lived in the area of Beitar to the south of Jerusalem, in the northern Galil, and on the Golan Heights. When Beitar was destroyed during the Bar Kochba rebellion in the year 132, the Jewish population was concentrated in the north of the country. For another century, Torah life continued to flourish under pagan Roman rule. It was during this period that Rabbi Yehudah HaNasi compiled the Mishnah.

By the year 312 both Rome and Byzantium were under the rule of devout Christian emperors who persecuted Jews for religious reasons. Julian the Apostate, the last pagan emperor, came to power in 363. He gave permission for the Jews to rebuild the Temple and there was a flurry of excitement and activity. But

Julian's unexpected death ended all hope, and life in Palestine became ever more difficult.

In 614 the Persians invaded Judea. The Jews joined the Persian forces and fought against the Christian Byzantines, hoping once again to reestablish Jewish rule in the Holy Land. However, the Persians were defeated by the Christians and both Persians and Jews were severely punished and further oppressed.

The great Arab conquest of 638 brought the Holy Land under Moslem rule. As the general economic and political situation in the country improved, Jewish immigrants and visitors arrived, and new Jewish towns and villages were established.

I n 1099 Christian Crusaders from Europe invaded the Holy Land and divided it into several small Crusader states. (See *Sand and Stars,* Volume I, Chapter 21.) The French knight, Godfrey of Bouillon, crowned himself "King of Jerusalem" and evicted all the Jews from the Holy City. For two hundred years the Crusaders ruled Palestine. In 1187 Saladin, Sultan of Egypt, reconquered Jerusalem and officially invited the Jews to return.

LIFE UNDER THE CRUSADERS

The country at large and the Jews in particular had suffered greatly under Crusader rule. Conditions deteriorated and lawlessness reigned. It was during this period of time that the Spanish rabbi and poet Yehudah HaLevi arrived (in 1141) and according to popular tradition was killed by a marauding horseman as he bowed to kiss the holy ground. The Rambam's family tried to come to the Holy Land, but were prevented from doing so by the chaotic conditions. The worldwide traveler Benjamin of Tudela reached Palestine in 1170. He described in full the terrible condition of the people and the Land.

Nonetheless, the Jews never gave up hope. In the year 1210, three hundred rabbis, part of the the *Baalei Tosafos* of France and England, moved to the Holy Land. In 1242 a group of Jewish scholars, disciples of Rabbi Yechiel of Paris, accompanied King Louis IX of France on his Crusade to Palestine. They established a community and founded a large yeshivah in the city of Acre. In 1270 the Ramban left Spain, bought a house in Jerusalem and built his famous synagogue.

Conditions in the Holy City were so bad that he was unable to find ten Jews for a *minyan* (even though Saladin had invited the Jews to return eighty-three years before!). The Ramban brought families from Chevron, Shechem and Safed to Jerusalem, thus renewing the Jewish presence in the Holy City.

<table>
<tr><td>

THE MAMLUKS

</td><td>

The Mamluks were a military force, made up of slaves, who rebelled and seized power in Egypt in about 1250. They entered the Holy Land and in 1290 conquered the Crusader

</td></tr>
</table>

fortress at Acre, bringing the Christian kingdoms to an inglorious end. The great Crusader castles were destroyed; their stones were scattered across the countryside. For the next two centuries, the Mamluks ruled Palestine.

In 1315 Ashtori HaParchi left Italy for Palestine where he wrote his famous book *Kaftor vaFerach,* on the laws and geography of Eretz Yisrael. In 1350 a group of *talmidei chachamim* from Germany made aliyah and opened a yeshivah in Jerusalem. Tourists and pilgrims traveled to and fro and yearly celebrations were held at the grave of Rabbi Shimon bar Yochai in Meiron and at the grave of Shmuel the Prophet outside Jerusalem. In 1488, a Sefardic community was founded in Jerusalem by Rabbi Ovadyah of Bartinoro, the famous commentor on the Mishnah, and Ladino (a Judaicized form of Spanish) was heard throughout the city.

AFTER THE EXPULSION FROM SPAIN

As a result of the Expulsion from Spain, the Black Death, and the massacres and pogroms in Europe, a small but steady stream of Jews immigrated to Eretz Yisrael from the fourteenth to the sixteenth centuries.

By the year 1500 three hundred Jewish families lived in Safed. They were traders, craftsmen and scholars. Safed boasted eight synagogues, many schools, yeshivos and a blossoming economy. Most of all, it boasted a community of rare scholars and holy men. Rabbi Yosef Caro wrote the *Shulchan Aruch* — the Code of Jewish Law — in Safed, and Rabbi Yitzchak Luria (the Arizal) sparked a period of profound study of Kabbalah. Among his many outstanding disciples in Safed were Rabbi Chaim Vital, Rabbi Shlomo Alkabetz, Rabbi Moshe Alshich and the *Chareidim.*

There were now Jewish communities in Safed, Bet Shean and throughout the Galil; in Jerusalem, Shechem (Nablus) and Chevron; and on the coast in Jaffa, Gaza and Rafiach. As Jewish settlement in the Holy Land spread, there was even an attempt by some rabbis to reestablish the ancient Sanhedrin. Anticipation of the coming of the Mashiach grew. (See Sand and Stars, Volume I, Chapter 26.)

W hen the Ottoman Turks conquered Palestine from the Mamluks in 1516, a new period began. The Turks welcomed Jewish immigration, and waves of Jewish refugees fleeing from the Spanish Inquisition gratefully entered the Turkish Empire. Suleiman the Magnificent repaired waterworks, expanded agriculture, guaranteed the peace and gave legal standing to the Jews in his empire. In 1537 he rebuilt the walls of Jerusalem. Communications improved and trade routes from Europe to the Far East passed through Palestine. Christian and Jewish pilgrims arrived and Eretz Yisrael suddenly became a bustling

RETURN UNDER THE OTTOMANS

Drawing of 19th century Tiberias

Woodcut of a typical family in Jerusalem, c. 1600

commercial and religious center.

In 1561 Suleiman awarded his Marrano counselor, Don Yosef Nasi, title to the city of Tiberias. Don Yosef and his mother-in-law, Dona Gracia Mendes, rebuilt the walls of the city and encouraged Jewish settlement. They opened a yeshivah and supported the scholars of Tiberias and Safed. It was a golden era for the Jews of Eretz Yisrael. By the end of the next century, however, security declined and the profitable trade routes to the East no longer passed through Safed. An epidemic struck the community in 1747, followed by a strong earthquake in 1759. The glorious period of Suleiman was over and the center of Jewish life shifted south, to Jerusalem.

A large Jewish community developed in the Holy City. In the 1600's, Jerusalem supported three hundred scholars, twenty-one synagogues and a yeshivah. Ashkenazic, Sefardic, Provencal and Italian Jews all lived side by side. In the year 1700 Rabbi Yehudah Chassid (the Pious) traveled to Palestine from Poland, accompanied by as many as eight hundred followers. He bought a tract of land in Jerusalem but died a few days after his arrival. A hundred and fifty years later a large and beautiful synagogue was built on his land. It was known as Churvah R' Yehudah Chassid and was the main Ashkenazi synagogue in the Old City, until it was destroyed by the Jordanians in 1948. In 1746 Rabbi Gershon Kitover, brother-in-law of the Baal Shem Tov, came to Eretz Yisrael and founded the first Chassidic community in the country. For the next fifty years, groups of Chassidim followed him. In 1808 the first group of *Perushim*, stu-

Interior of the Rabban Yochanan ben Zakkai Synagogue

dents of the Vilna Gaon led by Reb Menachem Mendel of Shklov, made aliyah. Settling first in Tiberias and Safed, most eventually moved to Jerusalem. By 1845 three thousand Jewish families lived in Jerusalem. The earlier Sefardic, Ashkenazic and Italian Jews were now joined by Chassidim and Perushim. The social and religious tapestry of Jerusalem was woven in rich and multicolored threads.

THE OLD YISHUV

The students of the early Chassidim and the disciples of the Gaon of Vilna were called the *Yishuv HaYashan* — the "Old Community" in Eretz Yisrael. (The term *Yishuv HeChadash* — the New Yishuv — refers to the Zionist settlers who arrived in the early 1900's.) The Old Yishuv was a religious, Ashkenazic community whose members lived in the cities of Safed, Tiberias, Chevron and Jerusalem. They viewed themselves as a holy community and they

The Western Wall in the 1930's

lived a life of piety and simplicity. Shmuel of Salant was rav of the Old Yishuv in Jerusalem from 1841 to 1909 — almost seventy years!

By the nineteenth century, the entire Turkish Empire was in a state of decline. The Jewish community in Jerusalem was very poor and the possibilities of earning a living were limited. The Old Yishuv survived thanks to an international system of Jewish charity — the *chalukah* — which was collected and distributed to the Jews of Palestine.

Despite the grinding poverty and the difficulties of living under the harsh and corrupt Turkish rule, the Jews of the Old Yishuv carried their burden with pride. Charles Warren, the famous British archaeologist, wrote in 1876:

> "There is an irrepressible pride about this fragile, wayward people of Ashkenaz that I could not help but admire. Dressed in rags they stalk about the Old City with as much dignity as though they were dressed in the richest garments. They give way to no one. Years of oppression have in no way quelled their ancient spirit ..."

The Jerusalemites of the Old Yishuv were fiercely protective of the Holy City's sanctity. They felt responsible to be the guardians of Zion, who would preserve the Jewish presence in Jerusalem until the Messiah arrived. But before the arrival of the Messiah, the story of the New Yishuv and the Return to Zion would unfold.

FAMOUS EARLY ALIYOS	
1210	300 Baalei Tosafos from England and France
1270	The Ramban founds community in Jerusalem
1492	Aliyot of Spanish Jews after the Expulsion from Spain
1700	Rabbi Yehudah Chassid and Ashkenazi community in Jerusalem
1740	Rabbi Chaim Abulafia reestablishes community in Tiberias
1770's	Aliyah of Chassidim, Students of Baal Shem Tov
1800's	Aliyah of Perushim, Students of Vilna Gaon

19
The Return to Zion
(From 1800-1900)

THE NINETEENTH CENTURY

NEW CITY, NEW LIFE

*A*lthough Jews had always made their way eastward to Zion, during the nineteenth century the return to the Holy Land took on a different dimension. Jewish settlement suddenly came into the limelight. For many and varying reasons, the return to Zion gained the approval of European governments and the attention and support of Jews all over the world. As the Jewish Yishuv grew to unprecedented numbers, the Holy Land awoke to the touch of its children and once again came to life.

*M*odern history in Palestine begins with the establishment of the New City of Jerusalem. The honor of inaugurating the New City belongs to the famous English Jew, Sir Moses Montefiore (see Chapter 8). In 1855 Sir Moses built Mishkenot Shaananim, the first new neighborhood outside the city walls. The

Mishkenot Shaananim

Panoramic view of the Old City, c. 1920. The large imposing building is the Tifereth Yisrael Synagogue, also known as the Nisson Bock Shul.

large windmill, originally built to power a flour mill, still marks the site today.

Once begun, the building did not stop. As Jews moved out of the crowded Old City, neighborhood after neighborhood was established. Many — Yemin Moshe, Zichron Moshe, Kiryat Moshe and others — were named in honor of Montefiore. Two modern hospitals, Misgav Ladach and Bikkur Cholim, were built. The railroad was extended from Jaffa to Jerusalem. Houses, schools, businesses and roads appeared.

The Old City also grew. Synagogues and yeshivos multiplied. In 1841 Rabbi Shmuel of Salant was appointed rav of the Old Yishuv, although in his great modesty he did not exercise the authority of his position until much later. During the nearly seventy years of his leadership, the combined population of Old and New Jerusalem increased fivefold.

Yet life in the Old City, and in the country as a whole, was difficult. Poverty was widespread. Both Jews and Christians

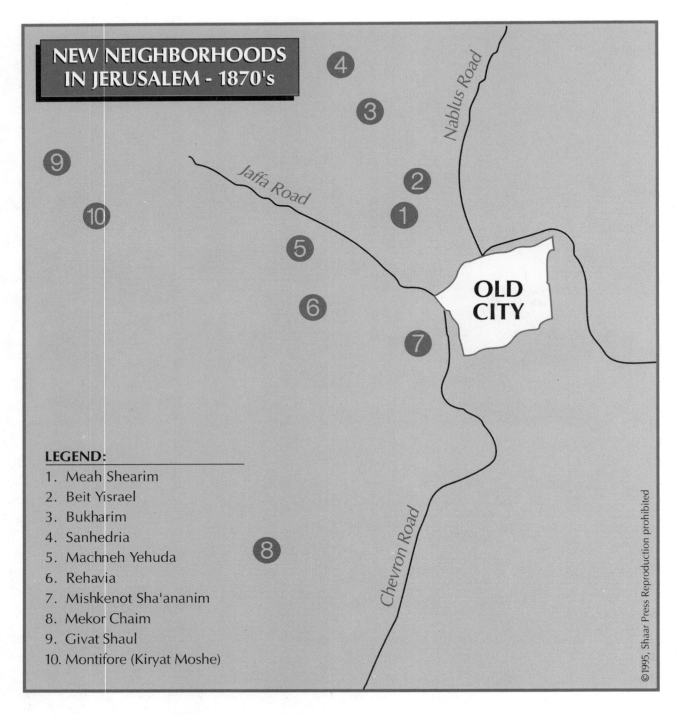

NEW NEIGHBORHOODS IN JERUSALEM - 1870's

Nablus Road

Jaffa Road

Chevron Road

OLD CITY

LEGEND:
1. Meah Shearim
2. Beit Yisrael
3. Bukharim
4. Sanhedria
5. Machneh Yehuda
6. Rehavia
7. Mishkenot Sha'ananim
8. Mekor Chaim
9. Givat Shaul
10. Montifore (Kiryat Moshe)

were considered infidels by the ruling Moslems and neither group enjoyed equal status or protection under the law. The persecution of the Jewish minority, however, was constant and especially cruel. In 1839 the British Consul reported: "... scarcely a day passes that I do not hear of some act of tyranny and oppression against a Jew." Yet Jews continued to arrive, great rabbis and simple people alike, drawn by the dream of living in the Holy City.

The first practical, widespread step in Jewish settlement came in the early 1880's. Rabbi Shmuel Mohilever of Bialystok convinced Baron Edmond de Rothschild, a wealthy French Jew, to support Jewish colonization in Palestine. Rothschild founded a network of settlements — Ekron, Gederah, Rishon LeZion, Zichron Yaakov, Rosh Pinah, Yesud Hamaalah and Metullah — which were known as the "Baron's colonies." Most of these colonies were populated by religious Jews, true pioneers who settled in dangerous, isolated places in order to reclaim the Land of Zion for the Jewish people. These early colonies were founded before the movement for political Zionism began. Today, all are thriving, respectable cities or towns in Israel.

Rothschild also founded the Carmel Wine Company. He invested over seventy million gold francs in the Land of Israel, and earned the name *HaNediv Hayadua* — the Famous Philanthropist. He and his

THE COLONIES OF BARON EDMOND DE ROTHSCHILD

R' Shmuel Mohilever

Baron Edmond de Rothschild

The Rothschild winery at Rishon LeZion

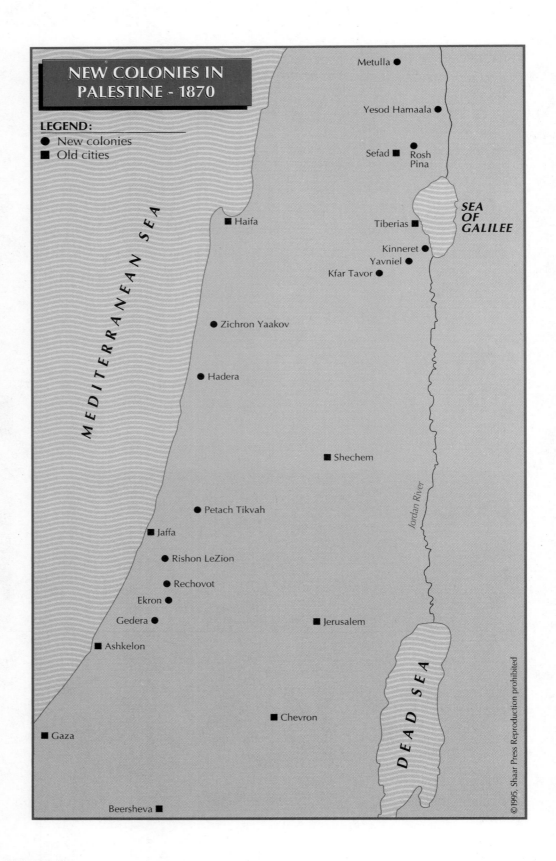

NEW COLONIES IN
PALESTINE - 1870

LEGEND:
● New colonies
■ Old cities

MEDITERRANEAN SEA

Metulla ●

Yesod Hamaala ●

Sefad ■ ● Rosh
Pina

● Haifa

Tiberias ■

SEA
OF
GALILEE

Kinneret ●
Yavniel ●
Kfar Tavor ●

● Zichron Yaakov

● Hadera

■ Shechem

● Petach Tikvah

Jordan River

■ Jaffa

● Rishon LeZion

● Rechovot

Ekron ●

Gedera ●

■ Jerusalem

■ Ashkelon

DEAD SEA

■ Chevron

■ Gaza

Beersheva ■

wife are buried in Ramat HaNadiv, a national park near his colony Zichron Yaakov.

From 1880 to 1900 the Jewish population increased rapidly. Additional villages — Rehovot, Haderah, Kfar Tavor, Yavniel, and Kinneret — were established. Factories were founded and new Jewish neighborhoods were built in Jaffa, Haifa and Jerusalem. The Land of Israel was filled with the sounds of rebuilding and rebirth.

I n the late 1870's a popular movement called *Chibat Zion* — Love of Zion — arose in Russia. Its members were called *Chovevei Zion* — Lovers of Zion. Its purpose was to support Jews in Palestine, to encourage emigration from Russia, and to help further Jewish agricultural settlement in the Land. Although the leader of Chovevei Zion, Dr. Leon Pinsker, and many other members were secular Jews, the movement was based on traditional Jewish foundations. It was supported by famous rabbis such as Rabbi Naftali Tzvi Yehudah Berlin of Volozhin (the Netziv), Rabbi Tzvi Hirsch Kalischer, and Rabbi Shmuel Mohilever of Bialystok. At first, the most prominent opponents of the Chovevei Zion were Rabbi Yosef Dov Soloveitchik and Rabbi Eliyahu Chaim Meisel, who objected to the movement's secular leadership. After 1890 the secularists, headquartered in

CHOVEVEI ZION AND THE FIRST ALIYAH

Chovevei Zion, 1880

The Levovitz family — members of BILU

Odessa, adopted policies that cost it the support of many more rabbinic leaders.

In 1881 a small group of Chovevei Zion called BILU (*Bais Yaakov Lechu V'nelchah* — House of Israel, Let Us Go Forth) immigrated to Palestine. This was the first ripple in what soon became a wave of Jewish immigration to Eretz Yisrael. Between 1881 and 1903, 20,000 Jews would leave Eastern Europe and settle in Palestine. This group is referred to as the First Aliyah. Between 1904 and 1914, 40,000 more would come as part of the Second Aliyah.

As secular and religious Jews arrived in the Holy Land, great questions divided them. Were Jews to continue in the old, Torah-true, traditional ways, or should they become modern, secular Jews? Was settlement in Palestine primarily a practical answer to anti-Semitism, or was it the fulfillment of a basic Torah commandment? Were Jews to become like all other nations, or should they remain a Chosen Nation, different and apart?

Rabbi Yehudah Elkalai of Bosnia saw the return to Zion as the beginning of Jewish Redemption. He called for *maaser* — tithing: Ten percent of the Jews in Europe should emigrate to the Land of Israel and ten percent of all Jewish wealth should be invested in the new settlements. He wrote in his book, *Raglei HaMevasser*, "All of the time limits for the arrival of the Messiah have already passed. Only the return of the Jewish people to the Land of Israel is lacking. The return will be the national *teshuvah* — repentance — of the Jewish people ... through the return, Israel will accept God's sovereignty and rule. Let us only return to our Holy Land." The message echoed in many Jewish hearts. But not all ...

מבשר טוב

HARBINGER OF GOOD TIDINGS,

AN ADDRESS TO THE JEWISH NATION,

RABBI JUDAH ELKALI.

ON THE PROPRIETY OF

ORGANIZING AN ASSOCIATION

TO PROMOTE THE

REGAINING OF THEIR FATHERLAND

LONDON.
PUBLISHED BY S. SOLOMON, 37, DUKE STREET, ALDGATE.
5612.—1852.
[*Price Six Pence.*]

Title page of Rabbi Elkali's Mevasser Tov

I n direct opposition to Rabbi Elkalai, the great Hungarian Rebbe, Rabbi Moshe Teitelbaum (known as the *Yismach Moshe*) wrote, "I am convinced that it is the will of God that we should not emigrate to the Land of Israel now, of our own volition. Rather we are to wait here in the exile until the day when our righteous Messiah will lead us to our land."

These two opposing views set the stage for a century of controversy. Would the Return to Zion bring Jewish Redemption or, God forbid, hasten Jewish destruction? The dispute continued to rage but the Jews continued to emigrate. Between 1883 and 1887, eight new suburbs (including Geulah and Meah Shearim) and Jewish Yemenite village were built outside the walls of Jerusalem, Petach Tikvah was founded by Jews from the old Yishuv, and ten new settlements were established. By 1890 the New Yishuv was an undeniable fact.

REDEMPTION OR DESTRUCTION

Artist's rendition of the Yismach Moshe

SHEMITTAH

The year 1889 was a *Shemittah* year — a Sabbatical Year — when the Torah commands that the Land of Israel must be allowed to rest. This was the first Shemittah in almost fifteen hundred years when large numbers of Jewish farmers had land in Eretz Yisrael to tend. There was widespread fear that the entire new and fragile network of settlements would collapse and that hunger would result if the land were left fallow for the year. The issue became a fiery topic of halachic discussion around the world. Despite strong opposition by many leading rabbis, including many supporters of the Chibat Zion movement, other leading rabbis gave a *heter* — halachic permission — to till the fields under carefully prescribed conditions. The question is still being debated today, over one hundred years later.

The issue of whether and how to observe Shemittah became symbolic of attitudes toward Eretz Yisrael. Should the settlement of the Land be accompanied by a relaxation of Halachah, or should there be no effort to accommodate the settlers? Many controversies of the future would revolve around this question.

The Return to Zion was a new road, filled with many serious, complex problems — physical, social, economic and religious. The solutions were not all apparent, but the Jews continued to return to Eretz Yisrael nonetheless.

Below:
Yoel Moses Solomon,
a founder of
Petach Tikvah
Right:
Early lithograph of
Petach Tikvah

20
Political Zionism
(From 1850-1900)

THE DREYFUS AFFAIR

The Chibat Zion movement in Russia had been fueled by the Jews' age-old love for Zion, but Political Zionism in Western Europe was originally sparked by the fires of anti-Semitism.

After the Napoleonic Emancipation, Jews entered all areas of French life. They were highly successful, but their success was a mixed blessing, giving rise to much jealousy and fear. "Jewish influence" was viewed as a dangerous threat to French society, and anti-Semitic literature was widely published and read.

In 1894 Alfred Dreyfus, a Jewish officer in the French army, was accused of having provided military secrets to Germany. Dreyfus was convicted on the basis of a secret document which later proved to have been forged. He was court-martialed and sentenced to life imprisonment on Devil's Island, a torturous colony in the Caribbean. Stripped of his sword and his honors, Dreyfus was paraded through the streets of Paris while the mob shouted "Death to the Jews!"

The degradation of Alfred Dreyfus: He is stripped of his army commission and his sword is broken.

Emile Zola, a popular, non-Jewish French journalist, demanded the release of Dreyfus. His famous front-page article, *"J'Accuse — I Accuse,"* was like a bomb exploding across the face of France. He accused the French army and government of falsely charging Dreyfus in order to cover up the crimes of others. For the next ten years, the Dreyfus case became a worldwide affair and a national French obsession. It divided all of French society, almost pushing the country to the edge of civil war. The army would not publicly admit its error, but eventually a second trial was held and Dreyfus was pardoned and released, although not acquitted of guilt.

The pardon was a direct result of the concentrated, united efforts of the Jews and the Liberal Left. While the Jews and the Liberals considered this a great victory, the anti-Semitic Right considered it further proof of international Jewish power. Anti-Semitism laced with anger soared in the supposedly free, liberal countries of Europe.

An Austrian journalist by the name of Theodore Herzl was present at the Dreyfus trial. Herzl was a wealthy, thoroughly assimilated Jew whose knowledge of Judaism was almost non-existent. Although he had celebrated his Bar Mitzvah, he

THEODORE HERZL

DER

JUDENSTAAT.

VERSUCH

EINER

MODERNEN LÖSUNG DER JUDENFRAGE

VON

THEODOR HERZL

DOCTOR DER RECHTE.

❧

LEIPZIG und WIEN 1896.
M. BREITENSTEIN'S VERLAGS-BUCHHANDLUNG
WIEN, IX., WÄHRINGERSTRASSE 5.

Title page of Herzl's Judenstaat, The Jewish State

knew no Hebrew and was ignorant of the most basic Jewish customs. Nonetheless, when he saw the humiliation heaped upon Dreyfus and heard the outpouring of anti-Semitic hatred that was hurled at all Jews, he reached a crucial turning point in his life.

Herzl returned from the trial and wrote his famous book, *The Jewish State*. He wrote that Jews must have their own homeland where they would no longer be subject to shameful scenes such as the one he had witnessed in Paris. He described his ideal Jewish state as a beautiful, modern, secular country — a replica of Vienna or Paris — whose language would be German, or possibly French. Poor, persecuted Jews could come there and live free, productive lives. He was sure that if the Jews left the countries of Europe, the problem of anti-Semitism would disappear. Herzl called for a meeting of Jewish leaders to discuss his idea. Using his great organizational skills and financing the venture with his own money, he succeeded in arrang-

The second Zionist Congress

ing the first Zionist Congress. On August 29, 1897, delegates from sixteen countries met in Basel, Switzerland.

Dr. Theodore Herzl

The meeting of the Zionist Congress electrified the Jewish world. The Congress defined its goal as the creation of a national home for the Jewish people in Palestine. A combination of forces made this an idea whose time had come. Nationalism was in style; many of the smaller European nations were fighting for political freedom and national independence. Secondly, there seemed to be no place for the Jews in Europe. Eastern Europe no longer offered much hope of peace or security, and after the Dreyfus trial, even the assimilated Jews in Western Europe were badly shaken. Finally, the renewed immigration to Palestine and the creation of Rothschild's colonies had turned Eretz Yisrael from a dream into a practical possibility.

Combined with the age-old, religious longing for Zion, the secular Zionist plan became a real and compelling idea. Many religious Jews rejected the entire Zionist concept; others agreed with the idea but not with Herzl's view of a Jewish state. Reform and assimilated Jews rejected his idea completely. despite the opposition, Zionism became a powerful force in Jewish life.

Herzl was a highly intelligent, charismatic man. He was an imposing figure, a man who inspired confidence. Many of the persecuted Jews of Eastern Europe adopted him as their king; his picture hung in Jewish homes across the continent. Unfortunately, his connection with his Jewish background was fatally weak. He had so little understanding of the deep connection between the Land of Israel and the people of Israel, that he was willing to establish his Jewish state anywhere in the world. He did not realize that for the vast majority of Jews, even secular Jews, a Jewish state could only exist in Zion, in the land of their fathers.

Herzl dedicated the next ten years of his life to the Zionist cause. He traveled around the world, met with every important leader of the time, wrote, published, lobbied, organized and tried to find land for a Jewish state. When England, for reasons of its own, offered to found a Jewish colony in East Africa, in Uganda, Herzl saw this offer as the realization of his dream. The Zionist movement, however, rebelled and split in two. The Eastern European Jews, led by Chaim Weizmann (who would later become the first president of the State of Israel) revolted. To the Jews of Russia and Poland, Zionism had only one meaning — Jerusalem and the Land of Israel.

Herzl threatened to resign if the Congress did not accept the Ugandan proposal. The crisis affected him deeply. He had spent his large family fortune on the Zionist cause and now his health was failing. His energy was sapped, he suffered from heart disease, his marriage had suffered, his money was gone. He died in 1904, when he was only forty-four, before the next Congress could vote on the choice of Uganda. Towards the end of his life he realized that "Palestine is the only land where our people can come to rest."

Herzl is buried on Mt. Herzl in Jerusalem. He was a highly devoted man who had the welfare of his people at heart and who spent ten years of his life, unlimited energy, and his entire fortune on their behalf. He once said, "At Basel I founded the Jewish state." He exaggerated, but there was, nonetheless, a kernel of truth in the statement. Herzl indeed fathered the idea of an independent, secular Jewish state. The existence of the State of Israel today is proof of the appeal of that idea.

Zionism captured the Jewish imagination. Although only a small percentage of Jews actually immigrated to Palestine, young and old alike were caught up in the dream of Eretz Yisrael. Herzl's political Zionism would change the course of Jewish history, leading to phenomenal successes and to unforeseen problems.

ORTHODOX OPPOSITION

Many great rabbis opposed the new Zionist movement. Even though Zionism itself was founded upon a religious idea — the Return of Am Yisrael to Zion — political Zionism was basically a secular, haskalah-oriented movement that sought to create a secular, Jewish state. There was also opposition to the leaders of the Zionist movement, many of whom were maskilim, assimilationists, even atheists. Rabbis insisted that salvation could not come to Israel through leaders who did not believe in the Torah, ate non-kosher food and desecrated the Sabbath.

There was also a great fear that this new movement would sweep away the masses on a wave of messianic expectations, as in the time of Shabtai Tzvi. Herzl did not believe in the Messiah, but many Jews saw the return to Zion as the fulfillment of God's promises and the beginning of the process of Redemption, even though it was being carried out by secular Jews. Many rabbis agreed, and in 1909 Rabbi Jacob Reines, a graduate of the Volozhin Yeshivah, founded the Mizrachi organization for religious Zionists.

The highly charged dispute continued. The issues could not be resolved and religious Jewry remained divided on essential questions: Was the Return to Zion the beginning of the Redemption or simply a practical solution to anti-Semitism? Should a Jew return to Palestine or wait patiently in the Exile until the coming of the Messiah?

THE SECOND ALIYAH

The immigrations between 1904 and 1914 are referred to as the Second Aliyah. Over 40,000 new immigrants from Europe arrived in Palestine. Most were secular, socialist, and very idealistic, and they left a permanent mark on the future development of the New Yishuv. Determined to create a new society, a new nation and a "new Jew," these *olim* made extreme efforts to break with the old Jewish past. The theme of the Second Aliyah was Jewish labor. Unlike the Jews of the First Aliyah who had employed Arab labor (thereby greatly raising the Arab standard of living and bringing a huge influx of Arabs into Palestine from surrounding Arab lands), the pioneers of the Second Aliyah spurned the Arabs. They created the socialistic kibbutzim, based on collective living, ideas of social justice and equal rights. They built Degania, Ein-Harod, Givat Brenner, Nahalal and other settlements with their own sweat and blood. They drained swamps, planted trees, cleared rocks, plowed and planted. They invested superhuman efforts in settling the Land. The Shomrim — the Society of Watchmen — guarded and defended the Jewish settlements. The price for Eretz Yisrael was high. Many of

Top: a group of Shomrim
Bottom: Groundbreaking for the city of Tel Aviv

these pioneer settlers paid with their lives — they died of malaria or were killed by Arab marauders. In 1909 the foundation stone for a new city, Tel Aviv, was set in place outside of Jaffa. It has since become the largest Jewish city in the world.

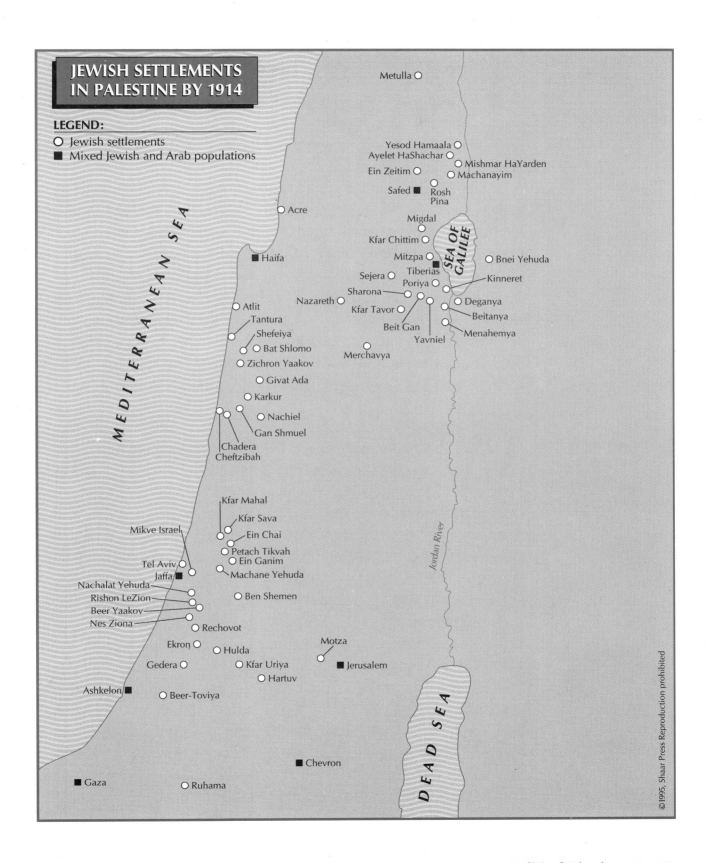

JEWISH SETTLEMENTS
IN PALESTINE BY 1914

LEGEND:
○ Jewish settlements
■ Mixed Jewish and Arab populations

Metulla ○

Yesod Hamaala ○
Ayelet HaShachar ○
○ Mishmar HaYarden
Ein Zeitim ○   ○ Machanayim
Safed ■   ○ Rosh Pina

MEDITERRANEAN SEA

Acre ○

Migdal ○
Kfar Chittim ○

SEA OF GALILEE

Haifa ■

Mitzpa ○   ○ Bnei Yehuda
Sejera ○   Tiberias ■
Sharona ○   Poriya ○   Kinneret ○
Nazareth ○   ○ Deganya
Kfar Tavor ○   ○ Beitanya
Beit Gan ○   ○ Menahemya
Yavniel ○

Atlit ○
Tantura
Shefeiya ○   ○ Bat Shlomo
○ Zichron Yaakov

Merchavya ○

○ Givat Ada
○ Karkur
○ Nachiel
○ Gan Shmuel
Chadera
Cheftzibah

Jordan River

Kfar Mahal ○
○ Kfar Sava
○ Ein Chai
Mikve Israel ○ Petach Tikvah
○ Ein Ganim
Tel Aviv ○   ○ Machane Yehuda
Jaffa ■
Nachalat Yehuda
Rishon LeZion   ○ Ben Shemen
Beer Yaakov
Nes Ziona
○ Rechovot   Motza ○
Ekron ○   ○ Hulda
Gedera ○   ○ Kfar Uriya   ■ Jerusalem
○ Hartuv
Ashkelon ■
○ Beer-Toviya

DEAD SEA

■ Chevron

■ Gaza   ○ Ruhama

©1995, Shaar Press Reproduction prohibited

THE JOURNEY FOR REPENTANCE

The fiery idealism and unlimited sacrifice of the Second Aliyah was combined with disdain for the Jewish past. Children on the new kibbutzim grew up knowing nothing of the Sabbath or Yom Kippur, of Jewish prayer or kosher food. The Bible was respected as a work of literature, but all religious ritual was scorned and abolished.

In 1913 the rabbis of Palestine organized a "Journey for Repentance." Led by Rabbi Avraham Y. Kook, then rabbi of Jaffa, and Rabbi Yosef Chaim Sonnenfeld, leading rabbi of the Old Yishuv in Jerusalem, they visited many of the kibbutzim and settlements and spoke to the people about Torah and Jewish tradition. In some places they were warmly received; the settlers agreed to open kosher kitchens and synagogues. In other places they were spurned. Rabbi Sonnenfeld was shocked and saddened at what he saw, but Rabbi Kook remained optimistic. He firmly believed that the settlers, or their descendants, would eventually repent and return to Torah.

HEBREW AS THE NATIONAL LANGUAGE

What language were the Jews of Palestine supposed to speak? Today, Hebrew seems the obvious choice. Yet, at the time, Hebrew was not a spoken language. Jews studied and prayed and corresponded in Hebrew, but they did not use it for their everyday needs. Herzl suggested an international language such as German or French for the Jewish state, but the Sefardi Jews in Palestine spoke Ladino, the Ashkenazi Jews spoke Yiddish and the Arabs and officials of the Ottoman Empire spoke Arabic.

Nonetheless, Hebrew became the spoken language of the Land. This amazing feat was due in great measure to the efforts of one man, Eliezer ben Yehudah. Ben Yehudah was a stubborn Lithuanian Jew, a former yeshivah student turned maskil. To him Hebrew was not a Holy Tongue, the God-given Language of the Torah, but a secular, national language that would unite the Jews of the world in their old-new home. He was strongly opposed by religious Jews of the Old Yishuv who considered the revival of Hebrew to be another anti-religious, Zionist ploy. Whether or not to speak Hebrew became a burning issue in the Yishuv.

Eliezer ben Yehudah

Ben Yehudah turned the adoption of Hebrew into a lifelong crusade. He insisted that his family speak only Hebrew and he was the first teacher in the country to conduct classes only in Hebrew. He chose to use a modified Sefardic dialect rather than one of the European, Ashkenazic pronunciations. In 1910 he published his *Complete Dictionary of Ancient and Modern Hebrew*. Slowly, Hebrew caught on. In 1919 it was given equal status with English and Arabic; in 1948 it became the official language of the State of Israel. Today, Hebrew is a vibrant, living language spoken by the five million inhabitants of Israel and by Jews (and many gentiles) throughout the world. One man had incredibly turned the linguistic tide for a nation.

Ben Yehudah himself was an extreme and virulent opponent of Jewish religion and tradition. Yet, he succeeded in making Hebrew, the language of Torah and Jewish life in the Holy Land.

GROWTH IN THE SHADE OF WAR

The settlement of the Jews on the soil of Palestine quietly progressed. The entire country was dotted with agricultural colonies. The Jewish National Fund, a non-profit organization funded by contributions from Jews all over the world, was estab-

Aerial view of present-day Tel Aviv

lished to purchase land in Palestine. Their blue and white collection boxes were on the shelves of Jewish homes all over the world and were a daily reminder of the eternal connection between Eretz Yisrael and the Jewish people. As Jewish immigration increased, Palestine responded to the loving touch of Am Yisrael. The Land blossomed and gave forth its fruits. A desolate, abandoned country came miraculously to life.

The New Yishuv rapidly outnumbered and overshadowed the Old, and a new, modern, secular Jewish society emerged. Yet Torah in Eretz Yisrael did not disappear. Its defenders slowly grew in numbers and gathered strength. By the end of the Second World War, they would become an influential force in society. But before that, the Jews of Palestine would meet terrible challenges and undergo tremendous change. They would endure war, famine, pogroms, mass immigrations and war again. The old adage of the Sages remained true: *Eretz Yisrael nikneis b'yissurim* — the Land of Israel is acquired only through suffering.

21
Shores of Gold —
The Rise of American Jewry
(From 1850-1900)

*T*he Jewish people had an old and honorable history in the saga of the New World. Columbus' expedition was made possible by a large loan from two Marrano Jews and the patrons and officials involved in his expedition were all "New Christians" (Marranos). The first European to set foot on the shore of the new land was Colombus' interpreter, Luis de Torres, a Jew who had been baptized the day before Columbus set sail.

JEWS IN THE NEW WORLD

The first Jews to reach the New World were Sefardim or Marranos escaping from the long arm of the Catholic Inquisition. They settled throughout the West Indies under Dutch and English colonial rule. For the most part, they engaged in the import and export trade — in tobacco, sugar and wheat. The history of the Jews in these islands is

The Touro Synagogue in Newport, Rhode Island. Built in 1763, it is the oldest extant synagogue in North America.

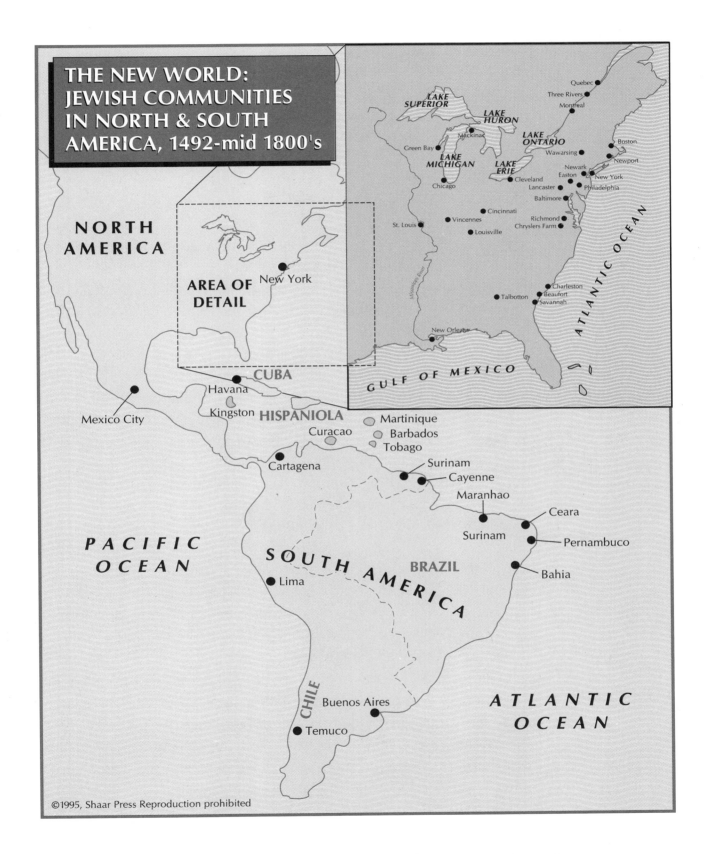

THE NEW WORLD:
JEWISH COMMUNITIES
IN NORTH & SOUTH
AMERICA, 1492-mid 1800's

NORTH
AMERICA

AREA OF
DETAIL

New York

CUBA

Havana

Kingston HISPANIOLA

Mexico City

Curacao

Cartagena

Martinique
Barbados
Tobago

Surinam
Cayenne

Maranhao

Ceara

Surinam

Pernambuco

Bahia

PACIFIC
OCEAN

SOUTH AMERICA

BRAZIL

Lima

CHILE

Buenos Aires

Temuco

ATLANTIC
OCEAN

Area of Detail:

LAKE
SUPERIOR

LAKE
HURON

Quebec
Three Rivers
Montreal

Green Bay

Mackinac

LAKE
ONTARIO

Boston

Wawarsing

Newport

LAKE
MICHIGAN

LAKE
ERIE

Chicago

Cleveland

Newark

Easton New York

Lancaster

Philadelphia

Baltimore

Cincinnati

Richmond

St. Louis

Vincennes

Chryslers Farm

Louisville

ATLANTIC OCEAN

Charleston
Beaufort
Savannah

Talbotton

New Orleans

GULF OF MEXICO

a fascinating story in itself. Very few of these early communities still exist, but their synagogues and cemeteries remain. In 1654 a small group of Jewish refugees arrived in New Amsterdam (later called New York) and the story of North American Jewry began.

Jews took an active part in the American War of Independence. Most famous, perhaps, was the Polish immigrant Chaim Salomon. Salomon helped finance the American Revolutionary War. He lent large sums of money, without interest, to members of the Continental Congress and to the war effort. Even after he was arrested by the British as a spy for the colonies, he continued to assist American prisoners and to serve the Revolutionary forces. He worked unceasingly for the rights of the Jews and contributed generously to Jewish causes and to the building of the synagogue Mikveh Yisrael in Philadelphia.

DURING AND AFTER THE CIVIL WAR

Until the Civil War, the Jewish population in the United States was small. In 1820 only 4,000 Jews lived in the country. They were officially recognized as a religious group in only seven of the original thirteen colonies.

The overwhelming number were German-speaking Jews from Western or Central Europe. Many began their lives in America as peddlers, but they were hardworking, earnest immigrants who quickly became prosperous citizens. They settled in northern New York and the Midwest — in Chicago, Detroit, Milwaukee and Cincinnati. In 1843 the first successful Jewish newspaper, The Occident, was published, and the Jewish Publication Society produced the first Jewish textbooks. The Jewish community had become respectable and well established.

During the Damascus protest, in 1840, American Jews banded together as a national group for first time. Afterwards, however, they continued to go their individual ways. Like all other Americans, Jewish Americans considered themselves to be Northerners or Southerners, for or against slavery. Over 10,000 Jews fought in the armies on both sides during the Civil War. Jewish organizational and financial skills came to the fore as they pro-

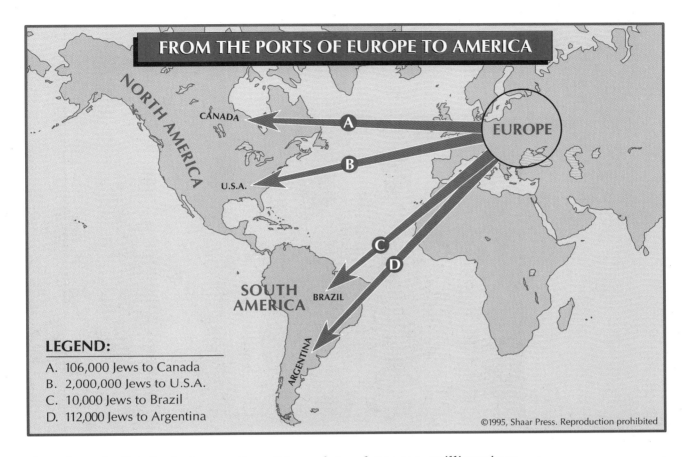

FROM THE PORTS OF EUROPE TO AMERICA

LEGEND:

A. 106,000 Jews to Canada
B. 2,000,000 Jews to U.S.A.
C. 10,000 Jews to Brazil
D. 112,000 Jews to Argentina

duced and distributed supplies. Many later became millionaires, owners of great firms and retail concerns. They were generous philanthropists, giving charity and funding magnificent institutions, both Jewish and general.

By the 1860's, New York had a Jewish community of 40,000. When General Ulysses S. Grant issued an order in 1862 expelling Jews from serving in the Treasury Department, the reaction was immediate. Within two weeks, President Lincoln ordered Grant to revoke the order.

Between 1881 and 1903 the American Jewish community underwent a drastic change. Two million Jewish refugees arrived as a result of the Czar's persecution and the pogroms in Eastern Europe. The refugees were Yiddish speaking, not German; they were Orthodox or Chassidic, not Reformed. Unlike

MASS IMMIGRA-TION IN 1881

their wealthy, sophisticated, American brethren, they were frightened, disoriented and desperately poor.

Yet the immigration from Eastern Europe revitalized the American Jewish community and caused it to blossom. A relief agency was set up on Ward Island by a young Jewish poet, Emma Lazarus. She came from an old and wealthy Sefardic family, but she gave her soul to the poor Ashkenazic Jews who were daily arriving at the ports of the New World. Her famous poem graces the Statue of Liberty. Originally written as a song of welcome to her fellow Jews, it became a symbol of America, a sign of light and liberty for the oppressed people of the world.

> Give me your tired, your poor,
> Your huddled masses yearning to breathe free,
> The wretched refuse of your teeming shore.
> Send these, the homeless, tempest-toss't to me.
> I lift my lamp beside the golden door.

The immigrants, sensing the warm welcome, wrote their relatives in Europe to pack their meager bags and come. They sent money, tickets and encouragement. They formed groups of *landsleit* — friends and relatives from the same town — to help their families and townsfolk. For the Jews, America indeed became the *Goldineh Medineh* — the Golden Land.

The majority of the new refugees settled on the Lower East Side of New York. The crowded tenements teemed with poor people trying to earn a living and create some semblance of an orderly life in a strange new world. Religious life suffered a severe blow. The immigrants were forced to work twelve to fourteen hours a day, six days a week; the Sabbath and holidays were often pushed aside. The level of Jewish education was abysmal. HIAS (the Hebrew Immigrant Aid Society) and a network of Jewish federations all offered aid and helped "Americanize" the new immigrants. The children went to public school (there were no day schools and very few yeshivos). Torah was forgotten. As a

JEWISH POPULATION AND IMMIGRATION TO THE UNITED STATES

1770	2,000
1820	4,000
1826	6,000
1840	15,000
1860	150,000
1880's	350,000 (200,000 immigrants from Russia)
1890's	700,000 (360,000 immigrants)
1900's	1,500,000 (800,000 immigrants)
1914	2,000,000 = Total Jewish Population

JEWISH LIFE AFTER 1881

The market on Orchard Street, on the Lower East Side of New York, c. 1900

result, great rabbis in Russia advised the Jews not to come to America, but their advice was ignored. The Jews of Russia voted with their feet, running away from the pogroms, the poverty and the horror of life in Czarist Russia. The famous Yiddish humorist, Sholom Aleichem, wrote:

> The word "America" was heard more often than any other ... it had a kind of magical meaning ... they imagined America to be a kind of heaven, a sort of Paradise.

New York soon became the largest Jewish city in the world. Six hundred thousand copies of Yiddish newspapers were sold daily. *The Jewish Daily Forward* was the largest and most influential Yiddish newspaper. It was socialist and anti-religious. Like most Yiddish culture of that time — art, theater, literature — its leftist outlook was a product of liberal, humanist, Haskalah views.

The East Side became a vast world unto itself. Poets, novelists, socialists, revolutionaries and great Talmudic scholars all lived and worked side by side, trying to earn enough to get through the week. Working conditions were horrendous. An entire Jewish-led labor movement would eventually emerge from the cauldrons of the East Side, to the benefit of all American society. Jewish parents worked their fingers to the bone so that their children might go on to colleges and universities and become doctors, lawyers and great industrialists.

I n the 1800's and the early 1900's, during the "German" phase of American Jewry, Reform Judaism was dominant. The "melting pot" theory of assimilating new immigrants and turning them into good Americans was very popular. Although religious freedom was guaranteed by law, the white, Anglo-Saxon, Protestant life-style was the norm and the goal. Reform Jews very much identified with everything it symbolized.

REFORM AND CONSERVATIVE JUDAISM

In 1875 Isaac Mayer Wise, head of the Reform movement, established the Hebrew Union College in Cincinnati. A writer, lecturer and talented organizer, he united the many Reform temples in the country into the Union of American Hebrew Congregations. Thus, by the beginning of the twentieth century, Reform Jewry was powerful, well organized and well financed, while Orthodoxy was still ill prepared and unable to deal with the new American reality.

At the first graduation dinner of the Reform Hebrew Union College, in 1883, shrimp was served. A furor ensued and many distinguished rabbis walked out in disgust. Shortly afterwards, both the Orthodox and the Conservative movements founded their own institutions.

In 1885 the Reform movement made its official break with many basic Jewish beliefs. In its Pittsburgh Platform, it declared that all Biblical and rabbinical laws were obstructions to modern life; that they no longer considered the Jews a nation, but a religious community; and that a return to Palestine, a future Temple, sacrifices, or any form of a future Jewish state had no meaning. They allowed Saturday services to be held on Sunday, and they canceled the requirement of circumcision for Jewish males.

Opposing the extreme changes made by Reform, a group of rabbis and laymen founded the Conservative Movement. In 1886 they established the Jewish Theological Seminary of America. At first the seminary was rather Orthodox, but this changed, especially after Professor Solomon Schechter of Cambridge University in England was brought to America 1n 1902, to head the Seminary. He was a respected scholar, but he did not believe in the Divinity of Torah and Jewish law. He was faced with the impossible dilemma of trying to preserve Jewish ideals, traditions and actions while denying their Divine origin. As a result, the seminary could not be considered Orthodox by any stretch of the imagination, and it became the spiritual center of Conservative Judaism.

ORTHODOXY

In 1880 ninety percent of America's synagogues had been Reform. By 1893, 316 out of 533 synagogues — more than half — were Orthodox. Scores of Jewish synagogues were opened — places where the Maharal of Prague, the Baal Shem Tov or the Vilna Gaon would have felt at home. But traditional Judaism was not yet ready to deal with America. It had no structure or overall organization. Every synagogue was an island unto itself. There was no community to provide education, supervise kashruth, or be responsible for general welfare. America was a mammoth melting pot into which all the immigrants were poured, willingly or not. The vast majority emerged as successful Americans, but less successful Jews. An entire generation of Jewish youth, tempted and molded by the great American dream of wealth and prestige, was lost to Torah.

Rabbi Jacob Joseph

In 1888 Rabbi Jacob Joseph, the famed Maggid of Vilna, accepted an invitation to serve as Chief Rabbi of the immigrant community in New York. One of the leading students of Rabbi Yisrael Salanter, he was a man of great talent, energy and scholarship. He struggled to control the integrity of the kosher poultry and meat business in New York, but to no avail. There were too many unscrupulous butchers, corrupt politicians and greedy laymen. He attempted to organize and structure Jewish religious life, but was unable to complete this task successfully. Rabbi Jacob Joseph suffered a stroke and died in 1902. His funeral was one of the largest ever seen in New York.

In spite of its rocky beginnings, Orthodox Jewry eventually began to organize. The Union of Orthodox Jewish Congregations of America was founded in 1898, and in 1902 the Union of Orthodox Rabbis (the *Agudath HaRabbonim*) was created. These organizations attempted to bring a sense of order and community into the chaos of religious life in America.

EDUCATION

It has been estimated that by 1906, a mere eighteen years after the first large wave of Eastern European immigration, ninety percent of the Jewish immigrants were no longer strictly observant. Jewish life was falling by the wayside and Jewish education seemed irrelevant. Hardly any day schools or yeshivos existed. Boys went to "Hebrew School" several times a week. At best, they were taught how to read and pray. Most classes were conducted in Yiddish. The quality of teaching was often poor; there was no set curriculum; the students were bored and anxious to be set free. Only a handful continued to study after they became Bar Mitzvah.

The first yeshivah in America, the Etz Chaim Hebrew School, was founded on the Lower East Side of New York in 1886. In 1897, Rabbi Moshe Matlin founded the Yeshivah Rabbi Isaac Elchonon, named after the great rabbi of Kovno, who had passed away not long before. This ionstitution was attracted mainly students who had a strong Talmudic background from Europe.

Rabbi Jacob Joseph founded the Beis Sefer Yeshivah in 1900, and after his death it was renamed Yeshivah Rabbi Jacob Joseph, in his honor. Mesivtha Tifereth Jerusalem was founded in 1907. All these institutions were located on the Lower East Side of New York, which was the main center of Jewish life for a few generations.

In 1915, Etz Chaim and Yeshivah Rabbi Jacob Joseph merged

Rabbi Bernard Revel

under the name Rabbi Isaac Elchonon Theological Seminary. That year Rabbi Bernard Revel became president of the institution. He bagan to include secular studies in the high school program and, in 1925, founded Yeshivah College.

NEW HEIGHTS

By the beginning of the First World War, American Jews already held positions of great prominence in American society. They included millionaires, diplomats, great businessmen, lawyers, doctors and industrialists. Benjamin Cardozo and Louis Brandeis would become Supreme Court Justices. Jews established publishing houses and newspapers; they took part in sports and the arts. They established great retail stores. Levi-Strauss, Macy's, Gimbel's, Sears-Roebuck, Bloomingdale's, and Altman's were all founded by Jewish immigrants who had begun their careers as peddlers. The times were filled with bright high hopes and American Jewry was fast finding a place in the center of the American dream. No one expected what the future would soon bring.

R.H. Macy's department store, 1888

22
Before the Storm
(From 1850-1910)

The years before the First World War were particularly chaotic (see Chapter 17). The belligerence of the German Kaiser, combined with the weakness of Austria, the instability of Russia, the turmoil in the Balkans, the corruption in Turkey, and conflicting British and French imperial interests kept the world in a state of constant agitation.

Science, psychology and philosophy were being transformed. Darwin changed the way man saw nature; Freud changed the way man viewed his inner self; and Einstein revolutionized man's understanding of the vast world around him — of time, space and physical laws. Urbanization, socialism, nationalism, the effects of the Industrial Revolution and fierce capitalism caused mass dislocations in society.

The furious intellectual, scientific, and political activity at the turn of the century caused a widespread feeling of bewilderment and anxiety. A famous novelist of the time wrote: "I am here. More than that I do not know; further than that I cannot go. My ship has no rudder and it is driven by the wind ..."

Anti-Semitism grew in Eastern and Western Europe. Pogroms in Russia became more savage. The anti-Semitic Black Hundreds held sway in the Pale of Settlement. Vienna elected an openly anti-Semitic mayor and France was still reeling from the Dreyfus affair. And the myth of the evil, all-powerful Jew was being exported to the Turks and Arabs in the Ottoman Empire.

The Jews turned in various directions for guidance and aid. The Return to Zion continued, the New Yishuv in Palestine grew and the Zionist movement persevered in working towards a Jewish homeland. Many secular Jews advocated other causes — anarchy, revolution, socialism, communism and democracy. Traditional Jewry, however, concentrated not on society as a whole, but on perfecting the building blocks of society — the individual person.

I n this period of great unrest and change, a saintly scholar by the name of Rabbi Yisrael Meir HaCohen Kagan lived in the village of Radin in Lithuania (which became part of Poland after World War I). He was a gentle, modest man, small of stature, yet he dominated his generation.

Rabbi Yisrael Meir is known as the *Chafetz Chaim,* which is the name of the book that he wrote on the laws of speech. Speech is communication, and communication is the way we shape our society. The Torah strictly forbids slander, gossip and verbal abuse, and it regulates what we may and what we may not say. Rabbi Yisrael Meir, a student of the Mussar movement, emphasized the ethical importance of speech, writing and other forms of communication. Proper communication leads to peace, social harmony and justice. Improper speech is a flagrant violation of the Torah's laws and spirit.

The Chafetz Chaim, right, in front of his home in Radin, speaking to his son , R' Leib. In back of them is the Chafetz Chaim's rebbetzin

Besides his great work on the laws of speech, the Chafetz Chaim compiled the six-volume *Mishneh Berurah* (a commentary on part of the *Shulchan Aruch*) and the *Likkutei Halachos* on many tractates of the Talmud. He also wrote other scholarly and ethical works. He was, however, concerned with the needs of all Jews, not only those of scholars. He wrote books and pamphlets for Jewish soldiers serving in the Czar's army, for Jewish immigrants to America, for Jewish women, for Jewish students. He preached hygiene, health, charity, welfare and the establishment of free-loan funds for the poor. He emphasized the rights of the laborer to fair wages. He fought for the sanctity of the Sabbath and placed the yeshivos at the center of the Jewish world. The Chafetz Chaim was a living example of pure, simple faith, love and humility. He exerted great influence on the Jews of Eastern Europe and was lovingly accepted as their teacher and guide.

In 1923 at the first congress of Agudath Yisrael in Vienna, the Chafetz Chaim was described in a secular Yiddish newspaper as "... a tiny, frail, old man; a venerable, hunched little man with a small white beard and a simple, poor black coat, a plain black scarf around his neck ... when you look more closely, you see the face of a servant of God .... The Divine Presence rests on that face and you must close your eyes because of the brilliance that shines from the small, wise, gray eyes ... He calls Jews to unity, to peace, to goodness, to piety, to love and to action ... From his eyes glows an entire world of wisdom and goodness."

The light of his "wisdom and goodness" still shines today, lighting the way for Jews who continue to walk in the path of Torah.

THE SFAS EMES

Another Jewish luminary was Rabbi Yehudah Aryeh Leib Alter, the Rebbe of the Chassidic Ger dynasty. He was known as the *Sfas Emes,* after his classic commentary on the Talmud and the collection of his discourses on the Torah and festivals. He was famous for his modesty, his humility and his disdain of power and luxury. The Sfas Emes was filled with a fierce sense of justice. Compelled by a never-ending search for truth and honesty, he inspired his tens of thousands of followers to self-improvement.

But the Sfas Emes was more than a philosopher. He was a practical and active leader. He encouraged political action and the publication of Orthodox newspapers. He organized a wide network of social institutions throughout Poland, where most of the Gerrer Chassidim lived. This work was continued and expanded under his successor, Rabbi Avraham Mordechai Alter, the *Imrei Emes*. The strength and loyalty of the Gerrer Chassidim were important factors in rebuilding Polish Jewry after the destruction of the First World War. Although Chassidic Jewry was less revolutionary and far less organized than the secular, charitable Jewish organizations, its peaceful programs for self-help and improvement were solid and long lasting.

Plaque marking the Sfas Emes' tombstone in Ger, Poland

AGUDATH ISRAEL

Troubled by the challenges of the times, representatives of major groups within traditional Jewry met in 1912 and founded the Agudath Israel. The Agudah was established as an international Jewish organization dedicated to the preservation of Torah tradition and values. Its leaders included followers of Rabbi Samson Raphael Hirsch of Germany, great Chassidic rebbes of Poland, and representatives of the misnagdic Lithuanian and the Hungarian communities. Rabbi Chaim Ozer Grodzenski of Vilna and Rabbi Avraham Mordechai Alter, Rebbe of Ger, were its spiritual leaders, while Jacob Rosenheim was its organizational leader and Nathan Birnbaum (an early Zionist leader who became Orthodox) was its philosopher. The great Chafetz Chaim gave the new organization his blessing.

Many different factions existed side by side within the Agudah. Although the movement viewed itself as the combined Torah voice of the Jewish nation, its members agreed that each community within the organization would retain

R" Chaim Ozer Grodzenski

its own life-style and traditions. Nonetheless, it did not receive universal support among religious Jewry. The Mizrachi, the Religious Zionist movement that had been founded by Rabbi Jacob Reines, enjoyed wide support among rabbis and religious Jewry. Since Agudah refused to recognize the secular Zionist organization as representing the Jewish people, it was opposed to the Mizrachi faction as well. The split within religious Jewry, between Mizrachi and the Agudah, would be deep and long-lasting.

There were also great rabbinic and Chassidic leaders who were opposed to the Agudah, especially among the Hungarian rabbis and some rabbis of the Old Yishuv in Eretz Yisrael. In their eyes, the new organization was too modern.

Agudah was weakened by the events of the First World War and by the widespread popularity of Zionism after the War. Its first Knessiah Gedolah — Great Congress — was scheduled for the summer of 1914, but due to the outbreak of the war it did not take place until 1923. Since then, Agudath Israel has developed into a great force in the rejuvenation of Torah and a vital component of Jewish life both in Israel and in America.

Leaders of the Mizrachi Party

First Knessiah Gedolah

THE RADICAL LEFT

A small but very vocal minority of the Jewish people joined the radical Left. Determined to create a new and universal world where a separate Jewish people would no longer be necessary, they paved a path of self-destruction. Everything old had to be erased. These self-hating Jews were prominent in every radical party and in every European country. They established a new Jewish stereotype: the Jewish revolutionary. In the eyes of Europe, the Jews became identified with the Bolshevik communists, with the anarchists, with every radical out to destroy society. This distorted perception would bring untold suffering to hundreds of thousands of

Jews who had no connection whatsoever with revolutionary forces. In the eyes of the capitalists, Jews deserved to suffer because "everyone" knew that "all" Jews were communists. (And in the eyes of the communists, Jews deserved to die because "everyone" knew that "all" Jews were capitalists!)

But not only Jews would suffer and die. Soon, millions of people, Jews and gentiles alike, would be pulled into one of the most ghastly wars in human history. It would change the face of the world and signal the beginning of the destruction of European Jewry.

A World at War
(From 1900 to 1948)

23
The First World War
(From 1914-1918)

THE GREAT WAR

The First World War began in the summer of 1914. It was called the "Great War" for it was the largest, the most horrendous, the bloodiest war the world had yet seen. Europe, Asia, parts of Africa and the United States were all engaged in a colossal slaughter which cost ten million lives. Millions more were maimed, and millions more were uprooted and turned into refugees. The war changed the map of Europe. It was the beginning of the end of European Jewry. It destroyed the foundation of Jewish life in Central and Eastern Europe and paved the way for the political upheavals that led to the Communist Revolution, the rise of Hitler, and the final destruction of European Jewry in World War II. It is striking that Germany declared war on Russia on the Ninth of Av, the traditional day of Jewish tragedy and mourning. That day of sadness was also the beginning of the destruction of European Jewry.

THE OUTBREAK OF WAR

Many developments led to the outbreak of the war. As a result of the Industrial Revolution, the factories of Europe were hungry for raw materials. Competition for natural resources was fierce. European powers built and guarded huge colonial empires in Africa, India, Persia, Egypt and other parts of the world in order to assure a steady supply of material for their industries. Russia, Great Britain and even the tottering Austro-Hungarian Empire all vied for influence and control of the Turkish Ottoman Empire. Known as the "Sick Man of Europe," the Ottoman Empire was weak and corrupt, but it still controlled vast wealth in Europe and the Middle East. An ambitious Germany also had its eye on Turkey, and German activity in the Balkans soon brought the Turks under German, rather than British, influence.

Another result of the Industrial Revolution was the development

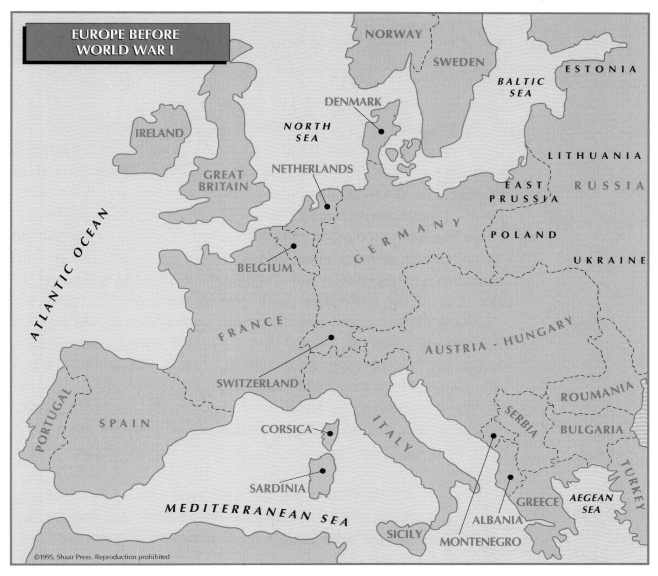

EUROPE BEFORE
WORLD WAR I

NORWAY
SWEDEN
ESTONIA
BALTIC
SEA
DENMARK
IRELAND
NORTH
SEA
LITHUANIA
NETHERLANDS
GREAT
BRITAIN
EAST
PRUSSIA
RUSSIA
ATLANTIC OCEAN
GERMANY
POLAND
BELGIUM
UKRAINE
FRANCE
AUSTRIA - HUNGARY
SWITZERLAND
PORTUGAL
SPAIN
ROUMANIA
SERBIA
CORSICA
ITALY
BULGARIA
SARDINIA
MEDITERRANEAN SEA
GREECE
AEGEAN
SEA
TURKEY
ALBANIA
SICILY
MONTENEGRO

©1995, Shaar Press. Reproduction prohibited

of powerful weapons. Europe became a great arsenal. Germany, whose plans included the conquest of France, spent ten years strengthening its armies and preparing itself for a greater, more powerful place in the world.

The general unrest and instability spread to Russia. In 1905 Russia had suffered a humiliating defeat in the Russo-Japanese War. Now the country was in a state of turmoil. Angry Russians and rebellious communists both threatened the rule of Czar Nicholas. In an attempt to turn attention away from Russia's many unsolvable problems, the Czar encouraged a brutal wave of anti-Semitism and a series of vicious pogroms. Jews fled from Russia in massive numbers — mostly to the United States, but also to Palestine.

Although no one but Germany was actually planning a war, Europe was a tinderbox, seething with conflicting interests and about to ignite. Suddenly, unexpectedly, the match was lit and Europe exploded. It was over a seemingly minor matter. In June of 1914, the Archduke Ferdinand, heir to the Austrian throne, and his wife were assassinated by a nationalist in Sarajevo, the capital of the Balkan province of Serbia. Austria threatened to attack Serbia. A complex web of alliances obligated Russia, France and England to come to Serbia's aid while Germany and Turkey sent their armies to fight with Austria.

It was thought that the war would be over in a month, at most. The Austrian chief of staff spoke about a "bright, brisk, little war," but the "little war" lasted four years. Germany invaded France, and England entered the war on the French side. Austria invaded Russian Poland. Russia attacked Prussia. Germany swept into Russia. During the first month of fighting, four years' worth of artillery shells were fired.

One year later, all the armies were stalemated. On both the eastern and western fronts, neither side could break through for a decisive victory. The casualties were horrendous. Europe was drenched in blood.

DESTRUCTION FOR THE JEWS

Hundreds of thousands of Jewish soldiers fought in the First World war. They fought in all of the different armies, which meant that they were forced to fight and kill one another. A sad joke described how a cease-fire was called one afternoon so that the Jewish soldiers from two opposing armies could join each other and form a minyan for the afternoon prayer service.

Eighty percent of European Jewry lived in Russia (which included part of Poland, the Ukraine and Lithuania) and in the Austro-Hungarian Empire (which then included Czechoslovakia, Galicia, Austria and Hungary). Many Russian Jews greeted the invading Germans as saviors from the hated Czar. The Russians, therefore, considered all the Jews traitors, even though hundreds of thousands of Jews served in the Czar's army. A new round of pogroms was

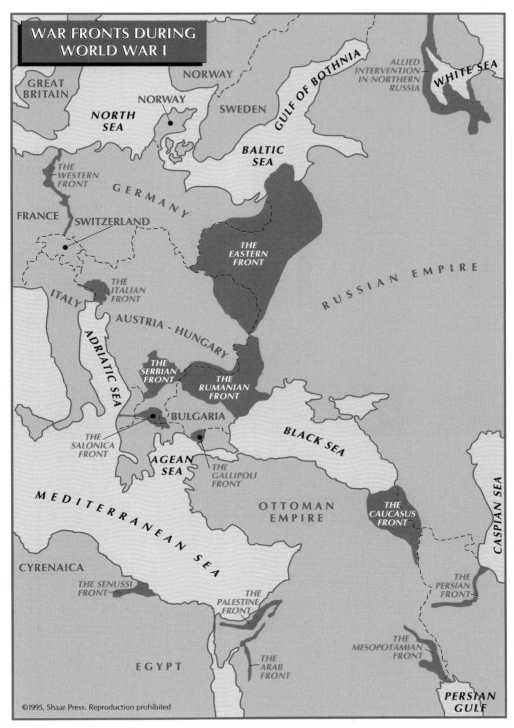

WAR FRONTS DURING
WORLD WAR I

GREAT
BRITAIN

NORWAY

NORWAY

SWEDEN

GULF OF BOTHNIA

ALLIED
INTERVENTION
IN NORTHERN
RUSSIA

WHITE SEA

NORTH
SEA

BALTIC
SEA

THE
WESTERN
FRONT

GERMANY

FRANCE

SWITZERLAND

THE
EASTERN
FRONT

RUSSIAN EMPIRE

THE
ITALIAN
FRONT

ITALY

AUSTRIA - HUNGARY

ADRIATIC SEA

THE
SERBIAN
FRONT

THE
RUMANIAN
FRONT

BULGARIA

BLACK SEA

CASPIAN SEA

THE
SALONICA
FRONT

AGEAN
SEA

THE
GALLIPOLI
FRONT

OTTOMAN
EMPIRE

THE
CAUCASUS
FRONT

MEDITERRANEAN SEA

CYRENAICA

THE SENUSSI
FRONT

THE
PALESTINE
FRONT

THE
PERSIAN
FRONT

EGYPT

THE
ARAB
FRONT

THE
MESOPOTAMIAN
FRONT

PERSIAN
GULF

unleashed after every Russian defeat; the "Zhid" was always the
guilty party. Great and ancient Jewish communities were destroyed
as hundreds of thousands of Jews were exiled from the Pale of Jewish

Jewish soldiers at the Seder during WW I

Settlement in Russian Poland. They were sent eastward, deep into Russia. The great yeshivos of Lithuania were disbanded as rabbis and Chassidic rebbes joined the stream of refugees. Poor, homeless and defenseless, thousands of Jews died on the roads.

The violence of the war convinced many that if they survived, they must break with the past and seek a new and different future. Those who could, emigrated to America or Palestine. Large numbers of younger people joined one of the socialist, communist or other radical movements, turning their backs on Torah in their search for a safer, happier, better world.

ENGLAND, TURKEY AND PALESTINE

The war continued. In 1915 England launched a sea attack against Turkey, hoping to march from Turkey to Austria. The British army, however, was pinned down on the Turkish coast and was unable to advance. Eventually, it was forced to retreat.

The failed attack convinced the British that holding territory in the Middle East was of strategic importance. This decision would have far-reaching implications for the Jews.

During World War I, 100,000 Jews and 500,000 Arabs lived in Palestine. 350,000 of these Arabs were new immigrants who had arrived from surrounding areas in the previous thirty years. The jobs and the higher standard of living that had been created by the new Jewish Yishuv were a strong drawing point.

The Jews in Palestine gave their entire support to England during the war; as a result, they were severely punished by the Turks. The Turks confiscated property, expelled Jews, executed others and hung their bodies on the walls of Jerusalem. Hundreds of Jews in Jerusalem died of starvation; many left the country. A small Jewish spy organization called "Nili" (initials for *Netzach Yisrael Lo Yishaker* — the God of Israel will not disappoint) was coordinated by the Aronson family in Zichron Yaakov. They surveyed the coast and provided information to the British, but they were caught and killed. Their graves were discovered fifty years later in Gaza, after the Israeli Army finally conquered that area in the Six Day War.

In 1917 British forces led by General Edmund Allenby invaded Palestine from Egypt and took the city of Jerusalem. With this victory, the four-hundred-year-old Ottoman Empire finally collapsed. The Jewish Yishuv was now free to openly aid the British war effort, and a Jewish legion was formed to fight for the Allied cause. The Jewish Brigade, or, as they were popularly called, the Zion Mule Corps, captured the Jewish imagination and created a nucleus of officers who would later help defend the Yishuv in Palestine.

AMERICA ENTERS THE WAR

America had managed to stay out of the war. In the presidential election of 1916, Wilson was reelected under the slogan: "He kept us out of the war." However, Germany brought the war to the high seas, interfering with the free passage of ships. Its submarines sunk more than four hundred allied vessels. The British luxury liner Lusitania was torpedoed without warning and twelve hundred people were killed. The unrestricted submarine warfare left Wilson no choice, and in 1917 an outraged America finally declared war.

RUSSIAN REVOLUTION

In February 1917 the hated Czar Nicholas abdicated and a popular democratic government was established. The Jews supported the new government fully, but eight months later the Bolshevik "October Revolution," led by Lenin and Trotsky, came to power. February had brought freedom and democracy to Russia, but October brought dictatorship and communism.

Jews in Russia, like all other religious individuals, were expected to abandon the faith of their fathers and accept the new Communist "truth." The Yevsektsia — the Jewish section of the Communist Party — was responsible for "re-educating" the Jews. They confiscated religious articles and closed synagogues and schools. Observant Jews were persecuted, rabbis were exiled or killed. Communist Jewish agricultural colonies raised pigs to prove that they had left their religion behind. All Zionist activity ground to a halt. Hebrew was forbidden, although Yiddish was permitted. The Revolution, which so many Russian Jews had worked and waited for, turned into a living nightmare.

In February 1918 the Revolutionary Government committed a singularly shameful, treacherous deed. Anxious to leave the general European war so they could continue fighting their own war for communism inside Russia, the Bolsheviks abandoned their allies and signed a separate peace treaty with Germany in the city of Brest-Litovsk (known to Jews as Brisk). Russia surrendered 34% of her population (which included three and a half million Jews), 32% of her farmland, 50% of her industry and 90% of her coal mines to Germany. After the War, most of this territory became part of the newly created Poland. It was later conquered by Germany during World War II, with unimaginable consequences for the Jews who then came under German domination.

With the Treaty of Brest-Litovsk, the Communists were free to devote themselves to their own bloody civil war. From 1917 to 1921 the Bolsheviks (as the Communists were called), the Mensheviks and the Monarchists slaughtered each other while attempting to gain control of the country. The Communists were victorious. They demolished all opposition, and whatever had survived of Jewish life in Russia after the First World War was now utterly destroyed.

THE END OF THE WAR

After Brest-Litovsk, Germany launched its last offensive in the West. By then, however, the United States had entered the war and Germany's efforts were nearing a bitter end. In the fall of 1918 the Kaiser abdicated and Germany signed an armistice agreement. The Great War was over.

History does not just happen. The Hand of God is always at work behind the scenes. At the beginning of the century, the German Emperor assured Theodore Herzl that a Jewish state could not possibly arise unless the Ottoman, Russian, German and Austro-Hungarian empires all fell. It seemed virtually impossible that such drastic changes would take place in the foreseeable future. Less than twenty years later, the impossible had happened.

Celebrating the end of the War in New York City

The Great War which began on Tishah B'Av brought horror and death to all of Europe. It marked the beginning of the destruction of European Jewry. Yet even while this destruction was taking place, seeds of hope were being planted. The war resulted in the fall of the Ottoman Empire and the proclamation of the Balfour Declaration. It led to the promise of Jewish return and the establishment of a Jewish homeland in Eretz Yisrael. The Hand of God was clearly at work.

24
The Aftermath of the War
(From 1918-1933)

By the end of World War I, Europe was in shambles. Germany was starving and exhausted; Russia was in the midst of a terrible civil war; France, England and Austria were trying to rally and recuperate. Ten million people had been killed, twenty million had been wounded. The "short, brisk war" had turned into an endless nightmare.

DREAMS AND DIS-APPOINT-MENTS

In 1919 a major peace conference met in Versailles, France. Woodrow Wilson, the American president, dreamed of a just and lasting peace. Indeed, the Treaty of Versailles gave equal rights to all of Europe's minorities, including the Jews. It established the English Mandate in Palestine, whereby England would prepare the Jews for sovereignty in their national homeland. It redrew the map of Europe, creating nine new national states, making territorial adjustments, and dismantling the German and the Ottoman Empires. Germany was punished severely and was made to pay for its aggressive role in the war. The German Rhineland, between France and Germany, was demilitarized and occupied by Allied troops.

Yet the Versailles Treaty was ultimately a dismal failure. The victors lacked the power to enforce their decisions and the treaty introduced twenty years of instability, hatred, violence and national wars. Germany seethed with rage and disappointment and dreamed of revenge against its "oppressors"; it blamed everyone but itself for its defeat in the war. This would lead to catastrophe for the world at large and for Jews in particular.

POLAND

The largest Jewish community in Europe outside of Russia was in Poland. Ten percent of Poland was Jewish. In Warsaw, Lodz and Cracow, the Jews comprised almost thir-

THE TREATY OF VERSAILLES

TERRITORIAL ADJUSTMENTS

- The German Colonial Empire is dismantled
- The Turkish Ottoman Empire is dismantled
- Italy, Greece, Belgium and Rumania are enlarged
- Germany returns Alsace-Lorraine to France
- England receives mandate to govern Palestine

NEW STATES CARVED FROM RUSSIAN AND GERMAN TERRITORIES

Finland	
Estonia	
Latvia	
Lithuania	
Poland	recreated as independent state

NEW STATES CARVED FROM AUSTRO-HUNGARIAN EMPIRE

Hungary	separated from Austria
Czechoslovakia	composed of Czechia and Slovakia
Yugoslavia	composed of several Balkan provinces

ty percent of the population. In 1917 Poland was reestablished as an independent state. "Poland for the Poles" became the national slogan. Polish independence, however, did not bring peace. Fierce battles between Poland's minority groups erupted immediately. Since the Jews were equally hated by all combatants, they provided a convenient scapegoat for whatever went wrong. In the battle between Poles and ethnic Ukrainians for the city of Lvov, both sides stopped fighting each other to indulge in a horrible pogrom. In the newly independent country of Lithuania, the battle for Vilna also offered an opportunity to massacre Jews.

The new and artificial border that was now established between Lithuania and Poland seriously disrupted Jewish life. Jews lived on both sides of the border. Once Poland and Lithuania began fighting, the Poles viewed these border Jews as Lithuanians while the Lithuanians insisted they were Poles. In general, the burning nationalism of the countless, small minorities throughout Eastern Europe was rife with anti-Semitism. Pogroms were a way of life. Jews tried to escape, and in the early 1920's, mass emigration from Eastern Europe reached epidemic proportions.

The most violent and vicious war took place in the Ukraine where Poland, the Soviet (Communist) Red Army and the anti-Soviet White Russian Army were all doing battle. The Ukraine exploded and Jewish blood flowed through the streets. Between 1918 and 1921,

more than two thousand barbarous pogroms took place. Half a million Jews were left homeless; 30,000 were killed; another 80,000 died as the result of wounds or illness. The once vibrant Pale of Settlement became a fiery grave.

In 1920 a permanent border between Russia and Poland was finally stabilized, but in the minds of most of the Polish, Russian, Lithuanian and Ukrainian masses, the Jews and the hated Bolsheviks were one and the same, even though the Jews suffered more than any other people under Bolshevik rule.

CZECHO-SLOVAKIA AND HUNGARY

The Treaty of Versailles called for the division of the once-mighty Austro-Hungarian Empire into several states: a greatly reduced Austria, a smaller Hungary separated from Austria; Yugoslavia, composed of several Balkan states; and Czechoslovakia, composed of Czechia and Slovakia. Large numbers of Chassidic Jews lived in Hungary and Czechoslovakia. Although the Jews received full and equal rights under Czechoslovakia's democratic president Tomas Masaryk in the 1920's, the closed borders and the constant border disputes caused many difficulties and disruptions in Jewish life.

More damaging was the close association between radical, leftist Jews and the communist regime. Bela Kun, dictator of the communist regime in Hungary, was a Jew; Kurt Eisner, leader of the communist uprising in Bavaria, was a Jew; and the most notorious communist revolutionary outside of Russia, Rosa "Red Rose" Luxemberg, was Jewish as well. These radical, international, totally non-Jewish Jews who turned on their own people with such vengeance were hated equally by both the Jewish and the gentile world. The anti-Semitism they engendered cost the Jewish people dearly and the guilt they bear for Jewish destruction is heavy. The fruits of Jewish assimilation were bitter indeed.

ANTI-SEMITISM BETWEEN THE WARS

Anti-Semitism was not restricted to Eastern Europe. The period between the wars saw a startling outbreak of anti-Semitism throughout the West. Conditions were highly unstable; there was a great longing for peace and security. But the fear of anarchy and Communism, fear and hatred of the Jews for their "connection" with communism, and fear of inflation and unemployment affected every corner of the liberal world. The collapse of the world economy and the arrival of the Great Depression in 1929 seemed to prove that the fears were well founded. Anti-Semitism flourished.

Communist anti-religious poster

In Russia, crowds roamed the streets during the Revolution screaming, "Beat the Jews! Save Russia!" The Jew was held responsible for the hated Bolsheviks. The Protocols of the Elders of Zion, a Russian forgery accusing the Jews of plans to dominate the world, gained wide acceptance and popularity, even in democratic countries like Britain. Anti-Semitism had deep roots in French culture and anti-Semitic groups and organizations were widespread in France. In the United States, anti-Semitism also reared its ugly head. The Ku Klux Klan arose. Henry Ford, one of the richest men in the world, subsidized anti-Semitic publications, including the infamous Protocols of the Elders of Zion. Jews were excluded from universities, clubs and hotels. The Bolshevik scare ended the American policy of unlimited immigration, putting an end to mass Jewish immigration at a time when it was most desperately needed. Everywhere, Jew and Bolshevik were considered synonymous terms.

The Versailles Treaty guaranteed Jews the right to vote in all European countries. In Central and Eastern Europe, the Jews formed their own political parties. The Bund and other leftist socialist parties represented one type of Jew; the traditional, observant Agudath Israel represented a second; and the Zionist parties, both religious and secular, represented a third. Unfortunately, the intense, internal disagreements of the Jewish parties probably caused more harm to Jewish society than any good the Jews were able to derive from voting.

Despite the constant persecution, Poland was a vibrant, thriving center of Torah education where traditional yeshivos existed alongside newer Chassidic institutions of learning. Secularism, nationalism and socialism had also become strong forces in Jewish life, and Zionism, both religious and secular, was widespread. Polish Jewry was a large and highly creative community, but it was insecure, its future unclear. Many Polish Jews emigrated to America until the U.S. closed its doors in the 1920's. Jewish immigration to the U.S. was reduced from 120,000 in 1921 to a mere 6,000 in 1924. Smaller numbers emigrated to Palestine.

Fifty thousand Polish Jews moved to Germany between the two wars. Although they helped bring new life to the German Jewish community, they were considered aliens and intruders, even by most of German Jewry. The post-war Weimar Republic, as the German government was called, was a catastrophe. It was a weak, democratic government, linked with defeat, a result of the Versailles Treaty. In the minds of most Germans, the Republic was associated with the Jews. Walter Rathenau, a Jew, was its first Foreign Minister. The Jews were pleased with the Weimar Republic, but the Germans were not.

Polish Jews leaving for Israel, 1922

Hatred, frustration, anger and violence seethed close to the surface. German Jews watched uneasily, waiting for the dark cloud to pass.

THE SPIRIT OF TORAH

Even in the midst of all the turmoil and uncertainty, Jewish life between the wars was dynamic. The yeshivos of Lithuania reestablished themselves and the old names — and new ones — became familiar. Slobodka, Mir, Kelm, Kletzk, Ponivezh, Kamenitz, Radin, Telshe, and Lublin became centers of Jewish learning. The numbers of students were relatively small, but Torah scholarship blossomed again. Students came from all over Europe, and even from America, to study. The Chassidic courts of Poland and Hungary teemed with life. Many would later be destroyed in the Holocaust of World War II, but Ger, Belz, Bobov, Munkacz, Satmar, Vizhnitz, Karlin-Stolin and others survived.

The Rebbe of Ger established and financed hundreds of yeshivos in Poland and the Chafetz Chaim and Rabbi Chaim Ozer Grodzenski of Vilna established the Vaad HaYeshivos (the Committee of Yeshivos) for Lithuanian yeshivos. Rabbi Meir Shapiro of Lublin organized the world-wide *Daf HaYomi* whereby, to this very day, Jews all over the world study the same page of the Talmud every day over a seven-and-one-half-year cycle until the entire Talmud is reviewed. The famous and beloved Sarah Schenirer founded the first Bais Yaakov girls' school in Cracow. Although some rabbis opposed her new concept of organized schools for girls, the Chafetz Chaim, the Rebbes of Ger and Belz, and others gave her their blessings and support, thus beginning a major revolution in Jewish life.

R' Meir Shapiro

In spite of the constant anti-Semitism, humiliation, taxes and restrictions which were its daily lot, religious Jewry persevered. The religious Jew did not expect salvation to come from the new, supposedly democratic governments. Nor was he surprised that the rosy promises of Versailles did not materialize. As always, he turned to the Torah for strength and satisfaction. Less traditional Jews, however, were shaken and depressed by the unexpected turn that events took after the war. The Jewish socialists, humanists, trade-unionists and others despaired of improving Jewish life in Europe. Many joined the Zionist movement, hoping that a national Jewish home in Palestine would provide a solution to their problems. To a great degree, the growth of the Zionist movement in the 1920's was the result of Jewish frustration and betrayal by the nations of the world.

25
The Yishuv In Palestine
(From 1900-1933)

*I*n the summer of 1917, World War I took an important turn. The British general, Sir Edmund Allenby, drove the Turks from Gaza, Beersheva, Jerusalem and then from all of Palestine. Unlike the German Kaiser who had proudly entered the gates of Jerusalem in 1898 astride his horse, Sir Allenby humbly entered the walls of the Old City on foot. It was seen as a gracious beginning of the relationship between England and the Jews of the Holy Land.

THE BALFOUR DECLARA- TION

British Prime Minister, David Lloyd George, and his Foreign Minister, Arthur Balfour, were highly sympathetic to the Jewish cause. Both men were friends of Dr. Chaim Weizmann, head of the Zionist movement. Weizmann requested a statement from the British government supporting the establishment of a Jewish homeland in

General Allenby and his troops entering Jerusalem, 1917

Palestine, and on November 2, 1917, the Balfour Declaration was delivered. It proclaimed:

> His Majesty's government view with favor the establishment in Palestine of a National Home for the Jewish people, and will use their best endeavors to facilitate the achievement of this object, it being clearly understood that nothing shall be done which may prejudice the civil and religious rights of existing non-Jewish communities in Palestine, or the rights and political status enjoyed by Jews in any other country.

The Balfour Declaration electrified the Jewish people. It was seen as a political commitment by England, one of the world's greatest powers, to the creation of a Jewish state. It had religious significance as well. Jewish tradition spoke of the need for the nations of the world to consent to the Jewish return to Eretz Yisrael. The Balfour Declaration meant worldwide recognition of the fact that Eretz Yisrael belonged to Am Yisrael and that Am Yisrael had the right to return.

With the fall of the Ottoman Empire in 1917, the Middle East was divided between the great powers. The League of Nations gave Britain the right to govern Palestine, stipulating that the British Mandate was to be administered according to the terms of the Balfour Declaration. The dream of Zion was no longer a private, Jewish dream. It had achieved recognition under international law.

The Balfour Declaration

THE NEW YISHUV

Britain set about ruling Palestine. The Jewish Agency for Palestine was established to represent Jewish interests and policy. Hebrew (along with Arabic and English) was recognized as an official language. In 1920 a prominent English Jew, Sir Herbert Samuel, was appointed High Commissioner of Palestine. Although Samuel officially represented Britain and not the Jews, he was the first Jew in over one thousand years to rule in Eretz Yisrael. The Jews in Palestine greeted him with great enthusiasm.

The Jewish Agency became the governing body of the yishuv; although Great Britain ruled the country, it gave certain important powers to the Agency. Through its foreign financial support, cooperation from the British, control of the press and emergency relief supplies, it dominated and controlled the Jewish community in Palestine, even in places like Jerusalem, where a majority of the population was religious.

Typical Tel Aviv street scene, 1920's

In 1919 the Third Aliyah began to arrive in Palestine. It consisted of over 36,000 East European Jews, most of them secular Jews with socialist leanings. They became the backbone of the New Yishuv. In time, many of these people would become the leaders of the Jewish state. Other Jews, from places as far away as New York and India, also came. The Jewish population of Palestine almost trebled in a mere ten years. Jewish suburbs sprang up; Tel Aviv was established on sand dunes outside Jaffa and rapidly turned into a thriving, bustling city. Large tracts of land that had been purchased as from Arab owners had to be repurchased again and again as Arabs seized their former properties from the new Jewish owners. Sometimes the same land had to be bought three or four times over, and at very high prices. Chaim

Weizmann said the soil of Palestine was "covered with Jewish gold."

Much of the land was malaria-ridden swamps, useless and unhealthy. But idealistic Jewish pioneers from the cities and villages of Eastern Europe drained the swamps, opened settlements, built cities, established businesses, orchestras, schools, libraries and a university. Modern agriculture was introduced and the sweet, heavy scent of Jaffa orange blossoms filled the land every spring. The country was slowly reforested by the Jewish National Fund and a growing carpet of green covered mountainsides which had lain bare since the time of the Romans.

A living miracle took place in the space of a few decades as an empty, abandoned country that had been desolate for almost two thousand years suddenly came to life. More than anything else, many people considered the blossoming of the Land a sign of miraculous times. The prophet Yechezkel had written (36:8):

> And you, O mountains of Israel, you shall send forth your branches and yield your fruit to my people Israel, for they have come close.

THE ARAB REACTION

First to reap the benefits of Jewish settlement were the Arabs. Throughout the 1920's, they flocked to Palestine from the surrounding countries, attracted by hopes of a better livelihood and a higher standard of living. According to available figures, two Arabs followed in the footsteps of every Jew coming to the Holy Land.

Despite the improved standard of living, the Arab reaction to the growing Jewish yishuv was hatred and violence. Jewish immigrants were viewed as enemies. When large numbers of refugees, fleeing the pogroms in the Ukraine, arrived in Palestine in April 1920, Jewish settlements were attacked in the Galil. Yosef Trumpeldor and the defenders of the northern settlement at Tel Chai were killed. Additional Arab riots and a pogrom in the Old City of Jerusalem followed. Anxious not to be accused of favoring the Jews, Sir Herbert

Samuel bent over backwards to favor the Arabs. The result of his neutrality was more terror.

In May 1921 Arab rioters in Jaffa killed twenty-seven Jews and wounded over one hundred more. As the riots spread throughout the country, the Jews began to arm. Hoping to appease the Arabs, Sir Herbert refused entry to three boatloads of Jews who had escaped the massacres in the Ukraine; the boats were sent instead to Turkish ports. Sir Herbert then ordered a temporary halt to all Jewish immigration and appointed the violently anti-Semitic Haj Amin el-Husseini as Grand Mufti of Jerusalem. The position of Grand Mufti was created by the British to provide an official leader of the Arabs, but the choice of El-Husseini was tragic. He was responsible for constant terror and death and would later cooperate with the Nazis in supporting Hitler's "Final Solution" for the Jewish people.

THE FIRST PARTITION

There were now several groups in charge of affairs in Palestine. Britain controlled the police and immigration policies. The Zionist organization governed the Jewish community through the Jewish Agency, the Haganah (the Jewish self-defense militia), and the Histadrut (the trade union organization). The Jews of the Old Yishuv and the Agudath Israel governed themselves. The Arabs formed a powerful Supreme Moslem Council under the Mufti. The English attempted to work with and balance these conflicting groups.

Although the Balfour Declaration had recognized the Jewish claim to the entire Palestine, Britain reneged on its promise and divided the country. In 1921 the huge section east of the Jordan River — the Biblical portion of the tribes of Reuven, Gad and half of Menasheh — was awarded to Emir Abdullah, a Hashemite sheik who had revolted against the Turks and aided the British during the war. Thus was born Transjordan (later called the Hashemite Kingdom of Jordan), a country which had never existed before.

The Jews felt that this division of the historical Eretz Yisrael was a betrayal, but there were so many other overwhelming problems for them to deal with that their protest was weak.

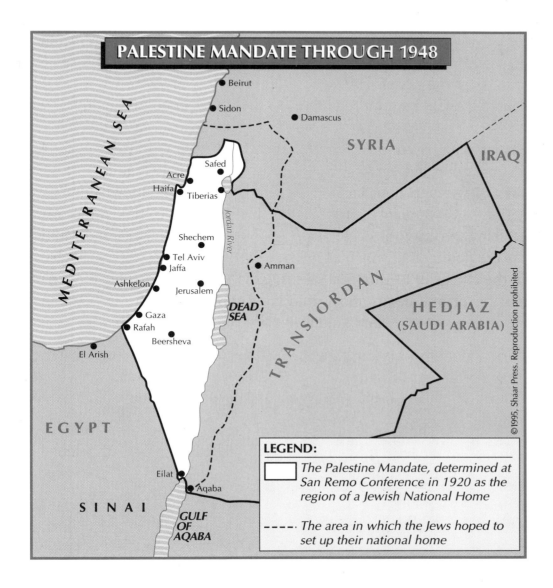

PALESTINE MANDATE THROUGH 1948

MEDITERRANEAN SEA

Beirut
Sidon
Damascus

SYRIA

IRAQ

Safed
Acre
Haifa
Tiberias

Jordan River

Shechem
Tel Aviv
Jaffa
Amman
Ashkelon
Jerusalem

TRANSJORDAN

DEAD SEA

Gaza
Rafah
Beersheba

HEDJAZ
(SAUDI ARABIA)

El Arish

EGYPT

Eilat
Aqaba

SINAI

GULF OF AQABA

LEGEND:

The Palestine Mandate, determined at San Remo Conference in 1920 as the region of a Jewish National Home

- - - - The area in which the Jews hoped to set up their national home

JEWISH IMMIGRA-TION

In 1924 the ban on Jewish immigration was removed and 50,000 new immigrants arrived, mostly from Poland. This wave of immigration was called the Fourth Aliyah. The majority of these immigrants settled in the cities of Jerusalem, Tel Aviv and Haifa.

During most of the 1920's, Jewish immigration to Palestine had been free and open. The Jewish population doubled, and by 1930 Jews comprised twenty percent of the population. The total number of immigrants, however, was not more than 100,000 and a quarter of those who came, left. Many reasons were given for the small num-

ALIYOT TO PALESTINE	
First Aliyah 1881-1903	*20,000 immigrants; Biluim, Chovevei Zion; religious base; joined Old Yishuv and settled colonies.*
Second Aliyah 1904-1914	*40,000 immigrants, mostly from Russia. Secular, socialist; used only Hebrew labor; established fourteen agricultural settlements.*
Third Aliyah 1919-1921	*36,000 immigrants; trained, secular, socialist, political. Established twenty-eight kibbutzim, moshavim, towns.*
Fourth Aliyah 1924 & 1925	*50,000 immigrants; capitalist. (By 1931, 84,000 immigrants.) Mostly to towns and cities. Founded forty-four towns and settlements.*

ber of immigrants in the 1920's — the threat of Arab violence and the overwhelming attraction of the United States were but two — but history would soon show how mistaken these reckonings were. In the frightening 1930's, the bloody Nazi star began to rise and hundreds of thousands of Jews tried frantically to leave Europe. Yet in their desperate hour of need, most were unable to enter the Holy Land. In blatant disregard of the Balfour Declaration and the Palestine Mandate, the British severely restricted Jewish immigration to Palestine. The doors to the United States and to most of the Western world were also closed. By the late 1930's there was literally no place for Jewish refugees to go. The lack of a large immigration to Palestine in the 1920's was a missed opportunity and the making of Jewish tragedy.

JEWISH POPULATION IN PALESTINE					
1882	24,000	1916	60,000*	1938	400,000
1900	50,000	1922	80,000	1940	500,000
1914	85,000	1930	160,000	1947	600,000
*(Many Jews left or died as a result of famine and difficult conditions during the First World War.)					

C hevron, the site of the *Mearas Hamachpelah* (Cave of the Patriarchs), is one of the Four Holy Cities of Eretz Yisrael. For nearly eight hundred years, a Jewish community had continuously existed in Chevron. In 1924 Rabbis Nosson Tzvi Finkel and Moshe Mordechai Epstein brought one hundred students to Chevron to found a branch of the great Lithuanian Slobodka Yeshivah. Other yeshivos followed suit, spreading the seeds of Torah throughout the New Yishuv. Slowly, these seeds would take root, and amidst the physical rebirth of the land, the spirit of Torah would also blossom and grow.

As Jewish immigrants continued to arrive throughout the 1920's, the Arabs reacted. In 1929 they attacked the community in Chevron. Fifty-nine unsuspecting Jews, including twenty-four yeshivah students, were slaughtered by their previously friendly Arab neighbors. Most were stabbed and hacked to death in a cruel and brutal fashion. The yeshivah was destroyed. Jewish property

Students studying at the Chevron Yeshivah, prior to the 1929 massacre

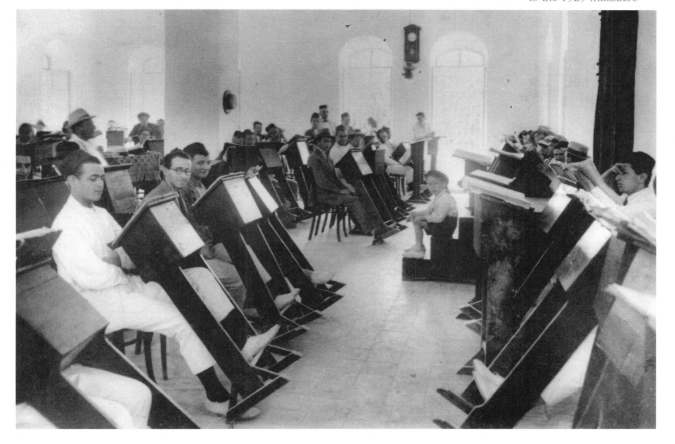

throughout the country was looted. The British announced that they were unable to guarantee the safety of the Jews in Chevron and the Jews were evacuated. Not until the Six Day War in 1967 would a new Jewish community be re-established in this ancient and holy Jewish city where Jews had lived for over fifteen hundred years.

POLITICS AND IDEOLOGY

The Jews of Palestine were divided into several ideological groups and the differences of opinion between them were deep and fiery.

The socialists, led by David Ben Gurion, wanted a secular, socialist state. Although willing to fight, they hoped for a peaceful solution to the Arab problem. The Revisionists, led by Zev Jabotinsky, wanted a Jewish, capitalist state. They were certain that the Arab problem would be solved only by force of arms. Many traditional Jews belonged to this camp. The General Zionists, led by Chaim Weizmann, wanted a secular, capitalist state, hopefully under the auspices and protection of the British Empire.

Orthodox Jews, of course, dreamed of a Jewish state run in accordance with the laws of the Torah, but their numbers and political influence were small. The Mizrachi and the Agudath Israel disagreed sharply as to the goals and policies of a political, non-religious state. The Agudah believed that a Jewish state was at most a practical and necessary physical haven for Jewish refugees, but the real and final Redemption would only come about when Jews repented and returned to Torah. The Mizrachi, however, believed that the return to Palestine and Jewish independence in Eretz Yisrael was a first, necessary step in bringing about the Redemption. These differences in outlook affected many matters and often prevented the religious parties from working together for common goals.

Last, there were other Jews who opposed any form of Jewish independence or statehood in Eretz Yisrael, even if it were religious. They believed that the Mashiach must come before any Jewish state could be established.

By the 1920's it was the secular socialists who were setting the tone and laying the foundation for the new Jewish society. Until the coming of the Modern Age — with Emancipation, Reform, Haskalah, and political Zionism — Jewish leaders had almost always been Torah scholars. Now, for the first time in Jewish history, secular leaders would stand at the helm of the Jewish ship. This development would further speed the process of secularization and assimilation which had begun in the eighteenth and nineteenth centuries.

POWER AND RELIGION

The Zionist Organization and the Jewish Agency were now in a position of power while the small Orthodox community in Palestine was virtually ignored. Faced with several difficult issues all at once, the Orthodox were disorganized and divided. How should observant Jewry react towards the Return to the Land? Were they experiencing the beginning of the Messianic Age or was that a dangerous illusion? How should religious Jewry relate to the secular Zionist movement? To surrounding secular society? Should they cooperate and adopt some of the new ways? Or should they turn their backs on everything new in order to guard the old? The challenges were taken up by Rabbi Avraham Yitzchak HaCohen Kook.

In 1904 Rabbi Avraham Yitzchak Kook came to Palestine from Lithuania to serve as the rabbi of Jaffa. He gained immediate fame as a great rabbinic scholar and a Talmudic sage, as a Kabbalist, philosopher, poet, organizer and political leader. He also served as counselor to the secular farmers and colonists in the new settlements. Rabbi Kook became the central figure of Religious Zionism. He believed that the Messianic Era had begun and that in time, all the complex problems would be dealt with and solved.

HARAV AVRAHAM YITZCHAK HACOHEN KOOK

By nature a shy and sensitive man, Rabbi Kook was, nonetheless, a man of strong principles. He was convinced that an all-encompassing love for the Jewish people would bring about the Redemption. He said:

Harav Avraham Yitzchak HaCohen Kook

Jerusalem was destroyed because of unwarranted hatred among Jews; it will be rebuilt because of unwarranted love among Jews.

In 1913-1914 he and Rabbi Yosef Chaim Sonnenfeld organized the famous "Journey of Repentance" (see Chapter 20). His personal relationship with Rabbi Sonnenfeld and with other rabbis of the Old Yishuv and Agudath Israel was warm, even though many rabbis of the Agudah and the Old Yishuv opposed his views. Rabbi Kook was thus involved in much controversy and was shamefully subjected to threats and abuse by irresponsible zealots.

In 1921 the mandatory government decided to establish an official rabbinate to govern Jewish affairs. Rabbi Kook was elected Chief Ashkenazic Rabbi. Many rabbis supported and joined the Chief Rabbinate; others opposed it. Some said it was a political, Zionist institution; others answered that it would guarantee that Torah and Jewish law become a legal, accepted part of life in the future Jewish state. The existence of the Chief Rabbinate thus became another point of controversy among religious Jews.

Rabbi Kook established a yeshivah, Mercaz HaRav, in Jerusalem. Today it is one of the largest in the country and the "Mother Yeshivah" of Zionist yeshivos. He also campaigned vigorously for the right of Jews to pray at the Western Wall, for free immigration of Jews to Palestine, and for matters of social justice between Jews and Arabs. He denounced the Grand Mufti and his terrorist policies and supported Jewish defense efforts.

A kind, pious and gentle soul, Rabbi Kook found himself engaged in difficult disputes until the end of his life. Nonetheless, he remained friendly and on good terms with almost all the great rabbis of his time. The Chafetz Chaim, the Rebbe of Ger and others corresponded with him regularly. He never lost his deep, kabbalistic belief that secularism was merely a passing phase in Jewish life and that one day the Jewish people in the Land of Israel would return to the Torah.

26
Jews East and West
(From 1900-1933)

PHILAN-THROPY — THE AMERICAN MITZVAH

*A*t the beginning of the twentieth century, the Jews of Europe were trying to protect themselves from the ravages of the new Communism and the old anti-Semitism. In Palestine, they were attempting to strengthen the Yishuv through hard labor, blood and tears. In America, they were passionately dedicating themselves to the American dream.

By the middle of the 1920's, over four-and-one-half-million Jews were living in the United States. Most were foreign born immigrants, insecure, self conscious, and anxious to work their way up the ladder of success. In their great rush to become Americans, they left behind much of Jewish life and practice. Nonetheless, they organized, belonged to and contributed to Jewish causes and communal life. One mitzvah they faithfully performed, and which came to characterize American Jewry, was the giving of *tzedakah* — charity — to both Jewish and general causes.

At the end of the First World War, when Jewish Europe was in a state of dire need, American Jewry stepped forward to help. The Joint Distribution Committee, composed of three relief organizations including the Orthodox Central Committee for the Relief of Jews, was created. The Joint distributed millions of dollars in aid and welfare, providing food, clothing and medical help. Ezras Torah, a smaller organization, was organized by the Union of Orthodox Rabbis to offer help to poor rabbis and scholars.

Charity became, to a great degree, the expression of American Judaism. Jewish education and the practice of halachah suffered greatly in the turbulent twenties, but the attitude of solidarity towards other Jews, the Jewish "heart" and open hand, helped unite American Jews. Later, the State of Israel would become the major focal point of American Jewry, but in the 1920's, charitable work on behalf of European and Palestinian Jewry formed the foundation of the American Jewish community.

The 1920's saw the rise of a massive entertainment industry in America. In the era before television, American culture was spread primarily through the movies. A weekly or bi-weekly trip to the movies was as American as apple pie and the Fourth of July. Hollywood and the major movie studios wielded a powerful influence on American life. Dreams and expectations, public opinion and values — all were created, shaped and packaged in Hollywood, and Hollywood was created by Jews. The largest, most powerful studios — Twentieth Century Fox, Metro-Goldwyn Mayer, Universal Studios, Columbia Pictures and Warner Brothers — were owned by ambitious, immigrant Jews who were determined to realize the "American Dream." They rejected their Jewish past and plunged into the present. Assimilation and success were their goal, and they were more than willing to abandon their faith to reach it. Traditional Judaism, while it might have had emotional, nostalgic value for them, was definitely not the key to their American future.

Despite their great wealth and influence, Hollywood Jews were very insecure. From 1933 to 1945, Hollywood led the country in opposing Hitler and Nazism. They used the movies to support the war effort and to arouse American patriotism. Yet they were completely silent about the Holocaust and Hitler's Final Solution for the Jews. Since being a good American in Hollywood required total and rapid assimilation, the great studios did not want to appear overly concerned with Jewish issues. No movie during the war dealt with the destruction of the Jews.

Most American Jews in the 1920's were merchants or laborers, but they were determined to give their children a higher education. Jewish parents had once dreamt of "My son, the scholar"; now "My son, the doctor (or the lawyer)" became the American Jewish dream. Quotas limited the numbers of Jewish students in many prestigious universities, especially medical schools, but masses of young Jews streamed to the colleges and universities which were open to them.

THE MEDIA AND THE AMERICAN DREAM

Jews began to enter professional life, and three Jewish judges, Benjamin Cardozo, Louis Brandeis and Felix Frankfurter (in the 1920's and 30's) were appointed to the Supreme Court. But it was the Jews of Hollywood, the radio (the founders of RCA and NBC radio and the chairman of CBS were all Jews), famous composers of popular music, and Jewish actors and comedians who first put their imprint on American life.

INSECURITY AND ANTI-SEMITISM

In the midst of the race for assimilation, anti-Semitism reared its ugly head. After the War, Jews were accused of causing the loose morals of the wild Roaring Twenties and were considered fomenters of dangerous change. A "Red Scare" swept across America in the early 1920's when huge numbers of Russian Jewish immigrants, feared to be communists or anarchists, entered the country. Americans were also afraid that the great wave of Jewish immigration would "Judaicize" America. In 1921 and 1924, Congress passed two restrictive immigration acts, aimed largely at Jewish immigrants.

In the midst of all this turmoil and pressure to Americanize, the Conservative Movement prospered. Its Jewish Theological Seminary was recognized as a leading school of Jewish scholarship; even many observant rabbis sent their sons to study there. Orthodoxy seemed doomed while Conservative Jewry seemed to offer hope for some sort of Jewish-American future.

SEEDS OF TORAH REVIVAL

Jewish education, the guarantor of continued Jewish existence, had almost disintegrated in America. Struggling to earn a living and find their place in the New World, Jewish parents had little money, time, or strength to invest in Jewish education. Most sent their sons to a European-type *cheder* for a few hours a day, after their public school classes, to learn how to read and pray. These "schools" were poor, unfurnished and disorganized. They were usually not conducive to education. Many of the teachers knew little English and even less about American children. The curriculum had little connection with real life in public school or on the street, and the students waited impatiently each afternoon to be set free. Jewish education rarely continued past a boy's Bar Mitzvah. Practically no provisions were made for girls. Little wonder that so many left Jewish tradition behind the moment they were able to leave the cheder.

Mesitha Tifereth Jerusalem

But even while Orthodoxy was in disarray, the seeds for a Torah revival were being sown. Yeshivas Rabbi Jacob Joseph and Mesivtha Tifereth Jerusalem had been established on the Lower East Side in New York in the early 1900's. The Rabbi Isaac Elchanan Theological Seminary appointed Rabbi Dr. Bernard Revel as its head. He founded Yeshivah University and paved a new path. It combined a traditional yeshivah education with the university studies considered necessary in the United States. Yeshivah Torah Vodaath and Yeshivah Rabbi Chaim Berlin were established in Brooklyn soon after World War I. The Hebrew Theological College, the first major yeshivah outside New York, was founded in Chicago in 1921.

Perhaps the leading figure in Torah education was "Mister" Shraga Feivel Mendlowitz. (He had received *semichah* for the rabbinate,

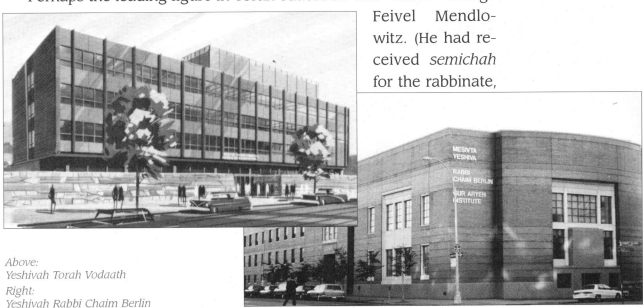

Above:
Yeshivah Torah Vodaath
Right:
Yeshivah Rabbi Chaim Berlin

R' Shraga Feivel Mendlowitz

but refused to use the title "Rabbi.") Mr. Mendlowitz came to America from Czechoslovakia as a young man. He taught for several years and then headed the small Yeshivah Torah Vodaath in Brooklyn. As his yeshivah grew, he sent his students to help establish the new high school division of Yeshivah Rabbi Chaim Berlin in Brooklyn, Telshe Yeshivah in Cleveland, Ner Yisrael in Baltimore and Beth Medrash Govoha in Lakewood. He helped found day schools outside New York and he created Torah Umesorah — the National Society for Hebrew Day Schools. His influence reached as far as Jerusalem, where his son-in-law established the famous Boys Town yeshiva-vocational school. He can justly be called the father of Torah education in America.

European rabbis, small in numbers but great in stature, came to teach in American yeshivos; English translations of prayerbooks and Talmudic works were published and more and more English speaking Orthodox rabbis were ordained. The Young Israel, a national movement with branches across the country, introduced thousands of young American Jews to traditional Jewish life.

At the time, Orthodox activity seemed no more than a drop in an ocean of ignorance and assimilation, but its ripples would spread into larger and larger circles of Jewish commitment.

Above:
Campus of Yeshivah Ner Yisrael in Baltimore, Maryland
Right:
Campus of the Telshe Yeshivah in Cleveland, Ohio

I n the seventeenth, eighteenth and nineteenth centuries, the main stage of Jewish history was concentrated in Europe and the West. It was only in the twentieth century that Ashkenazic (Western) and Sefardic (Eastern) Jewry would meet and converge, partially as a result of the Second World War, but mostly during the great return to Eretz Yisrael.

At the beginning of the First World War, close to one million Jews lived under Moslem rule. The majority of Sefardic Jews were loyal, pious Jews who had protected their customs and traditions for centuries. Some of them had maintained a Jewish presence in the Holy Land from the time of the Destruction of the Temple until the return to Zion in the 1800's.

Jews in Moslem countries did not suffer from the same type of open anti-Semitism experienced by European Jews. The Moslem policy of *dhimma* proclaimed that all non-Moslem subjects were considered inferior, but they were nonetheless protected by law. Jewish life tended to be poor and somewhat primitive in Moslem countries, but it was more stable and secure than in Europe. With the decline of the Ottoman Empire in the nineteenth century, the situation changed. The Arabs were no longer proud members of a great empire. They became pawns in the hands of the Christian West. One result was that European anti-Semitism was planted and found fertile soil in the lands of the East.

THE JEWS IN THE EAST

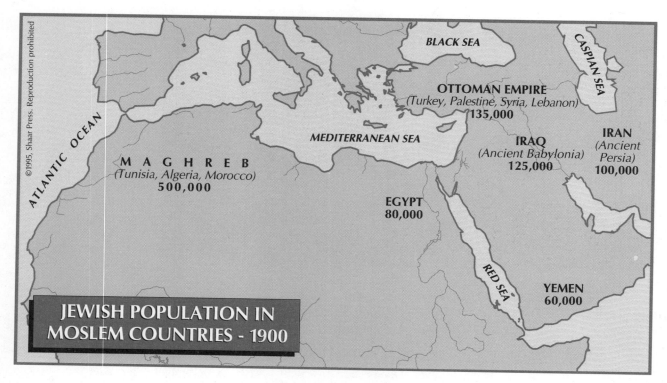

JEWISH POPULATION IN MOSLEM COUNTRIES - 1900

France and England dominated the Moslem world after the First World War. The French ruled in North Africa, Lebanon and Syria; the British were in Iraq, Egypt, Jordan, Palestine and parts of Arabia. A wave of modernization and secularization swept through the Islamic countries, yet beneath it lurked a deep hatred of Western values.

The Jewish-Arab conflict in Palestine brought this hatred into sharp focus and further undermined the security of Jewish communities in Islamic countries. The Arabs and their other Moslem brothers never differentiated between Zionist and Jew; their hatred towards Zionists was directed at all Jews everywhere. The Jewish return to Palestine would hasten the end of ancient Jewish communities in the Moslem world. It would bring the Jews of the East to Palestine, with all the problems that would entail.

THE EVE OF WAR

On the eve of the Second World War, the Jewish world was in disarray. Russian Jewry was enslaved in the throes of the Communist Revolution; Polish and Lithuania Jews were struggling to survive the upheavals caused by the First World

War; American Jewry was young and weak, rushing forward into a
sea of assimilation; the Jews in Palestine were fighting to retain their
hold on the land of their fathers. The religious and social divisions in
the Jewish world were deep and bitter. In the midst of this turmoil,
darkness was about to descend.

27
The Second World War
(From 1933-1945)

World War II was not just another, perhaps larger, war in the sad litany of mankind's wars. It was not just the story of one more tyrant determined to acquire more power, more land, more wealth. Nor was it just another attack, one of many, on the Jews. It was, rather, the first time in history that one of the world's greatest powers dedicated its entire might and being — military, financial, scientific, industrial, legal and cultural — to the vicious, insane, complete and utter destruction of the Jewish people.

THE FORCES OF EVIL

The Holocaust was not just another war. It was an unholy war, fought to destroy the people who represent the Divine Light and the Force of Good in this world. It was a war fought by the Forces of Evil.

Before approaching the Holocaust — the German war against the Jews — we must first look to Germany and Europe to try and understand how the Evil called Hitler came to power.

BACKGROUND OF THE WAR

At the end of the First World War, the German Kaiser abdicated his throne and the democratic Weimar Republic was established. But conditions in post-war Germany were difficult and chaotic. Germany resented the harsh and humiliating terms of the Versailles Treaty. Huge war reparations were demanded by the Allies. Military limitations and other punitive measures had been imposed. Strikes, unemployment and skyrocketing inflation plagued the country, and the savings of hundreds of thousands of middle class Germans were wiped out. The weak Weimar Republic had no solutions to offer.

Adolph Hitler was an Austrian veteran of the First World War. In 1921 he gained control of a small, extremist German party, the National Socialists ("Nazi" for short). After an attempt to overthrow the Munich city government, he was arrested and convicted, and while in prison he wrote his infamous book, *"Mein Kampf* — My Struggle."* Mein Kampf was a blueprint for Hitler's New Germany which would be dominated by pure, Aryan Germans. Hitler's book explained all of his racist theories — none of which had basis in fact — and described in detail how Jews and other "subhuman" races would be eliminated so that they could no longer "pollute" the Aryan race and German culture.

Cover of "Mein Kampf" with portrait of Adolf Hitler

Hitler promised to nullify the Versailles treaty and restore Germany its rightful place in the sun. With Hitler as its leader, Germany would conquer Europe and gain the *lebensraum* — room to live and expand — which it rightfully deserved. The Germans listened and liked what they heard. They gave their votes to their new Fuehrer (leader) and although they were not the majority of the electorate, the Nazis became the largest political party in the country.

The election in 1933 made Hitler the Chancellor of Germany. He promptly canceled all reparation payments and began rearming Germany, in direct violation of the Versailles Treaty. His rearmament program produced full employment and turned Germany into Europe's major industrial power after the Depression of 1929. He gave Germans jobs and economic stability while his security forces (the Black Shirts) and Secret Police (the Gestapo) destroyed all opposition to his rule. One of the world's most civilized and advanced states was now under the rule of an evil, demented man.

FIRST STEPS

Hitler wasted no time implementing his grand plans. In 1936 he invaded the Saar Basin, the rich coal mining region on the French-German border, and united it with Germany. He moved his army into the demilitarized sections of the Rhineland and then annexed Austria, which voted by over 90% to become part of Germany. The unification of Austria and Germany formed the German Third Reich which Hitler proclaimed would last one thousand years. He then moved on to claim the Sudentenland, the

German-speaking section of Czechoslovakia. At the Munich Conference in 1938, Britain and France bowed to Hitler's demands. Fearful of a second war so close on the heels of the previous war, they forced the Czechs to surrender the Sudentenland to Germany. The British Prime Minister Neville Chamberlain promised that appeasing Hitler would bring "peace for our time," but he was wrong. Hitler seized his opportunity. After receiving Sudentenland, he promptly invaded the rest of Czechoslovakia and prepared to invade Poland.

The Western democracies were still recuperating from the ravages of the First World War and the Great Depression. England and France did not take action, believing that Hitler was only flexing his muscles and that he would soon settle down peaceably; the United States had no desire to become involved in European affairs after the heavy casualties of World War I. Hitler was free to do whatever he desired; there was no one to oppose him.

In 1939 Germany formed the Axis Alliance with the Fascist Mussolini government in Italy. Somewhat later, Japan joined the Alliance. Mussolini attacked Albania; Japan attacked China; as Poland and Hungary fought each other for parts of Czechoslovakia, Hitler made plans to swallow them all.

First, however, he signed a non-aggression treaty with Stalin. By neutralizing Russia in the East, Hitler would be free to invade Poland. He did not expect any resistance. Russia was promised almost one third of Poland and the right to annex the small Baltic republics, Lithuania, Latvia and Estonia. Certain that England and France would not intervene, Hitler invaded Poland on September 1, 1939. He overran the country in only a month, and Soviet Russia moved in to gobble up its share. At that point, he finally met with resistance. England and France, both of whom had signed a treaty to protect Poland, now entered the ring. Once again, the world was at war.

THE WEST DECLARES WAR

The submissive British prime minister, Neville Chamberlain, was ousted and replaced by the spirited Winston Churchill, who became the spokesman for the free world against Nazi tyranny.

Germany invaded Norway in 1940 and English troops were sent to fight the Germans, but they were forced to withdraw before a wave of German victories. Germany marched on, occupying France, Denmark, Holland and Belgium. The German armies overran all of Western Europe in a mere six weeks. Three hundred fifty thousand French and British troops were successfully evacuated to England from the French port of Dunkirk, but as Winston Churchill said, "Victories are not achieved by evacuations." Germany seemed invincible.

For three months the German Air Force fought the Battle of Britain, bombing London and damaging the English defenses. The

The Blitz of London

"*blitz*" of London was a major turning point in the war; Britain suffered heavy casualties and destruction, but Germany lost 2,300 planes to the heroic British air force. Again, Churchill found the right words. He said of this air force, "Never have so many owed so much to so few." The war, however, was far from over. Hitler and Mussolini completed the conquest of Europe. They occupied Greece, Yugoslavia and Albania and were in control of Rumania and Hungary. Russia was next.

I gnoring its non-aggression treaty with Russia, Germany invaded Russian territory on June 22, 1941. Within four months, the German army was in sight of Moscow. Like Napoleon before him, Hitler was stopped not by human armies but by the forces of nature. Held up in his campaign, his troops were caught in snow and

GERMANY INVADES RUSSIA

EUROPE UNDER AXIS CONTROL

LEGEND:

Countries under Axis control

©1995, Shaar Press. Reproduction prohibited

sub-zero weather. In the spring, the German tanks sank in a sea of mud. While the German military machine was trapped by "General Winter," Stalin was single-mindedly rearming Russia. At the cost of great human sacrifice, Russia was molded into a vast industrial factory, producing planes, tanks and vehicles at a furious pace.

On December 7, 1941, Japan attacked the major United States naval base at Pearl Harbor, Hawaii. Hitler immediately declared war on the U.S. and America responded in kind. Hitler hated the

MAJOR EVENTS OF WORLD WAR II		
1939	September	Germans attack Poland
	September	England and France declare war on Germany
1940	April	Germany invades Denmark, Norway
	May	Germany invades Belgium and France
	June	Italy declares war on France and Britain
	September	Climax of air blitz on London
	September	Axis Alliance of Germany, Italy, Japan
1941	April	Germany invades Yugoslavia and Greece
	June	Germany invades Russia
	December 7,	Japanese attack Pearl Harbor; America enters the War
1943	February	Axis troops surrender at Stalingrad
	May	Nazi defeat in North Africa
1944	June 6,	D-Day — Allied invasion at Normandy
1945	April 12	Death of President Roosevelt
	May 1	Hitler's death announced
	May 7	Germany surrenders
	August 6	Atom bomb at Hiroshima
	September 2,	Japan surrenders

American President, Franklin Delano Roosevelt, whom he mistakenly believed was Jewish. Roosevelt responded to the Japanese attack by committing his country to winning the war.

THE TIDE TURNS

During the first half of 1942, the Allied Alliance of Great Britain, the Soviet Union and the United States was in a difficult situation. The German army controlled almost all of Europe and was deep inside Russia; the German General Erwin

Rommel and his Afrika Korps were in Egypt, poised to attack Palestine; the Japanese had overrun the Pacific. German bombers had bombed Tel Aviv, and the Jewish Yishuv in Palestine was in mortal danger. It was a time of prayer and fasting in Eretz Yisrael.

Then the tide began to turn. At the Battle of El Alamein, in Egypt, British Field Marshal Bernard Montgomery began an offensive that eventually drove the Italians and Germans out of North Africa. The Russians pushed the Germans westward out of Russia and began to coordinate their efforts with the Americans. Germany was subjected to heavy bombing, and finally, on D-Day, June 6, 1944, one million Allied troops stormed the beaches of Normandy in German-occupied France. On May 7, 1945, Germany surrendered.

Japan, however, continued to fight. On August 6, 1945, America dropped a cataclysmic new weapon, the first atom bomb, on the Japanese city of Hiroshima. A few days later another bomb destroyed Nagasaki. The Second World War came to its bloody end.

28
The Holocaust — The War Against the Jews
(From 1933-1945)

HITLER AND THE JEWS

For centuries Germany and the Jews had been inseparable. Germany was the first country in Europe to emancipate the Jews and offer them equal rights. It was the world's best educated, most civilized nation. It boasted the finest universities and the highest cultural and scientific achievements. Anti-Semitism existed, of course, but it was verbal and "civilized"; physical violence was unheard of. The Jews were part and parcel of German culture. They intermarried freely with the Germans, were highly assimilated, and participated in every phase of German life. They were patriotic citizens who loved their country. Twenty percent of the Jewish population fought in Germany's army in World War I. The "Fatherland" offered them everything a country could possibly offer a Jew. Germany and the Jews were a story of success.

The Germans, however, saw Jewish success in a different light. Even though the Jewish community was only one percent of the population, the hated Weimar Republic was considered a traitorous *Judenrepublik*, supposedly formed and run by Jews. Inflation and unemployment were considered the fault of the Jews. The Jews were said to be polluting German culture and stealing German wealth. According to many Germans, Jews controlled the country. They were dastardly and dangerous, the source of all of Germany's problems and humiliation, and the Germans strongly resented their presence. Communists called them capitalists and capitalists called them communists. Scores of nationalist folk organizations sprung up clamoring for Aryan purity, power and control. ("Aryan" was their name for pure-blooded, white North Europeans.) Adolph Hitler was the answer to their prayers.

Hitler was a madman with a mission. He promised to purify the Aryan race, cleanse Europe of its subhuman Jews and raise Germany to its rightful position as ruler of the world. Not only did he believe in his mission, he convinced an entire nation to follow and venerate him. His twisted theories gave anti-Semitism pseudo-scientific backing and academic prestige. Jewish professionals were thrown out of hospitals, universities, courts, theaters and orchestras. (German universities even invalidated Einstein's "Jewish physics"!) The Jews were boycotted, banished and defined as subhumans.

Jewish storefront with "Jude" painted on the plate glass window. Note the poster hanging above it urging Germans not to patronize Jewish businesses.

History books describe the strategies and battles of the Second World War and mention Hitler's anti-Jewish activities only as a secondary matter. Yet the Jews were the very heart of Hitler's plans. His sick, passionate hatred and lifelong obsession with destroying the Jews was the driving power behind the war. He did not kill Jews as part of the war; he fought the war in order to destroy the Jews, even when their continued destruction weakened his forces and worked against him. Not only did he say so himself, he proved it by his actions. While his army begged for reinforcements on the Russian front, Hitler ignored their pleas and sent German trains to Hungary to bring Jews to their death in Auschwitz.

EMIGRATION — A FIRST STEP

Hitler's war against the Jews began the day he assumed power. It began with violent attacks on Jewish professionals and intelligentsia. Doctors, lawyers, professors, scientists, musicians and others were beaten and arrested. In March 1933, Dachau, the first concentration camp, was opened. On April 1, 1933,

Jews being forced to scrub the streets of Vienna under the supervision of Hitler Youth members

all Jewish shops in Germany were boycotted. In May, mass book-burnings began. Jews were dismissed from the universities, the press, from doing scientific work. Jews throughout the world demonstrated and protested these actions, but German Jews kept their heads low, hoping the evil times would quickly pass.

Germany encouraged its Jews to emigrate and by August 1935, over 75,000 Jews had left the country. Some went to Eretz Yisrael and some to the United States. But by this time, Britain was severely limiting Jewish immigration to Palestine and America was restricting immigration, especially of Jews. Only about twenty percent of the legal American immigration quota was filled from 1933-1945, but the State Department made it very difficult for Jews to enter the country. Many German Jews were forced to settle in other European countries. When Germany overran Europe, these refugees would again find themselves under Nazi rule.

In November 1935, Germany passed the infamous Nuremberg Laws, stripping German Jews of their citizenship and denying them all civil rights. Jews who had intermarried or been baptized were forced to separate from their families; Jewish property was taken away. Jewish children, almost all of whom were studying in German schools, were excluded from the school system. In 1938 another 10,000 Jews managed to flee.

After the Anschluss union with Austria in 1938, Adolf Eichmann established an "Emigration Office" to help cleanse the Third Reich and make it *Judenrein* — free of Jews. Jews from Austria, Moravia and Bohemia were terrorized and beaten — 145,000 of them — thus "encouraging" them to emigrate. Thousands fled for their lives. Those who remained behind were later killed.

O n November 9, 1938, the Nazi government incited a massive country-wide pogrom which swept through Germany and Austria. It was called *Kristallnacht* — the Night of Broken Glass. Three hundred synagogues and over a thousand homes and shops were destroyed, filling the streets of German cities with shattered glass. Hundreds of Torah scrolls were desecrated and

MORE TERROR

Nazi soldiers strolling down the street past a burning Jewish building

Jewish cemeteries were vandalized. Thirty thousand Jews were arrested and sent to concentration-prison camps. The Jews were then fined one billion marks (about $400 million dollars) to pay for the damage! The world was aghast. The United States relaxed its strict enforcement of immigration laws for a time, allowing a larger number of Jewish refugees into the country.

As a result of the treaty between Germany and Russia, both countries invaded Poland — Germany from the west and Russia from the east. For the Jews of Poland, the result was a catastrophe. Chaos reigned in the Russian-held East. Many Jews fled across the Polish border to Lithuania; yeshivos escaped to Vilna with instructions to travel on the Sabbath in order to save their lives. From Vilna, nearly the entire Mirrer Yeshivah escaped to Japan and then to Shanghai, China. Great rabbis who managed to leave Europe in these few hectic months were later able to help rebuild the world of Torah after the war. Rabbi Chaim Ozer Grodzenski, head of the Vilna rabbinical court, worked heroically to help the refugees. The American rabbinate, Ezras Torah, and the Joint Distribution Committee offered major relief.

After the invasion of Poland, Hitler changed his tactics. There were now 3,250,000 Polish Jews under his control. Emigration was

Interior of the Mirrer Beis HaMidrash in Shanghai, 1941

Nazi soldier cuts off a Jew's beard while his cohorts look on

no longer sufficient to make his dominion *Judenrein*. There were simply too many Jews. At this point, the mass killings began. In the first fifty-five days of the German occupation of Western Poland, over five thousand Jews were murdered. All Jews were brutalized and humiliated. Beards were shaved, ear-locks pulled off; women and children were attacked. The Poles did not watch passively; most of them enthusiastically helped the Germans. German anti-Semitism was racist, based on Hitler's insane, pseudo-scientific theories; Polish anti-Semitism was religious, rooted in the teachings of the Catholic church. Either way, the hatred led to death for the Jews. Six thousand Polish Jews had died as soldiers in the Polish army; hundreds of thousands more would be killed by the Poles themselves.

But no matter how many were killed, there were still too many Jews. The Nazis began to gather the Jews of Western Poland into medieval-like ghettos, situated near railway junctions so that "future measures" could be accomplished more easily. The Nazi killing machine was being readied for its monstrous work.

The Germans established Jewish town councils — the *Judenrat* — in every ghetto. The Judenrat supposedly gave the Jews some community control, but in effect, they were merely tools for the Germans who used them to collect taxes, hostages and slave labor. Most members of the Judenrat conscientiously tried to help and protect their fellow Jews. When they finally realized that they were only pawns doing the work of the cursed Germans, many committed suicide. In the end, all Judenrat members and their families were exterminated.

The ghettos grew. Walls were built to assure that Jews could not leave. An identifying badge, a Yellow Star with the word *Jude*, had to be worn by every Jew over the age of six. Contact with the outside world was forbidden. As more and more Jews were concentrated in the ghettos, the ghettos were made smaller. Food supplies were cut. The houses were overcrowded. The streets were filled with terror. The people were hungry, sick and afraid.

Yet in the midst of all this suffering and horror, the Jews in the

THE GHETTO

Children in the Warsaw Ghetto

Jews spending Shabbos together in a shul in the Warsaw Ghetto

ghetto did not give up. They opened secret synagogues, yeshivos and schools. They gave lectures and conducted concerts. Somehow, they printed newspapers and even books. Amazingly, they kept their hopes alive: hope that France and England would be victorious against Germany ... hope that the nations of the world and their fellow Jews would not forget them ... hope that they would survive, and belief that the God of Israel would not abandon them.

Tiny numbers of Jews managed to join the partisans fighting the Nazis; a few (including the Rebbes of Ger and Belz, the Rabbi of Brisk, and the Rosh Yeshivah of Mir) managed to reach Palestine. Here and there, righteous gentiles — even among the notoriously anti-Semitic Germans, Poles and Russians — tried to save Jews at great peril to their lives. But the righteous were a tiny drop in a raging sea of blood and fury. Unarmed, terrorized, starved, surrounded by enemies, the Jews had no place to go; escape was virtually impossible. Germany dominated Europe; America had strict quotas for refugees; the world was at war. Even the gates to Eretz Yisrael were closed, because the British White Paper severely limited legal Jewish immigration to Palestine. The British had decided it was more important to appease the Arabs than to save the Jews. The doors to freedom were closed and locked. It seemed as though God had turned His face away, abandoning His people to their doom.

In May 1940, Germany invaded France, Denmark, Holland and Belgium. In six weeks the German army overran all of Western Europe. Jews who had fled from Germany to other countries now found themselves under Nazi occupation. The Balkan states,

Hungary and Rumania, together with their hundreds of thousands of Jews, came under Nazi rule. Each military success brought Hitler closer to fulfilling his dream of conquering Europe and making it *Judenrein*. The time for the "Final Solution of the Jewish Problem" was at hand. Only Russia, with its vast numbers of Jews, stood in his way. Hitler now turned his attention to the giant Russian Bear.

Flagrantly violating his non-aggression treaty with the Soviets, Hitler invaded Russia on June 22, 1941. He was soon in sight of Moscow. Russian losses were staggering and Hitler acquired control of two million Russian Jews.

One month after the invasion began, orders were given to the SS, Hitler's own private and vicious Security Force, to make preparations for the Final Solution in Europe. The biggest murder rampage the world had ever known was about to begin.

The first attempt at mass murder was made by killing units who worked with fanatical and cruel zeal. These SS units followed on the heels of the army, and together with local citizens and militia, they

KILLINGS AND SLAVE LABOR

One of many Jews being summarily executed at the mouth of a mass grave

managed to kill 1,250,000 Jews according to a precise plan. Victims were ordered to dig large trenches and then were lined up and shot. As they fell into their own graves, new lines of people were brought up and killed, until the trenches were filled. Perhaps most famous of these killings is the one which took place at Babi Yar, near Kiev, in the Russian Ukraine. On September 29, 1941, 35,000 Jews were machine gunned by the SS and left in a ravine. Within two years of Nazi occupation, the ravine had become the mass grave of almost 100,000 Jews. Very fittingly, a heroic statue of Chmielnicki, another great butcher of Jews, stands in nearby Kiev.

After eight months of constant killing in Lithuania, Poland, White Russia and the Ukraine, it was decided that the mobile units were too slow and inefficient for the vast numbers of Jews who had to be killed. They were too expensive as well, because they used up at least one bullet per person. And they were too gruesome; many German officers complained that ordinary soldiers were upset at such mass, cold-blooded murder. It was decided that the slaughter would take place in death camps, away from the public eye. Old trucks were converted into mobile gassing units. The victims were herded into the backs of the trucks and gassed to death with the carbon monoxide exhaust from the engines. But this, too, proved unsatisfactory. The Germans needed to kill more people faster. They worked on designing huge gas chambers and poison gas, with gigantic crematoria to burn the bodies. This was the perfect instrument for murder on such a colossal scale.

While they awaited a more scientific, efficient death, hundreds of thousands, if not millions, of Jews, Russian prisoners of war and other "subhumans" were worked to death as slave laborers for German industries and factories. These major corporations, many of which still exist, paid a small fee to the German government for each slave they received. Obviously, they were not concerned with the welfare of their workers, nor were the workers paid anything at all. No matter how many workers perished, the firms could always order more. Nine hundred labor camps were established where Jews were sent to be worked to death. Two camps — Auschwitz (which was divided into a labor camp and a death camp) in Poland and

Mauthausen in Austria — were the most infamous. Human inmates were used in place of heavy, metal machinery. The "welcoming" sign above Auschwitz read: *Arbeit macht frei* — Work Makes Man Free. Death, indeed, brought them freedom. Inmates rarely survived more than a few months. After the war, not one German firm, corporation, factory or industry agreed to pay compensation to the few surviving workers for the inhuman use of their labor.

Like Napoleon before him, Hitler's military campaign was stopped by a savage Russian winter. At the same time, the Russians began their counterattack and the United States finally entered the war. But even as he fought to conquer all of Europe and then the world, Hitler was determined to complete his War Against the Jews. In January 1942, high officials of the German government gathered at Wannsee, a suburb of Berlin, to receive instructions for the Final Solution. Eleven million Jews were still alive in Europe. They were to be shipped to the East and destroyed in the six major death camps. All camps were conveniently located in Poland, the center of Jewish Eastern Europe.

The largest camp was Auschwitz. Its highly efficient gas chambers were working to capacity. Auschwitz boasted of being able to kill 60,000 people a day if its murder apparatus worked a full twenty-four hours. For many months, during the years 1942, 1943 and 1944, the Nazis were killing over 100,000 Jews a week, in camps such as Auschwitz and Treblinka. Think for one moment, how horror stricken the world would be if a thousand people were killed in an accident. It is virtually impossible to imagine 100,000 being killed. And 100,000 a *week*, month after month? The numbers are so overwhelming that our minds are incapable of absorbing them. Even when desperately short of transport for his army on the Russian front, Hitler used Germany's superb train system to deliver Jews to their death rather than to send supplies to his soldiers.

Rabbi Michael Dov Weissmandl, son-in-law of the Rav of Nitra, Rosh Yeshivah of the Nitra Yeshivah and a leader of pre-war Slovakian Jewry, spent every moment trying to save Jewish lives.

THE FINAL SOLUTION

Top: Entrance to Auschwitz

Center: Electrified, barbed-wire fence surrounding the camp, patrolled by SS guards accompanied by German shepherd guard dogs

Bottom: A transport of Jews arriving at a concentration camp. Note the yellow Stars of David they are wearing which identify them as Jews.

During his work, he was arrested and shipped to Auschwitz, but he escaped from the train. Though he broke his leg in the fall, he went right back to his rescue work. By bribing important SS officers, Rabbi Weissmandl succeeded in stopping the deportations of Slovakian Jews for two years. Later he convinced the Nazis to consider a plan to stop the killing of a million Jews, for a price. But the negotiations failed.

In 1944 he besieged American and British officials with requests to bomb the railways from Hungary to Auschwitz. At the very least,

NAZI CONCENTRATION AND DEATH CAMPS

LEGEND:
Camps whose names appear in boxes were death camps

©1995, Shaar Press. Reproduction prohibited

this would slow the death march of Hungarian Jewry. His requests were ignored. The American government claimed that planes were not available, even though American bombing raids were conducted a few miles from Auschwitz, and American pilots reported seeing the smoke from the chimneys of the crematoria. Saving Jewish lives was not a high priority issue on the war agenda.

Many Jews died on the trains before they even reached the camps. Forcibly collected in the ghetto and then shut into closed cattle cars and sealed freight trains without water, air or sanitation, they perished on the way. Those who survived the hellish trip arrived hungry, thirsty, weak and terrorized. They were met by dogs and whips and shootings, and were then subjected to "selection." Old, young and weak were sent to their deaths in the modern, scientific gas chambers; the others were used as slave laborers until they, too, were released by death.

The Nazis had use even for dead Jews. Gold fillings were extracted from their teeth; their hair was cut for use in mattress stuffings; Jewish skin was used to make lampshades, and body fat was melted down into soap. Their clothing and goods were collected and distributed throughout Germany. In one six-week period, 222,269 men's suits, 192,652 women's dresses and 99,922 sets of children's clothes were collected from Auschwitz alone and distributed to German citizens. The Germans kept accurate records of all their atrocities, down to the last gold filling.

During the 1930's, close to 9,000,000 Jews lived in Europe under direct Nazi control. The Nazis killed 6,000,000, or sixty-six percent. The six big death camps were the center of organized, scientific, wholesale, mass murder. Three million Jews, about ninety-seven percent of Polish Jewry, were killed. Ninety percent of German, Austrian and Baltic Jews were killed. Seventy percent of the Jews in Bohemia, Greece and the Netherlands were killed. Fifty percent of the Jews in White Russia, the Ukraine, Belgium, Yugoslavia and Rumania were killed.

The deportation and extermination of the Jews was done in the midst of populated areas and with the cooperation of the local people. Millions of Poles, Lithuanians, Latvians, Austrians, Rumanians, Hungarians and Frenchmen cooperated with the Germans. They knew what was happening to the Jews. They were in the militias, they helped and supplied the SS, they buried Jewish victims. Nine hundred thousand people served in the SS and 1,200,000 were employed by the German railroads. Millions more serviced the camps, moved into Jewish homes, took over Jewish businesses and stole Jewish property. They saw the unending, sealed trains roll across the countryside. They heard the cries of the Jews inside, day after day, month after month, year after year. They saw the smoke from the gas chambers. Let no one say that Europe did not know what was happening to the Jews.

There were those who tried to help. The people of Denmark were a shining example. When Germany

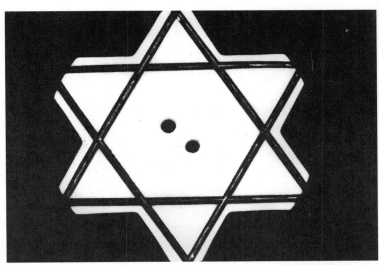

The infamous Yellow Star of David armband

invaded Denmark and ordered Danish Jews to wear the Yellow Star, the Danish king and many ordinary citizens donned the infamous badge, thus foiling German attempts to identify the Jews. When the SS was ready to begin the "Final Solution" in Denmark, the Danish people themselves organized a rescue effort. Using everything that floated, from small motorboats to large fishing vessels, the brave Danes ferried about seven thousand of the country's eight thousand Jews to safety in Sweden. Italy and Holland also tried to assist their Jewish citizens.

But civilized Switzerland turned away eighty-five percent of the Jewish refugees who reached her borders, and the International Red Cross refused to give aid to Jews anywhere. The Catholic Church heard no evil and saw no evil. Pope Pius XII refused to condemn the Nazis, and many of his priests saw no reason not to cooperate with the Germans. Thousands of Jewish children who were handed to the Church by desperate Jewish parents were not returned after the war. The doors to Palestine and America were closed. The list of countries who looked the other way is long. The Jewish people marched and mourned alone in the great blackness of the Nazi night.

29
Reactions
(From 1942-1945)

Between 1941 and 1945, a world was destroyed. European Jewry was shot and buried in the ravines of Europe or gassed in the death camps and burnt in the crematoria, its ashes scattered across the continent.

At first, the world had no idea how great a tragedy had taken place. When, despite the Nazi news blackout, the mind boggling news began to reach America in 1942, the first reaction was denial. When denial was no longer possible, American Jewish leaders honored the request of the State Department to suppress the news and keep silent for several months. But as reports started to pour in, the Jewish community began to organize and protest. The American government continued to stress that the only way to save the Jews was to first win the war. Even when the press reported, in November 1942, that two million Jews had been killed, the news was treated as a minor story, tucked neatly away on the inside pages of the newspapers.

By 1943 it was clear that Germany was going to lose the war. But even as the Nazis retreated from Russia, German fury with the Jews knew no bounds. The killings were speeded up and intensified. In spite of the slaughter that was taking place, England refused to relax its immigration quota to Palestine, America refused to open its gates to European refugees, and the Allies refused to divert their air power to destroy the death camps. President Roosevelt himself claimed to "understand" the complaints that Germans had towards the Jews in Germany. Most American Jews were afraid to push the "Jewish issue" for fear of seeming unpatriotic and inciting anti-Semitism in America. Instead, Jewish leaders decided sadly that rescue was impossible and that they should concentrate instead on establishing Palestine as a Jewish homeland once the war was over.

One prominent exception to this heartrending situation was the

Vaad Hatzalah (Rescue Committee) composed of Orthodox rabbis, laymen and many yeshivah students. Founded by the Union of Orthodox Rabbis, it had the cooperation of Agudath Israel, Mizrachi and Young Israel. The Vaad did heroic work, mostly through volunteers and with very little money. There were times when great rabbis drove on the Sabbath to collect funds that would save Jewish lives. As a small organization, the Vaad could save only small numbers of European Jewry, but it tried valiantly, night and day, to do whatever was possible.

Shortly before Yom Kippur in 1943, four hundred Orthodox rabbis marched to Washington to plead with the administration to begin rescuing Jews. Leaders of the general Jewish establishment, however, urged President Roosevelt not to receive the rabbis. Though they were met respectfully by Vice President Henry A. Wallace and leaders of Congress, the President sent his secretary to accept their message. Eventually, under pressure from Secretary of the Treasury Henry Morgenthau and Congress, the President grudgingly set up a War Refugee Board. Nearly all of its funding came from private donations with very little from the government, but the Refugee Board

The Rabbis' March on Washington

was able to save over 100,000 lives. How tragic that millions more who could have been saved were allowed to die.

DISBELIEF

The Jews of Europe themselves did not believe what was happening. When told they would be "resettled in the East" or sent to "work camps," they desperately believed this was true. No one could imagine that the Nazis truly intended to murder an entire nation — men, women, children, the elderly, tiny babies. At first, people were certain that the atrocity stories were wildly exaggerated propaganda. By the time they began to understand that the unbelievable horrors they were hearing were true, millions were dead.

JEWISH RESISTANCE

With the exception of Russia which reacted and reorganized to fight Germany, no nation in Europe offered any serious resistance to the Nazis. There were partisan groups who fought from the forest; here and there tiny numbers of people attempted to save Jews; and the Danes bravely stood up to the Nazis. Neither nations nor armies, however, were able to stop Germany's awesome military machine.

Unbelievable as it sounds, the Jews were probably the most heroic of all peoples in their resistance — both physical and spiritual — to the Nazis. Jewish partisans were active wherever they were allowed to fight. In the forests of Poland, anti-Semitic partisans often killed Jews who had escaped from the ghettos and volunteered to fight alongside the Polish partisans. Several ghetto revolts, tiny in size but incredible in terms of daring and bravery, took place.

Most famous of all was the Warsaw Ghetto uprising. In the spring of 1943, the Germans entered Warsaw, intending to liquidate the ghetto in a day or two. The Jews fought back with primitive, home-made weapons. After two weeks of defending itself, the astounded German army fell back and called for reinforcements. No uprising or resistance in Europe had ever held the Germany war machine up for two weeks, especially when its "soldiers" consisted of starving men and women with small homemade bombs and a few rusty guns. German reinforcements soon arrived and the Ghetto was duly and viciously destroyed. Other uprisings included a violent mutiny that took place at Treblinka in August of 1943 and a revolt by the Jewish Kapos of Auschwitz in October of 1944. Yet such resistance was like a fly attacking an elephant. It was doomed to failure.

The main Jewish resistance lay in trying to foil the Nazi plan of dehumanizing the Jews. Jews had a long history of dying nobly at the hands of their oppressors, but never had there been a chapter like the Nazi march in the Valley of Death. Yet the Jews guarded their faith and retained their kindness, love and sense of human dignity, even in the face of the Angel of Death. They shared their last crumbs of bread, offered helping hands on the way to the gas chambers, and sang *Ani Ma'amin* — I believe in the Coming of the Messiah — as they returned their souls to their Creator. The Divine Image covered their nakedness, its light illuminating the blackness of their indescribable suffering.

There is a story told of a small child in the Warsaw Ghetto who, in simple innocence and trust, said: "We are like Jacob and the

Germans are like Esau. I am glad. I don't ever want to be like Esau." Even those who had intermarried and assimilated — those who had not lived as Jews — died together with their brothers as Jews — holy martyrs all.

OTHER RESPONSES

The Arab Grand Mufti of Jerusalem spent the war in Berlin where he declared his fervent hope that "the solution of the Jewish problem as advocated by Hitler would be applied in the Middle East as well." Yet the English refused to allow the Jews to arm themselves or to aid in the war effort. Only in 1944, when the British were desperately short of manpower, were the Jews of Palestine finally allowed to form a Jewish Brigade and to fight as part of the British army.

As the German General Rommel and his feared Afrika Korps stood at the gates of Egypt and German bombers bombed Tel Aviv,

The Grand Mufti of Jerusalem reviewing German troops

the Yishuv fasted and prayed. At the same time, Rabbi Yosef Kahaneman laid the cornerstone for the great Ponivezh Yeshivah in Bnei Brak. He was planning for the future of Torah and the Jewish people in Eretz Yisrael. God, he said, would not forsake His Land. People thought his building plans were irrational, but history has justified his faith.

The Jewish Yishuv would expend superhuman efforts to save and help Jews after the war, but during the Holocaust they felt helpless. Even so, Jewish parachutists from Palestine landed in occupied Europe in 1944-45 to try and help their Jewish brethren. They were captured by the Germans and tortured to death.

By 1944 it was clear that Germany would lose the war. Nonetheless, the Germans installed Adolph Eichmann to destroy the Jews of Hungary — the last large Jewish community in Europe. With typical German efficiency, the German railroads transported 12,000 Jews a day to Auschwitz, even though the German army desperately needed the trains to supply their soldiers on the Russian front. In an attempt to find more transport, Eichmann offered to free one million Hungarian and Rumanian Jews in

· *Holocaust memorial wall in Cracow, Poland. It was built from the remnants of tombstones found in the old cemetery located in the courtyard of the Rema Shul.*

return for 10,000 trucks. The offer was made through the heroic Rabbi Weissmandl.

The Allies, however, refused to send the trucks. Aside from refusing to aid the enemy, the British openly said that if so many Jews were freed, "Where would we put them?" Where indeed, when they had closed the doors to Palestine.

AN END AND A BEGINNING

It was 1945. The Jewish world was shocked and numb, in mourning for six million dead. How does one mourn six million people? Fathers and mothers, brothers and sisters, babies and grandparents, aunts, uncles, cousins? Rabbis and yeshivos, friends and workmates, entire villages and communities? How can one mourn an entire world destroyed?

A remnant survived. A quarter-million Jews were housed in the

A group of Jewish orphans in Rumania

Displaced Persons camps set up after the war. Another 200,000 refugees wandered through Europe. But Europe was little more than a cemetery; there was no place a Jew could return to and live. Of the 250,000 survivors in the Displaced Persons' camps, two-thirds insisted on going to Palestine. It was clear to them that a Jew could only be safe in a Jewish land.

The Yishuv sent hundreds of people to the camps to organize Jewish immigration. A Jewish state would rise from the smoking ruins of Jewish Europe, and the light of Torah would be relit from the burning embers of destruction. The Jewish people would live.

SECTION VII

Israel — The Jewish State

(From 1945 to 1980)

30
Birth of the State
(From 1944-1949)

NEW BEGIN-NINGS, NEW HOPES

The Holocaust had been the greatest disaster in Jewish life since the Destruction of the Second Temple. In terms of sheer numbers, it was the greatest destruction the Jewish people had ever known. Yet even in the midst of its mourning, Am Yisrael was already engaged in a new beginning. By 1945 the process that would end in the birth of a Jewish State had begun. It would be a painful, difficult and costly process, but it would result in new life. The God of Israel had not turned His back on His people or His Land. His Presence would hover over them and bring them miraculous successes. But before they merited His miracles, the people of Israel had to do their part.

RESTRIC-TIONS AND REPRESSION

Even after the end of the Second World War, the British government kept the gates to Palestine tightly shut. In May 1946, a United Nations Inquiry Commission recommended that 100,000 Jewish refugees be immediately admitted to the country. The British refused to comply. As illegal boats full of Holocaust survivors continued to arrive, armed clashes between British forces and the Jewish population became more frequent. On "Black Saturday" in June 1946, thousands of Jews, including the heads of the Jewish Agency, were arrested for opposing the British.

Two Jewish military movements actively resisted the British. They were *Etzel,* known as the Irgun, and *Lehi,* which the British called the Stern Gang. Refusing to join or take orders from the more moderate Haganah (the Jewish Agency's defense force), they attacked the British in highly successful and publicized acts of sabotage. On July 22, 1946, they blew up the British government headquarters in the King David Hotel in Jerusalem. Despite prior warning, the British did not evacuate the hotel and many soldiers and civilians were killed. In

Chief Rabbi of Palestine, R' Ben Zion Meir Hai Uziel, speaking at an anti-British rally

דברו דבר ולא יקום כי עמנו אל!

a daring jailbreak, Etzel and Lehi freed two hundred Jewish prisoners held by the British in the massive Acre fortress. The British hung seven Jews in retaliation; Etzel and Lehi hung two British sergeants in return.

The British intercepted eighty-five percent of the "illegal" refugee boats. They sent tens of thousands of immigrants, newly freed from

THE GERMANS DESTROYED OUR FAMIL... ...MES—DON'T YOU DESTROY OUR HO...

An "illegal" refugee boat

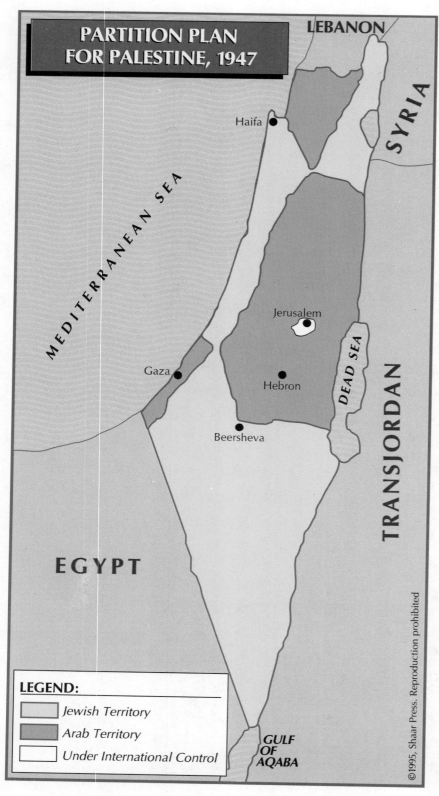

PARTITION PLAN FOR PALESTINE, 1947

LEBANON

SYRIA

Haifa

MEDITERRANEAN SEA

Jerusalem

DEAD SEA

TRANSJORDAN

Gaza

Hebron

Beersheva

EGYPT

GULF OF AQABA

LEGEND:
- Jewish Territory
- Arab Territory
- Under International Control

the Displaced Persons' camps in Europe, to new internment camps in Cyprus. When the ship *Exodus* arrived with 4,500 refugees in July 1947, it was not allowed to dock. It returned to France, but the immigrants refused to disembark and the boat was towed to Germany. The passengers were forcibly removed and left on German soil. This horrendous incident had a profound effect on world opinion. Jewish immigration to Palestine was now looked upon more favorably. Meanwhile, as the Jews of Palestine desperately continued to search the world for arms, American Jewry began to send funds and material.

Britain again submitted the Palestinian problem to the United Nations and a second investigation committee suggested a new plan. One hundred and fifty thousand Jewish refugees would be admitted to Palestine, but the Jewish homeland (which had been reduced and partitioned to create Transjordan, later called the Hashemite Kingdom of Jordan) would be further divided into two independent states — one Arab, one Jewish. The Western Galilee and the entire center of the country would be given to the Arabs. The Jews would receive the Eastern Galilee and a long, narrow strip along the coast. The vast majority of Jewish land would be in the desolate, southern Negev. Jerusalem, despite its long standing Jewish majority, would become an international city.

Believing they had no choice, the Jews accepted the new plan with a heavy heart, but the Arabs vehemently refused to do so. On November 29, 1947, the United Nations passed the new partition plan by a vote of 33 to 13. The next day, the Arabs declared war upon the Jewish Yishuv. Israel's War for Independence had begun. As a result of Jewish victories, the Jews ended up with much more territory than they would have received under the Partition Plan. The God of Israel has His own ways of arranging borders.

O n November 30, 1947 — six months before a Jewish state was officially declared — the Arabs attacked. Seven Jews were killed in an ambush on the Jerusalem-Tel Aviv road, Arab snipers in Jaffa shot Jewish children walking to school, and an Arab mob set fire to Jewish stores outside the Old City in Jerusalem. Riots broke out throughout the country and murderous attacks were launched on defenseless Jews in countries throughout the Moslem world. In a typical display of British "neutrality," the English permitted full freedom to Arab armies and rioters while doing their utmost to prevent the Jews from defending themselves. In the four months between December 1947 and Passover 1948, almost one thousand Palestinian Jews were killed by Arab violence.

The Arab League began bringing soldiers from surrounding Arab countries into Palestine. At the same time, they gave orders to Arabs living in Palestine to "temporarily" evacuate their homes until the battle was over. Everything seemed to be in the Arab's favor — huge armies, a surplus of equipment, training, and the support of the British. The Arab leaders had no doubt the war would be short, bloody (for the Jews), and highly successful.

BORN IN FIRE — THE WAR FOR INDEPENDENCE

*Left: On guard duty at a
Jewish settlement
Right: A British soldier
inspects a Jew's luggage*

THE SIEGE OF JERUSALEM

In February 1948, Ernest Bevin, the anti-Semitic English Foreign Secretary, convinced King Abdullah of Transjordan to invade Palestine and annex the Arab sections of the country to his own kingdom. Jerusalem was the heart of the struggle. The Arabs cut off the Jerusalem-Tel Aviv highway to the west of the city, and for nine months Jerusalem was in a state of siege. Food, water, ammunition and medical supplies were in dangerously short supply. People gathered grasses and weeds for food. The city was close to starvation.

The main battle for Jerusalem was fought on the hills and in the valley where the road from Tel Aviv twists its way up to the Holy City. The Jewish forces tried several times to dislodge the Arabs from their positions along the road, but without success. In early April, a fierce battle was fought at the Kastel, an Arab village overlooking the highway. Casualties were high, but the Arabs finally retreated. A six-mile-long convoy was immediately organized and sent out to Jerusalem from Tel Aviv. Two-hundred-and-fifty trucks, loaded with nine-hundred-and-fifty lifesaving tons of food arrived in the city on the Sabbath of April 17. Jews left the synagogues, still wearing their prayer shawls, to unload the supplies.

But the road was soon blocked again, this time at Shaar HaGai, the valley at the entrance to the Judean hills. For another seven weeks, Jerusalem was isolated. When the road was finally reopened, the armored cars and trucks that had been shot down in the convoys were

Two defenders of Mt. Zion take careful aim at the enemy

left lying in place — as silent, rusted, blood-colored memorials to those who gave their lives to free Jerusalem. A stone tablet was placed near each vehicle, inscribed with the names of its driver and crew.

GUSH ETZION

To the southwest of the city, midway on the Jerusalem-Chevron road, lay Gush Etzion. It consisted of four kibbutzim, three of them religious settlements. Abdullah's Arab Legion surrounded Gush Etzion and blockaded the road. Despite bitter fighting, a convoy with reinforcements could not break through the Arab lines. On May 13, Gush Etzion fell. Although West Jerusalem was still firmly in Jewish hands, the Arab Legion was now able to enter East Jerusalem and the Old City from the southeast. The Jews in the Old City fought bravely, forcing the Arabs to take one house at a time. But they were sorely outnumbered, down to their last rounds of ammunition, and cut off from reinforcements. On May 25, the Jewish defenders of the Old City surrendered. The men were taken prisoner; women and children were evacuated to West Jerusalem.

The Arab Legion occupied Arab towns throughout Judea and Samaria, but the Haganah captured Ramle, Lod, Nazareth, Tiberias,

Safed, Haifa and much of the Galilee. In the fall of 1948, the Haganah conquered Beersheva, the Negev and the Sinai Desert. In March 1949, they secured Eilat. Each battle is a fascinating story unto itself, full of wondrous happenings and unexpected miracles. The rabbis teach us that when Jews are willing to offer their lives for the welfare of the Jewish people, Divine help is forthcoming. The story of these uneven, mismatched, yet amazingly victorious battles is surely proof of their words.

But despite the victories of 1949, the war was not yet over. The situation in Jerusalem remained grim, and the Jews of Palestine anticipated an invasion of the seven Arab states now massing on their borders.

ARAB FLIGHT

An incredible event of the time was the flight of almost 600,000 Arabs from Palestine. Driven away by Arab propaganda, fear, hysteria and promises of great rewards upon their return, entire populations fled their towns. Arabs from Jaffa, Tiberias, Safed, Beit Shean, Haifa and Jerusalem picked up their families and belongings and ran away. At first, the Jews tried to convince them to remain, but the mass flight was a blessing in disguise. With the Arabs gone, the overwhelming majority of the population in the new state would now be Jewish. Some 600,000 Jewish refugees were forced to leave surrounding Arab countries as a result of the war against the new Jewish state. They arrived as refugees in Israel. When the fighting began, they found empty Arab housing ready and waiting, just as the Jews had found when they entered the Land of Canaan during the Conquest of Joshua. Despite this even "population exchange," Israel carefully catalogued and kept records of Arab property in order to one day recompense the owners. The Arab countries did no such thing. Jewish property left behind in Arab lands was lost forever.

While the Israeli government systematically resettled all of the Jewish refugees, the Arab governments, with the help of the U.N., forced the Arabs refugees to live in wretched refugee camps, where they still remained half a century later. Rarely allowed to become citizens of the countries in which they were living, they were held as a form of human "ammunition" in the war against the Jews. These Arab camps were held up to the world as examples of *Jewish* cruelty, and the hate-filled young people in the camps became the source of future terrorists.

The majority of Palestine's Arabs had originally arrived in the country after 1880. They came as a result of the Jewish immigration and its higher standard of living. Before the Declaration of the State, the Arabs refused to be called Palestinians. They insisted that Palestine was a part of Greater Syria and that they were part of the great "Arab nation." Before 1948, the term "Palestinian" referred to the *Jewish* inhabitants of Eretz Yisrael. The Jewish Agency for Palestine, the Palestine Post (now the Jerusalem Post) and the Palestine Philharmonic Orchestra (now the Israeli Philharmonic) were all Jewish institutions. Even the British issued passports to Jews identifying them as "Palestinians." Only after the Six Day War in 1967 did the Arabs begin to view themselves as the displaced "Palestinian nation." It was an effective way to gain the sympathy of the world.

THE DECLARATION OF THE STATE

May 15, 1948 was the deadline for the British to leave Palestine, the day the twenty-eight year old Mandate would officially end. At the last moment, under heavy American pressure, some of the Zionist leadership wavered. Fearful of the dangerous military and diplomatic situation, they did not feel secure enough to declare an independent Jewish state.

Nonetheless, David Ben Gurion fought stubbornly and carried the day. On the fifth of Iyar, 5708 — Friday, May 14, 1948 — at 4:00 P.M., before the entry of the Sabbath, the new State of Israel was declared. Jews young and old danced in the streets, and in Jewish homes and synagogues across the world the people of Israel gave thanks. Ben Gurion said: "...The Jewish people have ... waited two thousand years for it to come. ...We know no other people that was exiled from its land and dispersed among the nations, hated, humiliated and oppressed without respite for hundreds of years, but has nonetheless ... persisted in its belief that the day would come when it would restore its independence in its own state."

The Palestine Post proclaiming the birth of the State of Israel

Ben Gurion viewed the State as a great historical accomplishment, but he made no mention of the God of Israel or the Torah in his speech. Religious Jews, however, did not lose sight of the fact that it was God and His Torah which had guaranteed Jewish existence throughout those two thousand difficult, landless years of exile. In humble thanks, many of the Jews of Eretz Yisrael recited the blessing *Shehecheyanu* to thank their Creator Who "... kept us alive, sustained us, and brought us to this time."

CONTINUED WARFARE

As the last British soldier left Palestine, six Arab armies from Transjordan, Lebanon, Saudi Arabia, Syria, Iraq and Egypt invaded. The War of Independence which had really begun six months earlier, was now official. Egyptian bombers attacked Tel Aviv and their soldiers moved up to Jerusalem from the south. Iraq and Syria began an offensive in the north. The Israelis fought fiercely. Despite their lack of numbers, money and arms, despite their lack of an air force or a navy, despite their young, inexperienced soldiers, many of whom were refugees fresh from the D.P. camps in Europe, the Jews of Israel were full of determination and *mesiras nefesh* — the willingness to sacrifice for the Jewish people.

Fighting against the combined armies of the six Arab states, the

Left: Tel Aviv synagogue destroyed by Egyptian bombers
Right: Elderly couple fleeing the Old City

Jews defended each and every Jewish town, yishuv, kibbutz, and *dunam* of land. They were overwhelmed by numbers alone, yet almost everywhere they were able to maintain their positions, and battle by battle, they slowly turned the tide.

Thousands of new immigrants were drafted into the army immediately upon their arrival in the country. Weapons were purchased with the help of world Jewry. Morale was high and the Arabs suffered mounting defeats. But when the Old City of Jerusalem fell to the elite Arab Legion on May 25, the people of Israel suffered a severe blow.

The road to Jerusalem was still closed, but a novel solution was found. An ancient Roman road into the city was discovered. This narrow path bypassed the Arab forces, and night after night civilians, working by hand, cleared and widened the passage. Called the Burma Road, it was paved by the end of June 1948, thus ending the siege on Jerusalem.

Top:
Building the "Burma
Road"

Bottom:
Jerusalem
divided

With the end of the siege, West Jerusalem was in Jewish hands, but the city was cut in two. The Old City with the Kosel and its many holy places was in Arab hands; its synagogues and yeshivos were demolished. The Hebrew University and Hadassah Hospital on Har Hatzofim (Mt. Scopus) were isolated; the ancient cemetery on Har Hazeisim

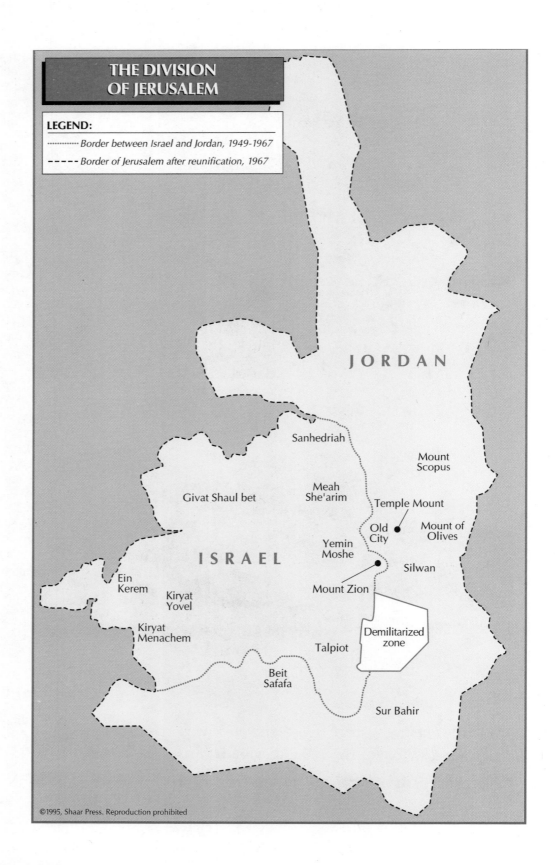

THE DIVISION OF JERUSALEM

LEGEND:

·············· Border between Israel and Jordan, 1949-1967

– – – – Border of Jerusalem after reunification, 1967

JORDAN

Sanhedriah

Mount
Scopus

Meah
She'arim

Givat Shaul bet

Temple Mount

Old
City

Mount of
Olives

Yemin
Moshe

ISRAEL

Silwan

Ein
Kerem

Mount Zion

Kiryat
Yovel

Demilitarized
zone

Kiryat
Menachem

Talpiot

Beit
Safafa

Sur Bahir

©1995, Shaar Press. Reproduction prohibited

(Mt. of Olives) was cut off. Jerusalem was divided by barbed wire and concrete walls. Other holy places — Beis Lechem, Chevron, Shechem, Judea and Samaria, the backbone of Eretz Yisrael — were now in enemy hands. There was joy and thanksgiving at the creation of the state, but the joy was mixed with sorrow. The heart of Eretz Yisrael had been left out of the new Jewish State.

On May 26, 1948, the Israeli Defense Force was established (in Hebrew, *Tzva Haganah L'Yisrael — Tzahal*). The resistance movements, Etzel (Irgun), Lehi (the Stern Gang), and the Jewish Agency's Haganah were all to be disbanded. Tzahal would now be the only army in the new state. Etzel and Lehi, however, were slow to comply. On June 20, the ship Altalena arrived, bringing ammunition and supplies for Etzel. When Etzel tried to dock the ship at Tel Aviv harbor, Ben Gurion declared: "There will not be two states; there will not be two armies. If Begin (the leader of the Irgun) does not give in, we shall open fire." Ben-Gurion's order was given and the ship was sunk; Jews were killed and the valuable cargo of ammunition was destroyed. At that point, unwill-

The shelling of the Altalena

THE JEWISH BATTLE FOR INDEPENDENCE

1946	**May 1**	Inquiry Commission recommends admitting 100,000 Jews from DP camps to Palestine.
	June 29	"Black Saturday." British arrest thousands and search country for arms.
	July 22	Etzel blows up British government offices in King David Hotel in Jerusalem.
1947	**Jan.-May**	Continuing acts of terror.
	May	U.N. recommends partition of country into Arab and Jewish states.
	July	Ship Exodus refused entry into Palestine.
	Nov. 29	U.N. votes to accept partition plan.
	Nov. 30	Arabs attack. Commercial Quarter outside Old City of Jerusalem looted and burned.
1948	**Dec.-April 48**	Over 1,000 Jews killed in Arab attacks.
	Feb. 2	Bombing of Ben Yehudah Street in Jerusalem by Arabs.
	April 3	Operation Nachshon clears road to Jerusalem.
	April 9	Etzel attack on Arab village of Deir Yassin.
	April 11	Arabs attack convoy of doctors, nurses and teachers en route to Hadassah Hospital on Mt. Scopus.
	April ll	City of Safed conquered.
	April 18	City of Tiberias conquered.
	April 22	City of Haifa conquered.
	May 13	Arab Legion conquers kibbutzim in Gush Etzion on Chevron-Jerusalem road.
	May 13	City of Jaffa conquered.
	May 14 (5 Iyar)	Declaration of the State of Israel.
	May 14/15	Egyptian air force bombs Tel Aviv.

1948	**May 25**	Jewish forces surrender Old City of Jerusalem to Arab Legion.
	May 26	Tzahal (the Israeli Defense Force) established.
	June	Burma Road into Jerusalem built.
	June 20	The ship Altalena sunk.
	July 8-18	Ten Days of Fighting: Lod and Ramleh captured; Nazareth and Lower Galil captured; Ein Kerem, southwest of Jerusalem, captured. Attempt to recapture Old City fails. Tel Aviv bombed. U.N. forces cease-fire.
	Oct. '48-Jan. '49	Continued fighting in southern Negev. Beersheva, the Negev and Sinai conquered.
1949	**Jan. 7**	UN negotiates temporary truces.
	March	Truce broken. Eilat conquered.
	July	Armistice agreements concluded.

ing to start a civil war, Menachem Begin disbanded the Etzel. Ben Gurion had prevailed.

In January 1949, the first Knesset (parliament) was elected. David Ben Gurion became prime minister and the aging Chaim Weizmann was elected the State's first president. During the Mandate, the

Right: David Ben Gurion
Left: Chaim Weizmann

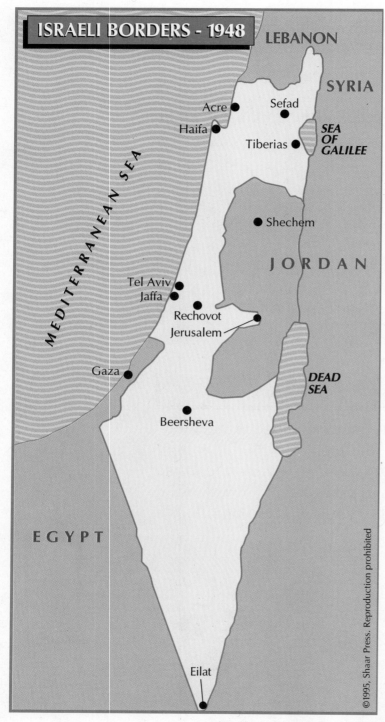

ISRAELI BORDERS - 1948

LEBANON

SYRIA

Acre

Sefad

Haifa

SEA
OF
GALILEE

Tiberias

MEDITERRANEAN SEA

Shechem

JORDAN

Tel Aviv
Jaffa

Rechovot
Jerusalem

Gaza

DEAD
SEA

EGYPT

Beersheva

Eilat

Jewish Agency (composed of the Labor Party, the Histadrut workers' union and the Haganah's Jewish Defense Force), had ruled the Jewish Yishuv. After the Declaration of the State, these same establishments and people remained in control. The Socialist Labor movement dominated much of the country — agriculture, industry, housing, health, education and immigration. It would leave its imprint on the entire face of the nation.

THE END OF THE WAR FOR INDEPENDENCE

Continued fighting through the end of 1948 and the beginning of 1949 brought Beersheva, the southern Negev region and the Sinai into Jewish hands. Then, just as the Jews were making important military gains, the United Nations insisted upon a cease-fire. Armistice agreements were signed between Israel and Egypt, Transjordan, Syria and Lebanon. The war for independence had lasted thirteen months; there were 6,000 Israeli dead. Israel assumed that peace treaties would soon follow the temporary cease-fire agreements, but the Arabs refused to discuss peace. Israel had survived its tumultuous birth and had won its freedom, but peace and security were still far away.

31
First Steps
(From 1949-1960)

The birth of the State of Israel was rich in miracles and full of feats of bravery, but the cost was high. Six thousand lives had been lost, one percent of the entire population. (This would be the equivalent of 2,650,000 American lives in 1995!)

Nonetheless, the population began to grow by leaps and bounds. One of the first laws enacted by the new State was the *Chok Hashvut* — the Law of Return. Any Jew wishing to immigrate to Israel from any country in the world was automatically entitled to citizenship upon arrival. Hundreds of thousands of refugees poured in from Europe. Large numbers came from the communist countries behind the Iron Curtain, especially from Rumania and Hungary.

As a result of the war in Palestine, Jews living in Arab countries

INGATHERING THE EXILES

Refugees arriving from Europe in 1949

were now subjected to great danger and violence, and ancient Jewish communities throughout the Arab world were forced to flee. The Jews of Iraq (Babylonia), Egypt and Morocco emigrated. Operation Magic Carpet brought most of the Yemenite community. The Yemenites viewed their move to Israel as following in the footsteps of the Messiah. Their plane flights to the Holy Land were seen as the fulfillment of the Biblical promise to arrive in Eretz Yisrael on "wings of eagles."

The voluntary Arab exodus from Israel was matched by the forced Jewish flight from the Arab lands: 500,000 to 600,000 Arabs fled from Mandatory Palestine; 567,654 Jewish refugees arrived in Israel from Arab countries. From Europe, the Middle East, Africa and Asia; entire communities from India, China, Yemen, Morocco, Iraq; small numbers from North and South America ... the Jews came. The world watched in amazement as the Children of Israel made their way homeward towards the tiny, new, struggling Jewish state.

JEWISH POPULATION IN ISRAEL					
1948	650,000	1960	1,800,000	1980	3,300,000
1949	1,000,000	1970	2,400,000	1995	4,500,000*
*An almost 700% increase in population in fifty years!					

PROBLEMS

Most of the new immigrants, whether from east or west, were poor refugees who arrived with nothing more than the clothes on their back. Those who came from Europe were survivors, their families scattered or destroyed. Those from Eastern Arab countries came with families but suddenly found themselves in an unfamiliar, Western world. Most of the immigrants had countless health problems. Moreover, they had come to a desperately poor country. During Israel's War for Independence, food was severely rationed and the housing shortage was widespread. The luckier immigrants were housed in abandoned Arab homes, but most were settled in mass tent-cities called *ma'abarot* (transit camps). The problem of providing housing, schools, clothing, med-

ical care, jobs and food all at once was enormous.

The policy of a secular government was to discourage the religious observance of the immigrants. The ruling Labor party believed that Zionism would now replace Judaism and they used their great political and economic power to influence the new immigrants and turn them into "modern" Israelis. Many children, especially those of Eastern origin, were removed from their families and sent to non-religious schools and institutions. Anti-religious activity was widespread, planned and purposeful. Tragically, it was successful to a great degree. Large numbers of religious parents saw their children leave Jewish tradition and observance behind.

Yet no one — neither secular nor religious — was properly prepared to deal with such massive numbers of refugees. Simply feeding, housing and providing minimal medical care was an overwhelming task. All in all, it was a time of great social upheaval.

RELIGION AND THE STATE

The conflict between the religious demands of the Torah and the demands of a secular, Zionist state was almost impossible to solve. As a secular, democratic state, Israel could not function according to the laws of the Torah. Yet without Judaism (and what was Judaism if not Torah?), Zionism had no legitimate basis. Therefore, it was imperative that some working compromise be found.

Chief Rabbis from left: R' Isaac Herzog, R' Ben Zion Meir Hai Uziel

The Israeli Prime Minister, David Ben Gurion, was a non-observant Jew as a matter of principle. Yet he understood that the Jewish religion had formed the Jewish nation and still played a central part in its life. Even though most Jews in the country were no longer religious, he realized that Judaism was the glue that held the nation and the State together. He therefore negotiated the Status Quo Agreement between the government and the religious parties which guaranteed four principles: 1) A separate religious school system would be established; 2) kashruth would be observed in all government, army and public kitchens; 3) the Sabbath would be observed as the country's official day of rest; and 4) all matters of personal status such as marriage, divorce and religious identity would be decided by the Chief Rabbinate.

The Chazon Ish

One of the first tests of the Status Quo was the question of drafting women into the army. The Chief Rabbi and most rabbinic leaders ruled that drafting women for army service was a violation of Jewish law and could not be allowed. A discussion with the Chazon Ish (Rabbi Avraham Yeshayahu Karelitz) in Bnei Brak convinced Ben Gurion that army service could not be imposed on religious women. The prime minister introduced legislation providing that religious women could be excused from the draft and volunteer instead for Sherut Leumi — national service in schools, hos-

pitals and institutions, or, if they wished, they could receive a complete exemption from all service.

Ben Gurion believed that in time religious observance would fade away. Meanwhile, he felt it was necessary to find a compromise which would guarantee the unity of the people and the survival of the State.

ISRAEL AND THE DIASPORA

On May 11, 1949, Israel was admitted to the United Nations. But the severe shortages of food, housing and medical supplies, the inflation and the lack of industry that plagued the new State would not be solved by the nations of the world. It was, rather, the Jews of the Diaspora who came to the aid of their brethren and began a worldwide commitment to the Jewish State. The United Jewish Appeal collected large sums of money to assist the needy, and the Israel Bond Organization raised funds for investing in the economy and the industry of the new country. The Jews of the world opened their hearts and their pockets. Through their generous contributions, they participated in the building of the new State.

American Jews demonstrate in favor of Israel

Israel became the focal point of world Jewry. The State served as a unifying force, and its support was seen as the obligation of every Jew. Guaranteeing Israel's survival became a prime "mitzvah" for Jews — both traditional and secular — in the Diaspora.

GERMAN REPARA-TIONS

The bitter issue of German reparations was raised in 1951. Germany had agreed to pay compensation for some of the financial damage done to Jews during World War II. It was understood that this would be only a partial financial payment for the robbery of Jewish assets — property, businesses and bank accounts taken away from Jews in Europe. The reparations would be made over twelve years. Since most of the Jews had been killed, the majority of funds would be given to the State of Israel, as heir and representative of the Jewish people. The money would be used for the development of the State.

Although accepting the reparations was intended as a purely economic agreement, the Jewish people were violently divided over the issue. Opponents argued passionately that it was immoral to allow Germany to "buy" forgiveness for its horrendous deeds. Those in favor of reparations agreed that the money could not absolve the Germans of their guilt, but argued that murderers and thieves should not be allowed to keep and enjoy the fruits of their evil. The State was, after all, giving new life to the refugees who had survived, and it was in dire need of assistance. It was their feeling that Germany should repay at least some of the money it had stolen.

The agreement was passed in the Knesset by a vote of 61 to 50. Menachem Begin, the leader of the opposition, was suspended from the Knesset for three months, due to "unruly and emotional behavior" during the debate. More than fifty years later, the question of the relationship between Israel and Germany still festers in the Israeli soul.

MIVTZA SINAI THE SINAI CAMPAIGN

Dissatisfied with the political system and its many small, political parties, confronted by religious and economic problems, and unable to control the government as he saw fit, Ben Gurion resigned as Prime Minister in 1953. Two years later he returned to power in order to deal with a new threat of war.

In 1955 the leader of the Arab world was Gamal Abdul Nasser of Egypt. Nasser had overthrown the corrupt King Farouk and now had dreams of becoming the ruler of a great Arab empire stretching from Morocco to Iran. Determined to destroy Israel, he employed Arab infiltrators — *fedayeen* — to commit terrorist acts against the country. From 1951 to 1955, there were 864 Israeli casualties due to the fedayeen. The Israeli army retaliated but was consistently condemned by the U.N. Under international law, government troops could not be used against another country as long as there was no official declaration of war.

Strengthened by his alliance with Russia and by enormous amounts of Soviet weapons, Nasser felt powerful and free. He blockaded the Straits of Tiran in the Red Sea and seized the Suez Canal from England. In blatant violation of international law, he closed both waterways to Israeli shipping. Understandably, Israel was anxious to topple Nasser, free itself of the fedayeen, and end the blockade on its ships.

Cover of Adolf Hitler's Mein Kampf in Arabic, found during the 1956 Sinai campaign

In the fall of 1956, Israel, England and France coordinated an attack on Nasser. Israel invaded the Sinai Desert and reached the Suez Canal; the British and French landed paratroopers and occupied the canal, intending to overthrow Nasser. The operation was a brilliant military success but a diplomatic disaster. The U.N. Security Council violently denounced the attack. England and France quickly evacuated their troops; Egypt was recognized as the legal owner of the Suez Canal; and Israel was forced, for the second time, to withdraw from the Sinai. (The first time had been during a forced cease-fire in the War for Independence.)

It was agreed that a U.N. international peace force would patrol the Egyptian-Israeli

border to prevent fedayeen from entering Israel, and U.N. troops were posted at Sharm el-Sheikh to guarantee free passage of Israeli ships through the Straits of Tiran. The Suez Canal, however, remained closed to Israeli shipping.

The war proved to be a mixed blessing. On the one hand, Israel gained a small measure of security and relief. It had also seized immense quantities of Russian vehicles and arms from Egypt. On the other hand, 171 Israeli soldiers were killed, several hundred wounded, and four Israelis taken prisoner. In other countries, these numbers might be considered insignificant, but Israel did not count its casualties like other countries. In Israel, each casualty represented a son of the entire nation, and the entire nation mourned.

TORAH IN THE JEWISH STATE

Beginning with the early 1900's, the size and influence of religious Jewry in Palestine dwindled. Increasing numbers of non-religious Jews arrived, creating new societal forces and influences. Yet the seeds for the future growth of the religious community were being sown. After the Second World War, the names of famous old yeshivos destroyed by Hitler were heard once again.

Ponivezh, Mir, Slobodka, Grodno, Ger, Lomza, Belz, Vizhnitz and Pressburg opened their doors in Eretz Yisrael. The Rebbes of Belz and Ger, both of whom had been miraculously saved from the Nazis, reestablished their courts in the Holy Land. Older Eretz Yisrael yeshivos such as Etz Chaim, Chevron, Chaye Olam and Porat Yosef grew side by side with newer institutions. In 1945 the yeshivos seemed small and insignificant. In time, they would grow and develop into a vibrant force in the fabric of the nation.

After the Declaration of the State, large parts of Orthodox Jewry had to reconsider their policies regarding a Jewish state. The Mizrachi, while disagreeing with the secular Zionists on many issues, nonetheless participated enthusiastically in the creation of the Jewish State. Many believed that even in its imperfect condition, the state heralded the "footsteps of the Messiah." Agudath Israel, the largest non-Zionist Orthodox group, rejected the Zionist philosophy but supported the desire to rebuild the Land. It viewed Jewish settlement in Israel as the fulfillment of the Divine commandment of *yishuv ha'aretz* — Settling the Land.

Even before World War II, Agudah had fought for the right of Jewish settlement in Palestine. Settlement was considered a physical necessity to help save the Jews of Europe. This attitude was endorsed by almost every leading Torah scholar of the century. Once it became clear that the Mandate was coming to an end and that the British would soon leave, there would be nowhere else for the Jews of Europe to go if Arabs took control of the country.

The Agudah had objected to an earlier partition plan, claiming that the Jews had no moral or legal right to change or reduce the historic, Divinely ordained borders of the Holy Land. Now, faced with the 1947 United Nation's resolution repartitioning Palestine once again and with the need to make a decision, they announced:

> ... Agudath Israel sees as a historic event the decision of the nations of the world to return to us after two thousand years a portion of the Holy Land, there to establish a Jewish state and to encompass within its borders the banished and scat-

tered members of our people. This historic event must bring home to every Jew the realization that the Almighty has brought this about in an act of Divine Providence which presents us with a great task and a grave test."

With this statement, the Agudah officially accepted the reduced borders, recognized the State, and began to participate fully in its political, social and economic life. Once the State existed, it had to be sustained, defended and developed. The founding of the State of Israel was not, however, identified by the Agudah as the forerunner of the Messiah. It was a practical response to a particular situation, and its acknowledgment by the Agudah implied only limited acceptance.

In the 1950's and 1960's, religious life in Israel continued to intensify and grow. Great Chassidic leaders and rabbis who had escaped from Hitler established new communities and yeshivos. Chinuch Atzmai, an independent Torah-school system, was created and hundreds of new schools were established. The large Sefardic community had a generally positive attitude towards Torah tradition. The underlying tension between the secular government and the religious community remained, but the seeds of religious rebirth were nourished and developed.

By the 1970's the fruits of this rebirth were visible to all across a broad spectrum. Religious education in the Mamlachti Dati system — the state religious schools — had been reinforced, and Chinuch Atzmai had flowered. An extended system of yeshivos reached across the country. Private religious schools and *chadarim* sprouted. Religious trade schools and high schools were established and Bar Ilan, a university under religious auspices, grew rapidly.

The older, established yeshivos continued to expand, and newer ones blossomed across the country. Whereas traditional yeshivos had once been few in number and centered almost exclusively in Jerusalem and Bnei Brak, such institutions began to take root and blossom throughout the country. Israel became a magnet for students everywhere, who flocked there for advanced Torah studies.

In addition, Mercaz HaRav, Rabbi Kook's Zionist yeshivah,

became a great center of Torah learning. Bnei Akiva (a Religious Zionist youth group) high-school yeshivos and the *hesde*r yeshivos, which combined Torah study with military service, changed the complexion of religious life in Israel. Hesder students distinguished themselves in the tank and parachute corps during the Six Day War (1967) and the Yom Kippur War (1973).

Lastly, year after year, thousands of girls entered the Bais Yaakov schools and seminaries and the Bnei Akiva Ulpanot (girls' high schools) and seminaries.

It would take another fifteen or twenty years for the accumulated effect of this vast educational network to be fully felt. Meanwhile, day by day, month by month, year by year, Torah was quietly being woven into the tapestry of Jewish life in the Land of Israel.

32
Six Days of Deliverance
(From 1960-1973)

I n 1945 the Allies established a War Crimes Tribunal in Nuremberg, Germany to bring Nazi criminals to justice. Over a period of six years, 5,025 Nazis were tried and convicted; 806 were sentenced to death, but only 486 were executed. The United Nations also prepared lists of war criminals, and Nazi collaborators were brought to trial in various countries. But most Nazis escaped detection and the majority of those accused were eventually released or pardoned. The rest received only light sentences. Out of the millions of people who had actively and knowingly participated in the Nazi death machine, only a tiny percentage were convicted of any crime and few of those were severely punished.

THE EICHMANN TRIAL

Adolph Eichmann seated in a bulletproof glass booth at his trial in Jerusalem

Both the State of Israel and individuals around the world were involved in the search for missing, key Nazis. In 1960 Adolf Eichmann, the SS commander in charge of the Final Solution, was found by the Mossad (the Israeli Intelligence) in Argentina. He was abducted and flown to Israel to stand trial for his crimes. For the next two years, the horror of the Holocaust was relived in a long, detailed, public trial. For the younger generation in Israel, it was an education in the Holocaust.

Adolph Eichmann was found guilty. He died on the gallows in the Ramle prison on May 31, 1962. It was the only time the State of Israel had ever executed a criminal for his crimes. Perhaps the most horrifying part of the trial was Eichmann himself. A seemingly normal, quiet, civilized man, this mass murderer, architect of millions of deaths, went to his own death calmly, stating and believing that he had only followed orders and had done nothing wrong. His body was cremated and his ashes thrown into the sea.

The State of Israel had been born under the shadow of the Holocaust. The highly publicized Eichmann trial brought to light, clearly and explicitly, what had happened to the Jewish people in the dark, long night of the War. For Germany, it brought home the unquestionable guilt shared by millions of Germans and their government. As a result of the trial, many militant Jewish groups and organizations, formed in the 1950's and 1960's, adopted the defiant motto "Never Again!" It was a statement — and a prayer.

HOSTILE NEIGHBORS

The Arab world of the 1960's was a sea of political, economic and military turmoil. Russia had entered the Middle East and become a patron of Egypt, supplying Nasser with massive amounts of arms. Syria constantly shelled the Jewish settlements from the Golan Heights in the north of Israel, causing Israelis to sleep in bomb shelters throughout the decade. Syria also began digging channels to divert the waters of the Jordan River away from Israel, but Israeli air power and artillery put an end to that project. When Israel announced the operation of its first nuclear reactor, Syria and Iraq pressured Egypt and Jordan to take a more aggressive stance against Israel.

The Catholic Church also took a strong anti-Israel stand. Pope Paul VI championed the Arab refugees. He wished to see Jerusalem made an international city and he questioned the right of the Jewish State to exist.

In Israel, the aging David Ben Gurion resigned for the second time as prime minister. He retired to Sdei Boker, a small kibbutz in the Negev, and was succeeded by Levi Eshkol. The country was growing and developing, but it was still struggling with social and religious issues, still building its economy, still very new. Its most pressing issue, however, was security. Israel was still threatened by violently hostile neighbors. Eshkol's government would prove incapable of facing the growing military challenge.

PREPARING FOR WAR

In May 1967, the Arabs began to mobilize. Even worse, they began a pageant of furious public announcements and declarations. Nasser proclaimed, "This time we will exterminate Israel." The President of Iraq declared, "Our goal is clear — to wipe Israel off the map." Carried away on a wave of hatred and rhetoric, Egypt moved 100,000 soldiers into the Sinai and demanded that the U.N. peacekeeping forces be withdrawn. To everyone's surprise, the U.N. promptly complied.

On May 23, Nasser again blockaded the Gulf of Aqaba, thereby closing Eilat to Israeli shipping. Despite its promises to keep the high seas open, the United States took no action. King Hussein of Jordan signed a military pact with his erstwhile Egyptian enemy Nasser, and Iraqi troops took up positions in Jordan. On May 28, Nasser announced that the Arabs intended to open a general assault against Israel, a total war, aimed at the destruction of the Jewish State.

For once, political rivalries were forgotten in the Knesset. A national unity government was formed. Even Menachem Begin, whose differences with the ruling parties were well known, was called in to join the new government. Moshe Dayan was made Defense Minister.

Israel mobilized its entire army. Originally founded as a small, standing army, Tzahal had a large reserve army in waiting. The reserves were now called up. Almost every eligible male between the ages of eighteen and sixty was drafted. As streets, factories and stores were emptied of men, the women of Israel stepped forward to keep the country running.

Troops were sent to all fronts, especially to the south. Night after night, endless lines of trucks and tanks filled with soldiers drove down to the Negev. The television screens of the world broadcast pictures of Arab mobs in Cairo, Damascus, East Jerusalem and Amman, howling for the death of the Jews. A feeling of disaster filled the air. In country after country, Jews hurried to the synagogues to pray. In a great outpouring of love and concern, they waited in line outside synagogues and Jewish organizations to contribute money to the defense of the Jewish State. Airlines canceled flights to Israel but El Al planes were filled to overflowing with people anxious to reach

the country before the outbreak of war. Renewed visions of the Holocaust drifted over the House of Israel.

THE SIX DAY WAR BEGINS

There were many Arab states; losing a battle — or even a war — would not destroy the Arab people. There was, however, only one Jewish state, which was very small and very vulnerable. It could not afford to wait for an attack.

Israel decided to strike first and hard. On Monday morning, June 5th, 1967, the Six Day War began. In a superbly coordinated and executed attack, the Israeli Air Force destroyed the Arab air forces in the first four hours of the war. Most of the enemy planes were caught while still on the ground. 452 planes were destroyed; Israel lost nineteen of its own. The Israeli tank corps then crossed into the Sinai (for the third time!) facing massive Egyptian forces. But without air cover, Egypt was doomed. By June 8, Israel was at the Suez Canal. Despite ecstatic announcements on the Egyptian radio falsely claiming that Haifa and Tel Aviv were in flames, Nasser had lost the war.

Israeli troops at prayer near the front

JERUSALEM AND THE PROMISED LAND

Israel notified King Hussein that it would take no action against Jordan if Jordan did not enter the war. Hussein, however, had visions of occupying all of Jerusalem. Misled by the Arab broadcasts, believing that Israel was losing ground, he attacked. Jordanian artillery shelled Jerusalem — its houses, apartment buildings, synagogues, stores and parks. The Jews in West Jerusalem hurried into makeshift shelters as Tzahal crossed over into East Jerusalem. Unwilling to bomb the eastern half of the city, the Israelis suffered heavy casualties as they fought their way, house by house, to the Temple Mount.

On Wednesday afternoon, the 28th of Iyar, 5727 (June 7, 1967) Tzahal entered the Old City of Jerusalem. The Jewish army took the Kosel HaMaaravi — the Western Wall of the Temple — and Har HaBayis — the Temple Mount. The holiest of all Jewish places had returned to Jewish hands.

It was a miraculous moment of faith. Like a bolt of lightning, it electrified the Jewish world. The feeling of elation was so overwhelming that afterwards Jews, both secular and religious, said they

would not have been surprised to hear the radio announce the arrival of the Messiah. It was a moment of great unity, great thanksgiving, great relief and great joy. Even before the six days of fighting

Rabbi Shlomo Goren, Chief Rabbi of Tzahal and later Ashkenazic Chief Rabbi of Israel, blows the shofar at the Western Wall upon its liberation

had ended, the Jews of Jerusalem streamed out of their shelters and into the Old City. A week later, on the holiday of Shavuos, there was a mass *Aliyah LaRegel* — a pilgrimage to the Western Wall. Tens of thousands wended their way up Mt. Zion to the Kosel. As if pulled by a Divine magnet, they were drawn to the site of the Beis HaMikdash.

By June 8, Israel had regained all of Yehudah and Shomron — Judea and Samaria. These areas contained Beis Lechem, Chevron, Shechem, Beis El — the heartland of Biblical Eretz Yisrael. King Abdullah of Jordan had illegally occupied the area in 1948. He called it the West Bank of Jordan although he never officially incorporated it into his kingdom. Now the land was again in Jewish hands. In the North, Israel stormed the Golan Heights. By June 10, the Israelis had pushed the Syrians back to a mere thirty miles from Damascus.

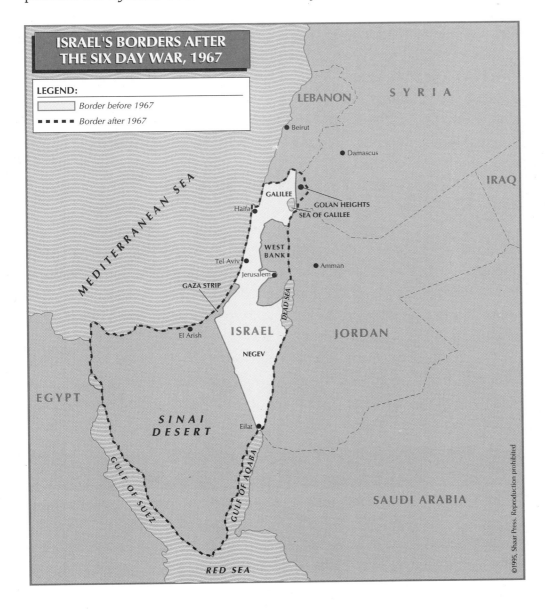

ISRAEL'S BORDERS AFTER THE SIX DAY WAR, 1967

LEGEND:
Border before 1967
Border after 1967

©1995, Shaar Press. Reproduction prohibited

In six days, Israel changed the face of the Middle East and with it, the face of the Jewish world.

The U.N. Security Council lost no time. The moment the Arab defeat became obvious, it hurried to limit the Israeli victory. It voted a cease-fire which the Arabs accepted and which Israel felt obliged to obey. Israel had suffered over 700 dead and twice as many wounded. It was a personal and painful loss for a tiny country where everyone was extended family. Nonetheless, the victories were a consolation. They were so large, so unexpected, so miraculous, that one had to be grateful.

Israel hoped that after their resounding defeat the Arabs would, at long last, make peace. They were wrong. At a meeting in Khartoum, Egypt, the Arabs adopted their famous "Three No's" — No peace, No war, No negotiations. As part of its own inner awakening and attachment to the Land, and as a matter of security, Israel began a policy of Jewish settlement in the Old City, in Eastern Jerusalem and in the West Bank.

The city of Jerusalem was officially united. The concrete walls dividing the eastern and western halves of the city were pulled down and the barbed wire which was stretched across its streets since 1948 was removed. Entire neighborhoods were added on to the south, north and west. In the following twenty years, the Jewish population in the city doubled in size.

The rebuilding of the Jewish Quarter in the Old City began. The Jordanians had destroyed the Quarter, its dozens of synagogues and yeshivos. Synagogues and yeshivos in other sections of the Old City had been used as animal shelters and storage houses. Tombstones

POPULATION OF JERUSALEM			
1945	164,400	1970	291,700
1961	237,400	1980	407,000
	1990	524,000	

from the ancient cemetery on Har Hazeisim (Mt. of Olives) had been removed and used to pave Jordanian streets, and a luxury hotel had been built over the graves on top of the mountain.

After Israel's victory in the Six Day War, the Jewish Quarter of Jerusalem was rebuilt and repopulated by families who had lived there before 1948, as well as by new inhabitants. The area in front of the Kosel was cleared and a huge plaza built where tens of thousands of Jews could congregate. Lower layers of stones from the Kosel were uncovered and the debris of hundreds of years removed so that the wall suddenly stood prouder and higher. Har Hazeisim was restored. Jerusalem came to life.

TERRORISM

The Palestine Liberation Organization (P.L.O.) was established in the early 1960's. Its purpose was to return the Arab refugees of 1948 to their homes in "Palestine" and to sponsor a war of liberation for the newly created "Palestinian nation."

"Liberation" was a code name for terrorism, and Yassir Arafat,

A PLO poster

who eventually rose to leadership of the P.L.O., turned terrorism into a science. Since it is easier to fight a war against civilians than against soldiers, Arafat introduced new methods and techniques to attack innocent, defenseless people. Hijacking airplanes, taking hostages, shooting children in schools, exploding car bombs in public places — all became the staples of P.L.O. trade. The terrorism was originally aimed at Israel, but it spread and became a tool of terrorist groups around the world. The P.L.O. made the entire world a more dangerous, frightening place to live in.

Israel refused to deal with the P.L.O. or to capitulate to its demands. It developed highly sophisticated methods to counteract this new evil, but Nasser, the P.L.O. and the Arabs continued to achieve diplomatic success in spite of their military defeats. Israel had won the war of 1967 and in so doing had lost the sympathy of the world. It seemed as though victory had turned the little Jewish David into a mighty Goliath, and defeat had turned the aggressive and violent Arabs into the new "persecuted underdogs."

THE CHALLENGE

The military victory of the Six Day War was a Divine gift for the Jewish people and the State of Israel. The war brought unhoped for successes and revived old dreams described in the Bible. For the first time since the Destruction of the Temple, the nation of Israel seemed secure in its Land. It had sensible, defendable borders; it had become a large, central power, not easily destroyed or, as the Arabs had so often threatened, "pushed into the sea." And Jerusalem, the entire city, was in Jewish hands.

The return of historical Eretz Yisrael led to Jewish settlement and

The Me'aras HaMachpelah in Chevron, built by King Herod over the original cave

development of the Land in Judea, Samaria, East Jerusalem and in the Gaza strip. By 1990, 145 settlements and over 140,000 inhabitants were living in "Greater Israel." Another 140,000 were in the new neighborhoods surrounding Jerusalem. Old Biblical sites — Chevron and Kiryat Arba, Beit El, Shiloh, Tekoa, Har Berachah next to Shechem — were now home to growing families and Jewish children. Towns from the time of the Maccabim or the Mishnah — Maon, Beit Choron, Modiin, Beitar, Susiya — were full of the sounds of Torah, of mothers with babies, of buses and ball games, of prayers, and renewed Jewish life in an old and holy homeland.

The war lit a worldwide spark of Jewish interest and led to a worldwide Teshuvah (Return to Judaism) movement. It saw the establishment of *baalei-teshuvah* yeshivos and yeshivos which specialized in the study of laws of the Beis HaMikdash. It brought about

Jews from all over the world at prayer on Chol HaMoed Succos, at the Western Wall

a revival of Judaism in Russia and encouraged the emigration of large numbers of Russian Jews to Israel. The challenges and possibilities inherent in the victory were enormous. Even the name of the Six Day War, suggestive of the Six Days of Creation, was alive with meaning. The question was: Would Israel be wise enough to take proper advantage of its miraculous gift?

33
A Time of Reckoning
(From 1973-1980)

**THE RISE OF
ANWAR
SADAT**

From the earliest days of the Jewish State, Russia had supplied massive arms, advisers and economic assistance to Egypt. When Nasser died in September 1970, he left Egypt in the throes of Russian domination and with a huge national debt. Egypt was also in the midst of a bitter and costly "War of Attrition" against Israel. The Israeli Bar-Lev Defense Line on the Suez Canal was shelled day after day and P.L.O. infiltrators crossed the borders, perpetrating many damaging attacks against Israeli towns and communities.

Anwar Sadat, Nasser's successor, looked for a way to end Egypt's obligations to Russia and to restore Arab pride after the many Arab defeats by Israel. In 1973 (after receiving a shipment of the latest Russian arms) Sadat expelled his Russian advisers and concluded a secret pact with Syrian dictator Haffez Al Assad. Syria and Egypt agreed to coordinate a surprise attack against Israel. Israeli intelligence reported the increased military activity in the two countries, and in a fight over the Golan in August 1972, the Israel Air Force shot down thirteen Syrian planes. Israel mobilized its army for several weeks until the danger seemed to have passed.

Trusting that Sadat would not dare to attack after the downing of the Syrian planes, Israel committed the unforgivable error of letting down its guard. Egypt had 800,000 troops, 2,200 tanks, 2,300 artillery pieces and 550 modern planes ready for battle. Syria had 50,000 soldiers including a large force protecting the road to Damascus, 1,500 tanks, 1,000 pieces of artillery, and Russian anti-aircraft missiles to use against the Israeli air force. Both countries were well trained and superbly equipped. Yet Israel somehow paid no heed to these facts. The Israeli defense line on the Suez was poorly equipped and vastly undermanned. On the Golan, Israel had fewer than sixty tanks facing 1,500 Syrian tanks. The moment of reckoning was near.

At 2:00 P.M. on Yom Kippur, 1973, Egypt and Syria simultaneously attacked Israel on two fronts. The Egyptian army crossed the Suez Canal and captured most of the Bar-Lev line. Syrian forces rolled across the Golan. Surprised at the lack of opposition, the Syrians stopped close to the city of Tiberias, expecting a surprise attack. They did not know that the road all the way across the country to Haifa was open and unprotected.

The heroism of the few defenders at the Bar-Lev line and on the Golan is legendary. Many of the fighters were young men in the tank core, students of hesder yeshivos. In the South the Bar-Lev line was broken, but in the North the Syrians were held back. A handful of young soldiers in the few remaining tanks kept the Syrians at bay for three days until reinforcements arrived. Then the Israelis forced the Syrians to retreat, pushing them back past their original lines and advancing until Israeli troops were within shooting range of Damascus. Casualties were high, but with their guns, their courage

YOM KIPPUR 5734/1973

Israeli tank crewman escapes from tank hit by enemy fire

and their prayers, a handful of soldiers saved the North. In both the North and the South, many paid with their lives because their government was unprepared.

Yom Kippur 5734 is remembered as the day sirens sounded across the country and men ran out of synagogues, still wrapped in their prayer shawls, to mount the trucks that hurriedly brought them to their units. Had the attack taken place any other day, it would have taken precious hours to find people. Because it was Yom Kippur, almost everyone was either in the synagogue or at home, and mobilizing the reserves was accomplished at lightning speed. Even Jews who had cast off the bonds of Jewish tradition spoke in hushed tones of the miracles that transpired. Miracles seemed to be the only explanation for the outnumbered, unprepared Israeli forces stopping the Syrian attack. Had it not been Yom Kippur, if the Syrians had continued to advance, if any one circumstance had been even a little different, the Syrians could, God forbid, have cut the country in two.

The battles continued throughout the holiday of Succos. Am Yisrael sat in their flimsy succos, vulnerable to the danger of enemy bombing and fire. The homes and cities of Israel were dark with the military blackout, but the sky was alight with stars. Side by side with the fear and the worry was the deep belief that *Netzach Yisrael lo yishaker* — the Eternal God of Israel would not forsake His people nor His Land.

An enormous amount of ammunition had been used at the outbreak of the war and Israel was desperately in need of supplies. On October 14, under the direct orders of President Richard Nixon, the United States began a military airlift to supply the Israeli forces.

On October 15, in a brilliant military maneuver, General Ariel Sharon stormed across the Sinai Desert, broke through the Egyptian lines, and crossed the Suez Canal. The road to Cairo was open and the Third Egyptian Army was surrounded and threatened with disaster. As the Israeli Air Force pounded the Egyptians, a massive Egyptian flight began. For miles and miles, Egyptian troops left a trail of abandoned equipment, vehicles, arms and clothing strewn across the desert.

The United Nations had watched silently when the war broke out and Israel was threatened with destruction. But the moment the Israeli victories began, it rushed in, as it had so many times in the past, to force a cease-fire, thus saving the Egyptian Third Army from the humiliation of defeat. Over the next few months, agreements were signed between Israel, Egypt and Syria. Israel again retreated from the Suez; Egypt received one-third of the Sinai; Syria received a small section of land and the city of Kuneitra on the Golan. Israel received a promise that the Arabs would fully observe the cease-fire and would return her prisoners of war.

For Israel, the Yom Kippur war had been a great salvation. The State could have easily been destroyed, God forbid. But the price of salvation was high; 3,500 soldiers had died. And although the Arabs lost the war, they felt that they had finally won a great victory. They "proved" that Israel was indeed vulnerable, that the Goliath of the Six Day War was only a little David after all. They missed the point; the strength of Am Yisrael lay in being David.

ANTI-SEMITISM AND TERROR

After the Yom Kippur War, the Arab oil-producing countries tripled the price of oil on the world market and began an oil boycott of the United States and other Western countries. Suddenly, there were long lines at gasoline stations, limited fuel for heating, and serious inflation. The American people were shocked and angry. The Arabs connected their oil-extortion policies to the "Israeli problem" and, illogical as it may seem, the world blamed Israel, not the Arabs, for its discomfort. Anti-Semitism always blames its victim.

Anti-Israel and anti-Semitic (the two are usually synonymous) literature and slogans spread throughout the world. The amount of anti-Semitic propaganda printed in Soviet Russia in the 1960's and 1970's almost equaled the amount of propaganda printed in Nazi Germany during the Second World War.

The supposedly international center of peace, the United Nations, welcomed Yassir Arafat, head of the world's largest terror organization, with tumultuous applause. He presented a speech in the General Assembly while demonstratively wearing his gun. Idi Amin, the "Butcher of Uganda" who had applauded the Nazis for destroying European Jewry, was also welcomed at the U.N. where he too denounced the "Zionist-American conspiracy." In November 1975, the U.N. General Assembly passed its infamous resolution stating that Zionism is racism. Anti-Semitism had been legitimized in the halls of the United Nations.

In October 1974, the Arab governments declared that the P.L.O. was the "sole legitimate representative of the Palestinian people." Arafat now had his credentials. He unleashed his murderous terrorists against Israel. More airplanes were hijacked, children were murdered at a school in the town of Maalot, and Israeli Olympic athletes were assassinated during the Munich Olympics in 1976. The response of the International Olympic Committee in Munich was typical. They refused to stop the games, even for a minute of silence in memory of the murdered Jewish participants.

World Jewry was stunned by this wave of modern anti-Semitism, but Israel fought back valiantly. Every terrorist attack was met with a response. On July 4, 1976, terrorists hijacked an Air France plane and brought it to the Entebbe airport in Idi Amin's Uganda. The one hundred Jewish passengers on board were taken aside to be killed. In a spectacular raid, Israeli forces flew across Africa to Uganda and rescued the hostages. One elderly woman was murdered by Idi Amin; all other hostages were saved. But the young Israeli commander, Yonatan Netanyahu, was killed. "Yoni," an American oleh, became a national hero and a symbol of shared Jewish responsibility.

BEGIN AND CAMP DAVID

The Israeli government appointed a commission to investigate the conduct of the Yom Kippur War. When it found the government guilty of being unprepared, the Israeli Prime Minister Golda Meir resigned from her post. In the elections of 1977 for the first time in the history of the State, the Labor party was defeated and Menachem Begin's Likud won the majority of seats in the Knesset. The Likud formed a coalition with the religious parties to set up a new government.

Golda Meir

Menachem Begin was a traditional, Eastern European Jew who valued the Torah and Jewish history. Unlike the secular Labor leaders who had governed Israel for the previous twenty-eight years, he believed that the Jewish past was the basis for the Jewish future. He put Jewish interests before all other considerations and felt no need to apologize to the Arabs or to the world for being in Israel. "We were granted the right to exist by the God of our fathers at the glimmer of the dawn of human civilization, nearly 4,000 years ago," he said. "That right has been sanctified in Jewish blood from generation to generation." A great orator, he held people spellbound for hours at a time. Large numbers of Sefardic and religious Jews were also attracted to his party.

Begin boldly invited the Egyptian ruler Sadat to Jerusalem. Sadat accepted and on November 9, 1977, amidst much fanfare, he arrived in the Holy City. In a dramatic presentation at the Knesset, he declared that Egypt was finally ready for peace with Israel. The following September (1978), Begin, Sadat and U.S. President Jimmy Carter met at Camp David, the presidential summer home, for a marathon thirteen-day session. Six months later an official peace treaty between Egypt and Israel was signed on the White House lawn, in front of the television cameras of the world. Proudly wearing a *yarmulka,* Begin recited the blessing *Shehecheyanu* before the eyes of the world.

As a result of this treaty, Egypt regained the entire Sinai peninsula, while Israel gained diplomatic recognition and peace with its largest adversary. Discussion of difficult matters such as the solution of the Palestinian refugee problem and the status of Jerusalem was postponed. Eighteen years later, Yitzchak Rabin and Yassir Arafat would wrestle with these thorny issues.

Begin felt strong enough to trade "land for peace" while Sadat, after the Yom Kippur War, felt secure enough to sign a peace treaty with Israel. Both men were awarded the Nobel Peace Prize for their efforts, but neither enjoyed the fruits of their efforts. Like many other Arab leaders, Sadat was soon assassinated for his moderate views while Begin lost much of his political support for having relinquished portions of the country to the Egyptians.

As Israel retreated from Sinai, it removed and uprooted everything it had built, invested in and planted since 1967 — oil wells, set-

Prime Minister Menachem Begin announces the historic peace accord with Egypt, as President Jimmy Carter looks on

tlements, homes, hothouses and fields. Protest rallies were held across the country. Jews had come to Eretz Yisrael to build, not to destroy; to plant, not to uproot; to settle, not to retreat. As Israelis watched the destruction of the beautiful desert city Yamit and its flowering settlements on their television screens, they were shocked and numb. It was a shattering experience both for Begin and for the country.

Nonetheless, Begin won another election. He waged a war to drive the P.L.O. out of Lebanon, thus making the cities and settlements in the north of Israel safe from murderous attacks. Standing up to scathing, worldwide protest, he bombed an Iraqi nuclear reactor which was developing atomic weapons to threaten Israel. (It would take several years until the world acknowledged how wise this attack had been.)

For many, Begin's finest hour was undoubtedly signing the Camp David Accord on the White House lawn. But for many others, his relinquishing parts of Eretz Yisrael which had been hard won and paid for with Jewish blood was a dangerous precedent. Eighteen years later, other politicians would use Begin as an example as they made their own concessions and still more controversial agreements.

THE RELEASE OF RUSSIAN JEWRY

Between 1967 and 1980 almost 150,000 Russian Jews arrived in Israel. The sudden awakening of Russian Jewry was a direct result of the Six Day War. The instinctive identification of Russian Jews with the Jewish State led to the study of Hebrew, Bible and Jewish history, in spite of the objections of the atheistic communist government. Secret, illegal Jewish study groups and yeshivos were formed in apartments. Simchas Torah celebrations at the Moscow synagogue became a time of Jewish solidarity. Jews who had been cut off from Judaism for the past fifty years (ever since the Russian Revolution in 1917) suddenly wanted to be Jews again. They wanted to study Torah and to return to the Jewish homeland. And they were willing to suffer for their cause. They were fired from jobs, hounded by the KGB (the secret police), imprisoned and made to wait long periods of time for a visa. The Russian Refuseniks became the latest in a long line of fighters for Jewish freedom. Partially due to American pressure (the result of active Jewish protest), Russia opened its tightly closed Iron Curtain and released several waves of Jewish immigrants. The State of Israel accepted them with open arms and open hearts.

Rabbi Eliyahu Essas, famous Russian refusnik, studying Torah with others in Moscow

The Jewish State had proved itself to be an anchor and a haven for the Jewish people. It had accepted responsibility for the physical welfare of Jews across the globe. It had become a focal point to which Jews around the world turned as a source of pride. Whether they considered themselves Zionists or not, whether they visited or cared about the Jewish State or not, in the eyes of the world — and most of its Jews — Israel was the Jewish homeland.

Despite all of its imperfections and problems, Israel was also becoming a vital element in the Torah world. Although the existence of the state did not yet fulfill Messianic expectations, it was nonetheless the source of much gratitude and joy. By the 1980's Israel had become the center of worldwide Torah study. Jews from around the world came to learn and study Judaism. Tens of thousands of students were in hundreds of yeshivos throughout the country. There had not been so many people studying Torah anywhere since the time of the Second Temple. Even the number of authentic converts to Judaism suddenly grew by astounding numbers.

The 1970's had been a turbulent time for Israel and for world Jewry. War and peace, terror and rescue, change and continuity intermingled. But under the tumultuous conditions, the basic, unsolved, underlying questions of modern Jewish life remained. How does one sustain Torah life and values in the modern age? How does one combine Halachah and democracy? How does one reach the vast majority of Jews who have lost contact with Jewish tradition? How "Jewish" should the Jewish State be? No easy answers were forthcoming.

SECTION VIII

The New Jewish World
(From 1950 to 2000)

34
American and Russian Jewry
(From 1950-1980)

TIMELINE

1938 *Founding of first Beth Jacob High School for Girls*
1960 *Eichmann Trial in Israel*
1963 *Assassination of President John F. Kennedy*
1967 *Six Day War; Jerusalem reunited*
1968 *Assassination of Dr. Martin Luther King*
1969 *First Landing on Moon*
1969 *War of Attrition at Suez Canal*
1970 *1,000 Russian Jews arrive in Israel*
1971 *14,500 Russian Jews arrive in Israel*
1973 *Yom Kippur War*
1976 *Entebbe Raid by Israeli forces*
1979 *Camp David Israel-Egypt peace agreement*

*A*fter the Holocaust, a revival of Jewish life took place in the East and in the West — in Israel and in America. Although American Jewry supported Israel wholeheartedly, only a small number of American Jews actually immigrated to Israel. The opportunities in America were so great and life was so promising that even committed American Jews chose to remain in the Diaspora.

**CHANGES IN
LIFE STYLE**

Jewish life underwent great changes after the war. Like their non-Jewish neighbors, many Jewish families left the cities and moved to the suburbs. Old, established, Jewish neighborhoods were abandoned, and synagogues, institutions and schools were sold. The Jewish population was now spread out over large areas. In most cities, there was no longer one central Jewish area where schools, synagogues, community centers, Jewish shopping and services were concentrated. Jews began to use the same services that were available to everyone else. Assimilation into American life came more quickly and easily.

If many first generation European Jews were Orthodox, the second generation was only traditional. They still kept a nominally kosher home even if they ate non-kosher food outside. They ate matzos on Passover and attended a synagogue (often Conservative) several times a year. But the third generation usually had little connection with Jewish tradition. They celebrated at a family Seder on Passover and they probably had a Bar or Bat Mitzvah. But they no longer had a kosher home. Many no longer even had a kosher circumcision for their sons. If they attended any prayer service at all, it was now most likely at a Reform temple. By the 1950's, most Orthodox synagogues were empty. The Conservative movement seemed to be the wave of the future.

Despite the empty Orthodox synagogues, the 50's saw the development of the Orthodox Day School movement. By the 1960's, the day schools had proven so successful that Conservative Jews established their own day schools (the Solomon Shechter schools), mostly at the elementary level. But Conservative Jewry continued to move further away from Jewish law. It issued divorces which were halachically unacceptable. It included women in a Conservative minyan and later granted recognition to women rabbis and cantors. It had been founded to "conserve" Jewish tradition while making it palatable for assimilating American Jews, but in practice the Conservative movement abandoned Halachah and moved closer to Reform.

THE CONSERVATIVE AND REFORM MOVEMENTS

The Reform movement was also undergoing important changes. Reform had originally been absolutely opposed to the Zionist movement. But after the Holocaust, many Reform Jews were not willing to turn their backs on the survivors or on a Jewish State which offered them a safe haven. The movement now rejected its extreme anti-Zionist position and Reform leaders such as Abba Hillel Silver and Stephen Wise worked for the establishment of the State of Israel. But it was not until the Six Day War in 1967 that Reform Jewry truly identified with the State of Israel.

Reform also made a catastrophic change in Jewish law. Many Reform congregants had children who were married to gentiles. In an attempt to keep these mixed-marriage families as members of their temples, and in opposition to all Torah law, the Reform leadership decreed that it was no longer the mother who determined the religious identity of her child. The child of any Jewish parent — whether mother or father — was now automatically considered a Reform Jew. It was the beginning of a serious breach within the Jewish people. Even the Conservative movement rejected this move.

Two major organizations — the United Jewish Appeal and the Israel Bond Organization — dominated American Jewish life in the 1960's and 1970's. They raised enormous sums of money on behalf of Israel and world Jewry. Their efforts were so suc-

THE UJA AND ISRAEL BONDS

cessful that it seemed as though American Jewry existed solely in order to supply funds for Israel. Afraid of endangering their all-important fund-raising activities for Israel, the UJA ignored vital projects such as Jewish education in America. This shortsighted and mistaken policy would bear bitter fruit. While American Jewish leaders were busy developing Israel, American Jewry was becoming more and more assimilated.

ASSIMILA-
TION

By the end of the 1970's, American Jewry represented 2.7 percent of the total U.S. population. Jewish impact on American society, however, was out of all proportion to its small numbers. American Jews lived and worked in the big cities. They were doctors, lawyers, teachers, professionals, politicians and public servants. They were in private business and in the public media. No longer the children of immigrants or outsiders, the small Jewish minority was transformed into an integral part of the American scene. No longer eternal strangers bargaining for favors, Jewish men and women saw themselves as full citizens with equal rights and obligations in all matters. They were totally integrated and assimilated into American life. Politically, economically, culturally — they were Americans.

In the 1980's, ethnic rights came into style. Knowing who you were and where your grandparents came from was considered a matter of ethnic pride. The idea of the Melting Pot which had so obsessed the immigrants at the beginning of the century was abandoned. Now Blacks, Hispanics, Asians and others all proudly claimed their national heritage. Many Jews also began to search for their roots. They felt wholly American, but a spark of Jewish consciousness refused to disappear. In the past, being Jewish might have been a source of embarrassment; in the 1980's, it became a source of pride.

Nonetheless, only a small percentage of Jewish children were receiving any Jewish education; of these, an even smaller percentage were in the day schools. Despite the rise in ethnic pride, millions of unaffiliated Jews were estranged from their religion. In frightening numbers, they were disappearing from the ranks of the Jewish people. Intermarriage rates reached over fifty percent; in areas with smaller Jewish populations, the numbers were even higher. While Jews in Russia and Israel struggled for physical and economic survival, the secure, affluent Jews of America were in danger of fading away.

T he Jew in Israel was living in the Jewish Homeland. The Jew in America and other Western lands was willingly assimilating into his adopted home. The Russian Jew was forcibly dispossessed of his Jewish heritage.

RUSSIAN JEWRY

Three and a half million Russian Jews were locked behind Stalin's tightly drawn Iron Curtain. Since 1917 they had lived under an anti-Semitic Communist regime. Denied any expression or practice of Judaism, they were cut off from all contact with world Jewry. Circumcision, the Sabbath, kosher food, Jewish calendars, holidays and prayer books were non-existent. It seemed as though this ancient branch of the Jewish people would disappear.

The establishment of the State of Israel was a turning point for Russian Jewry. When Golda Meir, Israel's ambassador to the Soviet Union, arrived in Moscow in 1948, she was mobbed by thousands of Jews who came to express their solidarity with the new Jewish State. Despite years of cruel suppression and vicious anti-Semitism, the masses of Russian Jewry had remained silent but loyal members of Am Yisrael. The Divine spark which lies within every Jewish soul had not been extinguished.

In 1967 the Six Day War electrified Russian Jewry. Many Jews defied Russia's anti-Semitic laws and began the illegal study of Hebrew and Torah. Each Simchas Torah, thousands gathered in front of the main synagogue in Moscow to identify with the Jewish people. A Baal Teshuvah movement began. A generation of "Refuseniks" arose — people waiting long years to make aliyah. New names were added to the list of Jewish heroes. Joseph Mendelevitch, Natan Scharansky, Eliyahu Essas, Yosef Begun, Ida Nudel, the Reiz family and others were hounded, harassed, exiled and imprisoned, but they did not surrender (see Chapter 33).

Yosef Begun being embraced by Natan Scharansky upon arriving in Israel

Leading Orthodox rabbis, scholars and laymen from Israel and the West paid thousands of visits to Russia to help train a core of Jewish teachers and activists. Prayer books, Bibles, Torah works, matzos, esrogim and other religious items were brought into the country in increasing quantities.

Anxious to avoid repeating the terrible mistake made during World War II, when they had remained silent in the face of Jewish persecution, American Jews reacted. They organized, protested, pressured, lobbied and marched. The result was strong American pressure on Russia to permit Jewish emigration. The first wave of emigrants arrived in Israel in the 1960's. In the 70's, more than 250,000 Jews left Russia; half settled in the United States. In the 1980's further waves of Russian emigration reached Israel and by the 1990's, more than 600,000 Russian olim, had emigrated to Israel.

Freer Russian emigration, however, was accompanied by a rise in Russian anti-Semitism. Jews, who had always been doctors, scientists, professors, engineers and musicians, were excluded from many of these professional areas and fired from their jobs. In 1977-78, not a single Jew was admitted to Moscow University. Virulently anti-Semitic works were published and widely distributed in Russia. One such book (*Judaism and Zionism*) contributed to the infamous U.N. decision of 1974 that Zionism is a form of racism. Russia was also involved in shipping huge amounts of arms and military advisers to Egypt and Syria. The country did everything in its power to destroy the security of Israel after the Six Day War. Russian anti-Semitism had long, deep roots and the age-old Russian hatred of the Jews defied all logic.

The year 1960 marked the beginning of sweeping changes in American society. The period began with the election of a young, vibrant, liberal, Catholic president, John F. Kennedy. The country's bright hopes for progress, however, were shattered when Kennedy was assassinated in 1963. The assassination was followed by two national crises. The first was the fight for minority civil rights and the second was the Vietnam War. These two issues engulfed the nation. They caused major turmoil and led to a rebellion against the established political and social order.

THE BREAKDOWN OF VALUES

The Jewish community was at the forefront of the Civil Rights movement. When Dr. Martin Luther King led the battle to end racial segregation, American Jewry gave him its full and active support. But as the campaign progressed, laws were violated, both in support of and against the Civil Rights movement. Dr. King was assassinated and his death led to riots, ghetto burnings and further lawlessness. Violence raged on the streets of America's cities. Scenes of looting and killing were beamed onto television screens in every American home.

The Vietnam War further accelerated the breakdown of law and order. The American involvement in that bloody, endless war become more and more unpopular. Those who opposed the war were the students who were being sent to Vietnam to fight. Widespread student protests turned violent and the fabric of society began to unravel. At times like this, anti-Semitism, always lurking in some dark corner, rears its evil head. Leftists and some blacks began attacking Jews, Judaism and Israel. The attacks were seemingly justified by the U.N.'s "Zionism equals Racism" decree.

Basic American values declined; permissiveness and immorality became open and acceptable. Drugs, alcohol, promiscuity and abominations forbidden by the Torah over 3,000 years ago became widespread. All were part of a mass culture nourished by advertising and the media and brought directly into American homes by television. Millions of individuals were caught up in the permissive activities of the times. Many people were emotionally maimed or left physically crippled for life. The divorce rate skyrocketed; families suffered. Religious groups, schools and communities attempted to deal with the sweeping problems of Western society, but the trend was clear. Modern America grew more immoral, more violent and more rebellious than it had ever been before.

American Jewry was also swept up in this struggle. Everyone was affected. The Orthodox reacted by turning to Torah and strengthening their community, schools and yeshivos. They became more involved in Torah Judaism, while secular Jews continued to assimilate.

35
The Revival of Torah
(From 1950-1990)

FOUNDERS OF A NEW WORLD

R' Moshe Feinstein

R' Joseph B. Soloveitchik

ifteen hundred years of Jewish life had been consumed in the flames of Hitler's furnaces. Six million sparks were extinguished. But the light of Torah did not go out. Throughout the 1930's and 1940's, great Eastern European Torah scholars and rabbis arrived in America and began to rebuild the world that had been destroyed. Many had been miraculously rescued from death. All believed that a strong, vibrant Torah life must be created in America. They believed they had been saved in order to help restore the Jewish people. These were men with a mission who would now dedicate their lives to Torah.

Rabbi Shraga Feivel Mendlowitz, founder of Torah Umesorah, was personally responsible for much of the development in Torah education. In 1940 Rabbi Aharon Kotler arrived in America and founded Beth Medrash Govoha in Lakewood, New Jersey. He became the dynamic leader of the drive for high-level Torah study. Lakewood became one of the great yeshivos of the world and the father of the *kollelim* — schools of advanced study for married men. Rabbi Joseph Breuer headed the German community in Washington Heights, New York and presided over its schools. He was succeeded by Rabbi Shimon Schwab.

Rabbi Yaakov Yitzchak Ruderman founded Yeshivas Ner Yisrael in Baltimore. Rabbi Yitzchak Hutner was head of Mesivta Rabbi Chaim Berlin in Brooklyn. Rabbi Reuven Grozovsky and Rabbi Yaakov Kamenetsky headed Yeshivah Torah Vodaath in Brooklyn and Rabbi Joseph B. Soloveitchik headed Yeshivah University in New York. Rabbi Elya Meir Bloch and Rabbi Mordechai Katz reestablished the Telshe Yeshivah in Cleveland, and their student Rabbi Nachum Z. Dessler, founded the Hebrew Academy of Cleveland, a pioneer day school. Rabbi Gedalia Schorr, whom Rabbi Kotler called "the first American *gadol*"

(great Torah scholar and leader) became head of Torah Vodaath, and another American gadol, Rabbi Mordechai Gifter, became the head of the Telshe Yeshivah.

The Rebbes of Lubavitch — Rabbi Yosef Yitzchak Schneerson and his son-in-law Rabbi Menachem Mendel Schneerson — developed a dynamic movement which reached out to tens of thousands of non-observant Jews. The great Chassidic Rebbes of Bobov, Klausenburg, Skver and others attracted large followings. When Rabbi Yoel Teitelbaum, the Satmar Rav, came to America in 1946, he had barely ten Chassidim for a minyan. Forty years later, Satmar had tens of thousands of Chassidim and dozens of institutions. The Satmar Rav set the tone for the explosive growth of Chassidic communities.

R' Mordechai Gifter

Last, but one of the most beloved, in this very abridged list of great men was Rabbi Moshe Feinstein. Known simply as "Reb Moshe," he arrived in America in the late 1930's. For nearly fifty years he served as head of the Mesivta Tifereth Jerusalem in Manhattan. Reb Moshe was the acknowledged master of Halachah in the world until his death in March 1986. A gentle, pious man, he carried the burdens of the Jewish people on his shoulders. Despite those burdens, he was always ready with a warm and genuine smile. His modest home, his deep wisdom and his unending kindness were available to all. More than 100,000 people attended his funeral in New York and 250,000 attended in Jerusalem the following day.

These rabbis, and others not mentioned here, created a quiet revolution in American Jewish life. They educated generations of

A sea of mourners. Over 100,00 people attending R' Moshe Feinstein's funeral in New York

American-born Torah scholars, strengthened Jewish education, kashruth and Sabbath observance, and helped shape a vibrant, proud, new Orthodoxy in America.

JEWISH EDUCATION AND THE DAY SCHOOLS

One of the major changes in American Jewish life was the Jewish day school. After a number of false starts, the Day School movement of today began in the late 1940's, when Reb Shraga Feivel Mendlowitz founded Torah Umesorah — the National Society for Hebrew Day Schools. Within a few decades, the population of the Orthodox day schools exceeded 100,000 students.

The day school was meant to provide a complete religious and secular education in one school under the guidance of observant teachers and principals. From Bangor to Boston, from St. Louis to Seattle, from New York to Miami, from Minneapolis to Memphis, from Columbus to Canada, day schools crisscrossed the continent.

A portion of the beis medrash in Beth Medrash Govoha in Lakewood where thousands of students study Torah

At first, there was staunch opposition to the idea of Jewish religious schools. Many felt that the graduates would be unprepared to deal with the gentile world. The system was somehow seen as "unAmerican." The Jewish Federations, which had donated millions of dollars for many projects, opposed the day schools and, in most cities, refused to support them. The financial plight of these schools in the 19██████ and 60's was very difficult. Nonetheless, they continued to grow. Yeshivah high schools, girls' schools and advanced yeshivos were founded in state after state, growing in size and scope, to accommodate the students graduating from the elementary schools.

The Bais Yaakov system of girls' schools and seminaries for college-age women also grew rapidly. The first girls' high school was founded by the famous Rebbetzin Vichna Kaplan around her dining room table in 1938. Today it is acknowledged that one of the main reasons for the widespread growth of Orthodoxy in America is the exceptional educational system established for girls and young women.

OLD AND NEW IN THE NEW WORLD

The 1950's and 1960's saw the growth of a large and strong Chassidic movement in the United States. Most Chassidic communities began in the New York area, but as time went on, they spread to other cities. The largest and most influential were the Satmar Chassidim in Williamsburg, New York. Satmar was a hard-working, active, strongly anti-Zionist group, not given to compromises of any sort. As a result of Satmar's influence, many Chassidic customs and clothing styles became widespread among Orthodox Jewry. Chabad-Lubavitch also prospered. Centered in Crown Heights in Brooklyn, Chabad operated student centers on college campuses and in cities around the world. Today, several Chassidic groups live in small towns throughout the United States where they have created communities free from the influences of the outside world.

In the early 1950's, Yeshiva University opened its Albert Einstein College of Medicine, the first Orthodox Jewish medical school in America. A doctor with a *kippah* on his head was a rare sight in the 1960's; by the 1980's it would become commonplace. Career choices for Orthodox Jews grew. Medicine, law, finance, engineering, even politics were opening up to religious Jews. Halachah was no longer an obstacle in professional life. Like the Chassidic and yeshivah population, the modern, professional, Orthodox Jew became more visible, secure and assertive of his rights. The intellectual leader of the M___ ___thodox (or "Centrist") community was Rabbi Joseph ___ He was one of the century's profound Torah scholars and thinkers, and the teacher of many thousands at Yeshivah Rabbi Yitzchak Elchanan.

Before the Second World War, the religious Zionist Mizrachi party had been the leading religious movement in the United States. After the War and the arrival of the European roshei yeshivah and rabbis, Agudath Israel became the official spokesman for parts of American Orthodoxy. By the 1960's, Orthodox Judaism, represented by the Union of Orthodox Jewish Congregations, Young Israel, Agudath Israel and others, had grown into a strong, well-organized force.

The thirty years from the 1950's to the 1980's were a time of ferment and change. Israel was still fighting for its physical survival, Russian Jewry was just beginning to awaken from a half-century nightmare of anti-Semitism and forced isolation, and the majority of American Jews were rushing into the deathly embrace of assimilation. America offered maximum freedom and professional opportunity, and American Jews eagerly seized their chance for success. At the same time, a strong Torah revival was taking place, but only a small minority of Jews — ten or fifteen percent — used their freedom and security as an opportunity for increased Torah observance. Higher standards of Torah knowledge and observance became the norm in all parts of the Orthodox community. For the rest of American Jewry, intermarriage skyrocketed, Jews observed fewer and fewer traditions and the family structure of Jewish America weakened.

RENEWAL, LOSS AND GAIN

Nonetheless, partially as a result of the Eichmann Trial and the Six Day War, a growing number of young, assimilated Jews began to search for a more meaningful life. Disillusioned with Western society, they turned back to their own Jewish heritage. The growing Baal Teshuvah movement was a welcome development in Orthodox life.

Ironically, the growth of the day schools, the yeshivos, the kollel movement, kashruth certification — everything necessary for the maintenance of Orthodox Jewish life — led to a more divided community. Traditional Jews became more traditional; secular Jews became more secular. Yeshivos grew and prospered while intermarriage and assimilation soared. American Orthodoxy was stronger than it had ever dreamed it could be, but millions of American Jews were estranged from their people and their God.

Yet all the while, the struggle for Jewish survival continued. In the Holy Land, in Russia and in the United States, an ancient people was at work renewing itself yet again.

36
Tomorrow —
Looking Toward
Redemption

**THE STATE
OF WORLD
JEWRY:
A SUMMARY**

The end of the twentieth century finds the Jewish people in a comfortable but challenging situation. The saga of Jewish Europe which began with Rabbeinu Gershom Meor HaGolah in the year 960 was almost ended by the flames of the Holocaust. The main stage of Jewish history has now shifted from Europe to America and Israel. In 1990 there were an estimated 14,000,000 Jews in the world. The three largest groups were living in the United States (5,835,000), in Israel (4,100,000), and in the former Soviet Union (1,800,000). It is impossible to know exactly how many Jews are in the United States and the former Soviet Union, because many people who are considered Jews are really children of non-Jewish mothers, who are not Jewish according to Halachah, while many others who are halachically Jewish consider themselves gentiles. Anti-Semitism continued to simmer, and often flare up, in the Western world, but it was not seen as a major, active threat. It was ignorance and assimilation which were weakening the fiber of the Jewish people.

AMERICA

Comfortably settled between the spacious and hospitable shores of the Atlantic and Pacific Oceans, American Jewry has experienced astounding material success. Even in the Golden Age of Spain, Jews did not reach the heights of achievement and acceptance which American Jewry has reached today. Spanish Jews of the fifteenth century were granted many valuable privileges; in twentieth century democracies, however, Jewish citizens possess their rights by law — not through special favors.

The small American Jewish minority has evolved into an integral part of American society. American Jews are not strangers from without, but members from within. Not only do they influence

JEWISH POPULATIONS THROUGHOUT THE WORLD IN 1991

AUSTRIA- 12,000
BELGIUM- 30,000
BULGARIA- 5,000
CZECHOSLOVAKIA- 12,000
NETHERLANDS- 25,000
HUNGARY- 90,000
ITALY- 35,000
YUGOSLAVIA- 5,500
SWITZERLAND- 18,300
SYRIA- 4,000

JAPAN
600

HONG KONG
700

AUSTRALIA
90,000

NEW ZEALAND
4,800

U.S.S.R.
1,800,000

GREECE
4,875

TURKEY
23,000

WEST GERMANY
28,000

RUMANIA
23,000

EAST GERMANY
400

IRAN
25,000

INDIA
6,000

ISRAEL
4,100,000

SOUTH YEMEN
1,000

ETHIOPIA
1,000

ZIMBABWE
1,200

POLAND
6,000

FINLAND
1,200

TUNISIA
3,500

KENYA
330

SOUTH AFRICA
120,000

SWEDEN
16,000

NORWAY
950

DENMARK
9,000

ALGERIA
600

ZAMBIA
85

IRELAND
2,000

GREAT BRITAIN
300,000

SPAIN
12,000

PORTUGAL
300

MOROCCO
13,000

FRANCE
535,000

COLOMBIA
7,000

VENEZUELA
20,000

BRAZIL
150,000

PARAGUAY
900

URUGUAY
44,000

ARGENTINA
228,000

CUBA
1,000

PANAMA
3,800

EQUADOR
1,000

PERU
5,000

BOLIVIA
600

CHILE
17,000

UNITED STATES
5,835,000

CANADA
330,000

MEXICO
35,000

GUATEMALA
800

American leadership, they are themselves part of this leadership, exercising lawful authority. They see themselves — including the Chassidim and the most Orthodox — as full-fledged Americans.

Yet despite its astounding success, American Jewry is struggling to maintain its existence. Success and a friendly environment pose their own dangers to Jewish survival. The growth of Torah in the United States and Canada is heartening, but mixed marriages and Jewish assimilation of over fifty percent of the non-orthodox population do not bode well for the future. This is perhaps the main challenge facing American Jewry in the twenty-first century.

EUROPE

By 1990, 1,200,000 Jews were living in Europe. Although active and well-organized Jewish communities exist in many European countries and most Western European Jews are successful professionally, European Jewry never recovered from the ravages of the Second World War. In 1990 most communities were small (by pre-war standards) and throughout Eastern Europe (except for Hungary) they tended to be elderly and poor. The level of Jewish observance varied from place to place, but in general it remained low. Small but vibrant Orthodox communities existed in Belgium, England, France, Switzerland and other countries, but even there, Torah scholarship was not yet widespread. Gateshead was the only major yeshivah and kollel in Europe. All the other great pre-war yeshivos had been destroyed or uprooted. In Europe as well as in America, the State of Israel served as a uniting force and a focus of Jewish interest.

The largest European Jewish community in the 1960's was in France. Since the time of Napoleon, French Jews had been highly assimilated. But in the 1960's, a huge influx of Sefardic Jews from North Africa transformed the French Jewish community, making it much more traditional and Zionistic. As bona fide citizens of their countries, the Jews of Europe enjoyed full protection of the law. Nonetheless, the venom of anti-Semitism continued to flow through the bloodstream of France and other European countries, even at the end of the twentieth century.

The Six Day War led to a widespread Jewish awakening across the world. Soviet Jewry, in particular, underwent a great transformation. The "Refuseniks" and Prisoners of Zion, the desire to emigrate to Israel, illegal schools for the study of Torah and Hebrew — all were part of the miraculous rebirth of Jewish life and interest in the Soviet Union. Still alive in 1990, even after seventy years of ruthless oppression, the Jewish soul was starved. The time had come for nourishment.

RUSSIA AND THE SOVIET UNION

In 1989 approximately 1,800,000 Jews lived in the Soviet Union; by 1995 about a third had emigrated to Israel. These 600,000 Soviet Jews made up the largest single immigrant group in the country. A further 120,000 Russian Jews emigrated to the United States. As was to be expected, many difficulties were encountered, both by the immigrants and by the host countries. Nor was it an easy matter, after seventy years of communism and constant anti-religious propaganda, to educate Soviet Jews in the ways of Judaism. Yet today, there are thousands of Russian Jewish families who are again practicing the faith of their fathers, both in the Holy Land and in the Diaspora.

In the former Soviet Union, Jewish education began to undergo vast development. In Moscow, Kiev and other large cities, yeshivos, girls' seminaries, adult classes and kindergartens were established. Synagogues were reopened and rebuilt. Rabbis, teachers and counselors from Israel and the Diaspora were sent to teach and work with the Jewish community. So far, only a small percentage of Russian Jews has been reached, but the results are heartening.

The Moslem countries of North Africa and Asia boasted great Jewish communities going back to the time of the Second Temple. Today, nearly all of them have disappeared. The first great wave of emigration began in 1948 in the throes of Israel's War for Independence. The Jews continued to emigrate — or were expelled — and by 1974, only 400 Jews remained in Iraq out of a community of 135,000; 350 remained in Egypt out of 75,000; and 4,000 remained in Syria from over 30,000. Since then, the great

NORTH AFRICA AND ASIA

A military transport plane en route from Ethiopia to Israel

majority of the Syrian Jews have been permitted to leave. Across North Africa and Asia, ancient communities returned to Zion. Thousands of people from Etiopia were dramatically brought to Israel in Operation Solomon in 1991.

For the Jew, the Land of Israel is the center of the world, the geographical focal point of all history, "a Land that Hashem, your God, seeks out; the eyes of Hashem, your God, are always upon it, from the beginning of the year to the year's end" (*Deuteronomy* 11:12).

Today, the existence of a Jewish state makes possible the large-scale return to our ancient and holy homeland. Thanks to the renewed Jewish sovereignty and independence, the Land of Israel has become not only a focal point of longing and dreams, but a physical reality. For the first time in two thousand years, we have the opportunity to try and create a Jewish state based on the laws and teachings of the Torah.

ISRAEL AND ITS ACCOM- PLISHMENTS

With all of its difficulties, complications, challenges and failures, Israel is nonetheless a reason for Jewish gratitude, love and pride. On a purely physical level, its accomplishments are awe inspiring. Eretz Yisrael has been transformed from an empty, desolate country into a Garden of Eden. Its agriculture is one of the wonders of the world; the country is self sufficient, feeding its own five million people and exporting food products across the world. Bare mountains have been reforested, deserts greened, and malarial swampland turned into fertile fields. A barren country has become a land of milk and honey.

Israel's population has grown tenfold in less than fifty years. Its people opened their arms, their hearts and their pockets, and lovingly gathered in over one million forsaken Jewish refugees whose survival was threatened. By the year 1995, 4,500,000 Jews, about one-third of the world Jewish population, was living in the Jewish State.

Hebrew, the holy tongue, is still the language of Torah scholarship, but in its modernized form it is now in daily use as a living language. Hebrew unites Jewish immigrants from Afghanistan to Australia and helps keep them one people.

In fewer than fifty years, a poor, undeveloped country has become a sophisticated state which launches satellites, exports state-of-the-art computer programs and researches remedies for cancer. A non-violent people now has one of the world's best armies, whose victories and battles are studied in military schools around the world.

And most fittingly, Eretz Yisrael has once again assumed its rightful position as the worldwide center of Torah. Throughout the land, the voice of Torah is heard as tens of thousands of students study in hundreds of yeshivos and kollelim, young women study in seminaries, and tens of thousands of younger students attend religious schools.

The Jewish State is a joint effort of Jews living in Israel and in the Diaspora. It has provided a measure of Jewish security in a dangerous, still anti-Semitic, world. The historian Cecil Roth has written, "Our generation is too near to appreciate, even now, the scale of achievement of the miracle of the rebirth [of the State]."

Today, Torah scholars in Israel are dealing with problems that no one has ever faced before. They are attempting to apply Jewish law to the life of an entire nation — to a modern, national economy, industry and security situation; to democracy, politics, education and welfare. How does one run a state, an army, a hospital, a factory according to the Halachah? How can one close the agricultural sector of an entire country on the Shemittah (Sabbatical)

THE CHALLENGE OF A JEWISH STATE

Year? How does one develop modern agriculture according to the Torah? How does one supply electricity, water and other services to an entire country on the Sabbath and Jewish holidays? How does one guarantee a minimal level of Jewish observance in matters of marriage, birth, death and conversions for the many people who are not observant?

In Israel, as in the Diaspora, another challenge looms large. What must be done (and how should it be done?) to bring Jews back to Torah values and observance? All Jews are the children of Avraham Avinu and Sarah Imeinu. As brothers and sisters, we are all mutually responsible for each other. Therefore, we must find a way into the minds and hearts of our fellow Jews and help them reclaim their heritage — the Torah. How can we best do this, especially when parts of the population believe that Israel should be a secular, democratic state where Torah has no legal standing?

Last is the pressing problem of national security. From its beginning in 1948 through the end of the century, Israel has lived under the threat of destruction by its Arab neighbors. Will the next century be any different? Will peace finally descend on the Middle East? Can peace result from the Jewish people relinquishing large parts of Eretz Yisrael, or is giving up part of our Divine heritage a sign of weakness? Will territorial compromose bring safety, or ever greater damage? The questions are difficult, the challenges great.

Thousands of Torah scholars across the country are wrestling with these problems, trying to find workable, halachic answers and solutions. But for the first time since the Destruction of the Temple, the Jewish People in Eretz Yisrael is responsible for applying Torah law to the entire spectrum of national Jewish life, including broad areas of life which we did not control and were therefore not responsible for in the Diaspora.

AN END AND A BEGINNING

This volume has told the story of Am Yisrael during the past five hundred years. The modern world has brought mixed blessings to the Children of Abraham, Isaac and Jacob. We are freer, more affluent and more influential than ever before in the history of the Diaspora. At the same time, we are also more assimilated, less knowledgeable, and more vulnerable than we have ever been.

Nonetheless, we face the future with faith and hope. Like "the stars of the heavens and the sand of the seashore," we are a blend of physical matter and celestial light, a blessed, enduring combination of heaven and earth.

The future is not ours to predict. Yet it is an article of Jewish faith that we are always moving forward towards the light of the future Redemption, towards a world of Torah and Godliness, towards a time of peace, joy and blessing for all mankind. Am Yisrael will return to Eretz Yisrael, the Beis HaMikdash will be rebuilt, and the Jewish people will once again be a Kingdom of Priests, a Holy Nation, and a Light unto the World. May it take place soon.

אָמֵן כֵּן יְהִי רָצוֹן!

Woodcut by Hans Holbein depicting the return from Exile

INDEX
GLOSSARY

INDEX

GLOSSARY

aliyah lit: "going up"; emigration to the land of Israel.

Ani Ma'amin the thirteen principles of Jewish faith as set forth by Maimonides

Anschluss the political union of Austria and Germany in 1938

apostate one who has abandoned his faith, religion or people

Arbeit Macht Frei lit.: Work makes man free; the inscription over the entrance gate of Auschwitz, the infamous Nazi death camp

ausstritt Rabbi Samson Raphael Hirsch's principle of communal separation from the non-orthodox community

Baalei Tosafos the 12th-13th century French and German commentators of the Talmud

Baal Teshuvah (pl: **Baalei Teshuvah**) a person who returns to traditional Jewish observance

Cantonist decrees laws promulgated in 1827 by Czar Nicholas I requiring Jewish communities in Russia to provide children for military service

Cantonists children conscripted for forced military service in 19th century Russia

Chadash asur min haTorah lit: The new is prohibited by the Torah; the motto used by the Chasam Sofer in his battle against the Reform movement

Chalukah lit: division; system of communal support used in Jerusalem's Old Yishuv

chassidim pious ones; adherents of Chassidic dynasties

Chassidism a new movement in Jewish life, founded by R' Israel Baal Shem Tov in 18th century Poland

cheder Jewish primary school

cherem excommunication

Chok Hashvut Israel's Law of Return, which guarantees every Jew the right to live in and be a citizen of the State

Daf HaYomi a study program in which participants study a folio-page of Talmud each day

Eretz Yisrael the Land of Israel

Goldineh Medinah lit.: The Golden Land; the term used by many immigrants to describe the United States of America

halachah Torah law

Haskalah lit: enlightenment; a movement which advocated the Jews' embracing of secular knowledge and mores, forerunner of the Reform movement

Judenrat Jewish community councils established by the Nazis and which were under their control

judenrein the Nazis' goal of making Europe free of Jews

Judenrepublik the Nazi term for governments they considered to be controlled by Jews

Kabbalah the mystical part of Jewish tradition

kehillah a formal Jewish community

Kibbutz (pl: Kibbutzim) communes in Israel

Kollel schools of advanced Talmudic study, esp. for married men

landsleit friends and relatives from the same town

Mamluks Egyptians rulers of the Land of Israel from the 13th to 16th centuries

Maskilim adherents of the *Haskalah*

Misnagdim opponents of *Chassidism*

mussar Jewish ethics and values; the movement established by R' Yisrael Lipkin of Salant which spread the study of these subjects

nusach the order of the prayers (e.g.: Nusach Ashkenaz - the prayer according to the Ashkenezic ritual)

Perushim lit: those who are separate; the Rabbis and their followers in the period of the Second Temple and the disciples of the Gaon of Vilna who settled in the Land of Israel

pilpul a complex method of Talmudic analysis involving bringing together and seeking to reconcile many different sources

pogrom an incited massacre of or attack on Jews

Rebbe leader of a chassidic dynasty

rebbi a rabbi, teacher, leader or guide

shechitah Jewish ritual slaughter of animals or fowl

Shemittah the sabbatical year, occurring every seventh year, during which the Land of Israel may not be cultivated

shochet ritual slaughterer of animals and fowl

shtetl small town in Eastern Europe

talmid chacham (pl: talmidei chachamim) Torah scholar

tzaddik (pl: **tzaddikim**) righteous person

tefillin phylacteries; small leather cases containing parchment scrolls with passages from the Torah; they are worn on the forehead and arm during morning prayers

Torah im Derech Eretz lit: the pursuit of Torah and the ways of the world; the pursuit of Torah study as well as the study of secular knowledge, as expounded by Rabbi Samson Raphael Hirsch

Tzahal acronym for "**Tz**va **Ha**ganah **L**'Yisrael", the Israel Defense Forces

Vaad Arba Aratzos Council of Four Lands; an independent, government-recognized court which ruled Polish Jewry from 1527 to 1764

Yishuv HaAretz the mitzvah of settling the land of Israel

Yishuv HaYashan the "old", pre-Zionist, settlements in Israel, especially those of the Chassidim and disciples of the Gaon of Vilna

Yishuv HeChadash the "new" settlements, established by Zionist settlers beginning in the early 1900's

THE
SHAAR
PRESS

THE JUDAICA IMPRINT
FOR THOUGHTFUL PEOPLE